KILLING IN THE NAME OF IDENTITY

KILLING IN THE NAME OF IDENTITY

A Study of Bloody Conflicts

Vamık D. Volkan

PITCHSTONE PUBLISHING
Charlottesville, Virginia

PITCHSTONE PUBLISHING
Charlottesville, Virginia

First hardcover edition, 2006
First paperback edition, 2019
ISBN: 978-1-939578-31-0

Library of Congress Cataloging-in-Publication Data

Volkan, Vamik D., 1932-
Killing in the name of identity : a study of bloody conflicts / Vamik Volkan.—
1st ed.
    p. cm.
Includes bibliographical references and index.
ISBN-13: 978-0-9728875-7-1 (hardcover : alk. paper)
ISBN-10: 0-9728875-7-1 (hardcover : alk. paper)
1. Ethnic conflict. 2. Genocide. I. Title.
GN496.V65 2006
305.8—dc22
                    2006004211

For my former colleagues
at the Center for the Study of Mind and Human Interaction

Nature's law,
That man was made to mourn.

Man's inhumanity to man.
Makes countless thousands mourn!

—Robert Burns, "Man was made to Mourn"

Contents

Preface to the Paperback Edition

The concept of identity—specifically, of large-group identity—is arguably more central to our current socio-political landscape than it was even in the years following the collapse of the Soviet Union or in the wake of September 11, 2001, when I wrote *Killing in the Name of Identity*. Indeed, at the present time, we are observing severe identity-based socio-political divisions across the globe, even in long-stable democracies and in countries with deeply rooted liberal traditions. Both Western and Eastern Europe countries have experienced a stark rise in support for right-wing nationalist and anti-immigrant political parties. In Turkey, the ruling party continues its open effort to purify the country by making it more religious. In the United States, the rise of the so-called alt-right and the election of Donald Trump as U.S. president acutely demonstrate the salience and power of large-group identity. My own adopted hometown of Charlottesville, Virginia, suffered a tragic case of "killing in the name of identity" in August 2017 that made international headlines.

All the while, civil wars and deadly political crises continue to occur elsewhere in the world, such as in Syria, Central African Republic, Yemen, Myanmar, and Sri Lanka. Although the social, cultural, religious, historical, economic, and political contexts of particular conflicts may change across time and space, the often-hidden substrate contaminating all large-group conflict—from local to global—remains the same: identity. Indeed, to understand the roots of societal divisions and political crises requires a serious study of identity—both its formation and its effects within and across groups.

In *Killing in the Name of Identity*, first published in 2006, I describe in detail my work in large-group conflicts and provide case studies to illustrate key concepts of large-group psychology. Not included in *Killing in the Name of Identity* is reference to some of my newer work, as detailed in my book *Enemies on the Couch: A Psychopolitical Journey Through War and Peace,* published in 2013. In that book, I discuss my involvement in a project in Turkey that attempted to find a solution to the so-called Turkish-Kurdish issue. I also write about the International Dialogue Initiative (IDI), which for more than a decade now has brought together psychoanalysts, political scientists, diplomats, and other professionals from eight different nations—the United States, Great Britain, Germany, Russia, Turkey, Israel, Palestine, and Iran—to apply psychologically informed perspectives for the study and amelioration of current societal conflicts. The IDI also runs training workshops in which participants study how societal, political, religious, and organizational conflicts become intertwined with both individual and large-group psychology. (For more, see www.internationaldialogueinitiative.com.)

All the while, I have continued studying large-group identity issues outside of my involvement in the IDI. For example, in 2015 I traveled to Malaysia to participate in a meeting with Dr. Mahathir Mohamad, before his second tenure as prime minister, in which he wanted to solicit ideas that might help prevent conflict among the various ethnic groups in his country and protect Malaysia from extremist Islamist fundamentalist movements. I was impressed by the desire of Dr. Mohamad and his close political circle to understand and consider a psychopolitical viewpoint.

I have also visited Bogotá, Colombia, twice in recent years—just prior to and soon after the Colombian government and the Revolutionary Armed Forces of Colombia (FARC) reached a peace agreement in the summer of 2016. My aim there was to assess how a fragmented population that had developed different large-group identities might start learning to live and work together physically and psychologically.

Through my ongoing work in large-group conflicts, I believe the observations, concepts, and lessons I first shared in this book in 2006 remain as relevant today as ever before—perhaps even more so as current events continue to attest.

Introduction

On November 19, 1977, then-Egyptian president Anwar el-Sadat, in a bold move, flew to Israel to give a talk at the Knesset, where he spoke about a "psychological barrier" between Egypt and Israel. During his speech, he declared that this barrier constituted 70 percent of the entire problem between the two countries. I was not aware of it at the time, but this event changed my life. I was then a member of the American Psychiatric Association's Committee on Psychiatry and Foreign Affairs. After Sadat's speech, this committee, supported by U.S. funds, was assigned to investigate the psychological barrier that Sadat had referenced and to explore possibilities of lowering it. We worked with influential Israelis, Egyptians, Palestinians, and others from 1979 to 1986, and thus I became closely exposed to psychopolitical and psychosocial aspects of large groups in conflict. Since then I have spent most of my professional life looking at many other troubled areas through a psychological lens while working in the field.

It was during my six-year involvement in the Arab-Israeli conflict that I met Joseph Montville, a career diplomat who for some years was also the head of preventive diplomacy at the Center for Strategic and International Studies (CSIS) in Washington, D.C. We have remained friends ever since. In 1983, through the efforts of Montville, I was included among a group of prominent psychoanalysts, political scientists, anthropologists, philosophers, and former diplomats to participate in an unusual, stimulating, and pleasurable activity. We, accompanied by our spouses or significant others, began spending one week each year with an aging psychoanalyst, Erik H. Erikson, and his wife Joan at the Esalen Institute in Big Sur, California. This project lasted for four years until Erikson's health would no longer allow us to continue meeting with him. Erikson died on May 12, 1994, at the age of ninety-one.

The Esalen Institute had been in the public spotlight for sponsoring programs in the sixties that encouraged new understandings of human nature. A lesser-known fact is that this institute also initiated citizen diplomacy with the Soviet Union in the eighties. Big Sur is a beautiful place with hot springs and gardens that provide food for the guests. We were given a house where we had many unstructured discussions with Erikson as well as among ourselves.

I am a psychoanalyst and had seen Erikson previously at some professional meetings, but I did not have any close contact with him until the Big Sur project. Erikson, of course, was a famous man. Among other things, he had explored societal and cultural influences on child development and defined the psychology of eight stages of human life from infancy to old age. He also made the concept of "identity"—a subjective and persistence sense of sameness—an area of psychoanalytic inquiry. I think that Sigmund Freud used the word "identity" only five times in his writings. It was not considered a psychoanalytic term until Erikson made it one.

In the beginning of the 1950s, as Senator Joseph McCarthy and his followers created a "paranoid" atmosphere in the United States, Americans were preoccupied with "Communists" and feared them. When professors at Berkeley were asked to sign the so-called "loyalty oath," Erikson, who was at Berkeley at that time, left the West Coast and came back to the East Coast. From May 1951 to September 1960 (on leave from October 1956 to February 1958), he was at the Austen Riggs Center, a small, nonprofit, open psychiatric hospital in Stockbridge, Massachusetts. A portrait of Erik Erikson, painted by Norman Rockwell who was also a resident of Stockbridge, hangs in the main entry hall of the Austen Riggs Center office building today, alongside portraits of other prominent clinicians who worked there in the past.

In 1994 the Austen Riggs Center founded an interdisciplinary research and teaching institute in the name of Erik H. Erikson. One of the efforts of the Erik H. Erikson Institute of the Austen Riggs Center is to bring the unique Riggs' experience—that of clinicians working with psychiatric patients in an open community context—to the larger challenges of contemporary society. Erikson had recognized that the individual could not be understood apart from a psychosocial and historical context.

In 2004 Edward Shapiro, the medical director and CEO of the Austen Riggs Center, and Gerard Fromm, the head of the center's Erik H. Erikson Institute, created a senior Erikson scholar position for me. This has allowed me, and will allow me, to spend some months each year in

Stockbridge. During the last two years, I was at Riggs for ten months and this gave me the opportunity to write this book. It is primarily based on the concept of identity that, as I mentioned earlier, for practical purposes was introduced to psychoanalysis by Erikson.

Besides focusing on an individual's identity, Erikson also showed interest in large-group identities. He defined a process he called *pseudospeciation*, in which, at the outset of human history, each human group developed a distinct sense of identity, wearing skins and feathers like armor to protect it from other groups who wore different kinds of skins and feathers. Erikson hypothesized that each group became convinced that it was the sole possessor of the true human identity. Thus, each group also became a pseudospecies, adopting an attitude of superiority over other groups. In this book, I deal with ethnic, national, religious, and some ideological large-group identities which are all formed in childhood.

My participation in the Arab-Israeli "unofficial" negotiation series introduced me to the importance of an abstract concept, "large-group identity," and its importance in international relations. My idea that large-group identity has to be studied carefully in order to understand world affairs from a different angle, received further support from my observations during dialogues that continued for many years between high-level representatives of opposing large groups besides Arabs and Israelis, groups such as Russians and Estonians, Serbians and Croats, and Georgians and South Ossetians. I also spent considerable time with various political leaders when they were actively protecting their large-groups' identities and trying to repair injuries to the shared sense of "we-ness" of the group to which they belonged. Furthermore, I visited refugee camps and traumatized societies where the concept of large-group identity becomes palpable.

Following Erik Erikson's description of individual identity, I describe large-group identity as tens of thousands, or millions, of people—most of whom will never meet one another in their lifetimes—sharing a permanent sense of sameness. In my book, *Blind Trust: Large Groups and Their Leaders in Times of Crisis and Terror,* I described a theory of how large-group identity (we are Arabs, we are Catholics) evolves, illustrated its various components, and examined how political leaders can manipulate their society's shared sentiments. In the present book, I focus on the relationship between large-group identity and massive traumas at the hand of enemies, such as what happened in the United States on September 11, 2001.

September 11, 2001, changed the world. After September 11 and the initiation of what is known as the "war on terrorism," and after the subsequent terror bombings in Madrid, Casablanca, Istanbul, Mombasa, the Red Sea resort of Taba, Egypt, and London, we can once more easily notice an echo of Erikson's pseudospeciation. Presently, in many parts of the world, there are severe "we" and "they" divisions and talk of a clash of religions or civilizations. Fantasized and/or realistic shared mental representations of old clashes, such as between Christians and Muslims during the Crusades, have been reactivated, and one group feeling superior to "others" has become routine.

This book is not about September 11 or the "war on terrorism." Instead, I focus on universal elements associated with large-group identity issues that, when converged, create an atmosphere for human tragedies. Under certain circumstances, human beings kill "others" without blinking an eye. In the name of identity, they initiate shared terror and massive trauma that produces decades or centuries of consequences. Humiliating and killing others can lead to the evolution of new political ideologies within the affected societies, poisoning existing cultural rituals and turning them into destructive ones, modifying large-group identity, and, in short, preparing a foundation for new massive tragedies decades or even centuries later. I hope that in studying such long-term processes and links between massive trauma, political ideologies, and new tragedies, we may be able to create an opportunity to look at the post–September 11 world from a fresh angle and allow ourselves to come up with new strategies for peaceful solutions to some of our international problems. I hope that some concepts described in this book may be useful in attempts to combat malignant aspects of pseudospeciation.

In this book people from many parts of the world, from Georgia, South Ossetia, Northern Cyprus, Israel, Germany, Kuwait, Estonia, and the United States, speak of their experiences and describe what people are capable of doing in the name of large-group identity and introduce us to the human struggle to maintain dignity under incredible conditions. This book is divided into three parts. The first part, "Georgia on My Mind," centers on moving stories of traumatized individuals and families from the Caucasus. I let these individuals and families, through their own words, introduce us to concepts of "massive trauma," "mourning," and "adaptation." When a massive trauma occurs at the hands of "others," the affected society responds predictably to it, just as individuals do. Part two of this book examines such societal responses, some of which, when not tamed, may lead to malignant outcomes. Others, such as the building of the Vietnam Veterans Memorial in Washington, D.C., help to heal societal wounds, as well as personal ones. Again, by telling the stories of people and large groups with whom I have worked, I illustrate the concept of "transgenerational transmissions" of trauma. The shared mental image of a massive tragedy that leads to shame, humiliation, helplessness, and difficulty in mourning over losses within a large group decades or centuries later may become the fuel for new infernos that are deliberately started by people in the name of identity.

Sigmund Freud was pessimistic about psychoanalytic contributions to the understanding of, and especially the solution for, large-group conflicts, mainly because of the presence of aggression in human nature. Over the last thirty years, I have slowly moved away from studying large-group conflicts by applying only what we know about the internal worlds of individuals to large-group processes. Since societies are composed of people, we do see derivatives of individual psychology in large-group activities, but such activities, I learned more and more, have their own special patterns. I have tried to understand the nature of large-group identity and how one large group relates to another one in peace or in war. I have become pessimistic about finding or establishing a peaceful world, not only because human beings are endowed with aggression, but also because large-group psychology, in its own right, includes the necessity to find enemies and allies, as I described in one of my previous books, *The Need To Have Enemies and Allies*, and this necessity is often accompanied by excessive destructive acts.

Despite attempts at democratization in massively traumatized places such as Iraq, having a democratic state in so-called underdeveloped societies—or in so-called developed states for that matter—is no guarantee that conflict will not continue to be "solved" by war or violent means. Various political systems come and go and identity issues continue to complicate things, especially, but not necessarily, when one large group lives next to another. I do believe large groups will continue to humiliate, maim, and kill human beings who belong to another identity group.

On the other hand, since my involvement in the Arab-Israeli dialogue series, I have become optimistic about using psychoanalytically informed insights and techniques to deal with and modify certain specific and limited international problems and establish nonviolent coexistence between groups with different identities. For this to happen, psychoanalysts must be willing to work steadily over long periods of time with historians, political scientists, diplomats, and others within an established team and also in the trenches of troubled locations of the world. Part three of this book describes a method, which I named "The Tree Model," a psycho-analytically informed years-long "unofficial" diplomatic effort, that may be a model for lowering the type of psychological barriers we see, such as the one that Sadat referred to in his Knesset speech.

I would like to thank Edward Shapiro and Gerard Fromm for providing me a supportive atmosphere at the Austen Riggs Center while I worked on this book. I also thank Rachel Vigneron, the librarian at Riggs' excellent library, and Liz Thomson for their technical assistance.

In 1987 I established the Center for the Study of Mind and Human Interaction (CSMHI) within the School of Medicine at the University of Virginia and I directed it until my retirement in 2002. Unfortunately, three years later, in September 2005, CSMHI was closed. The faculty of this center was composed of clinicians, former diplomats, historians, and others. In preparing this book I depended a great deal on my notes from my work as the founder and director of CSMHI at various locations throughout the world. I thank the former program director of CSMHI, Joy Boissevian, for her most valuable assistance in preparing these notes. Colleagues from CSMHI stood by me and helped me to observe many events described in this book. I acknowledge their support with gratitude.

I could not have finished this project without the diligent and intelligent help of my editor for the last two years, Dianna Downing of Monterey, Massachusetts, and the former editor of CSMHI's journal, *Mind and Human Interaction*, Bruce Edwards of El Cajon, California.

I would like to express my gratitude to all the people from different parts of the world, including the United States, whose stories are the backbone of my theoretical conceptualizations in this book. Lastly, I thank my wife, Elizabeth Palonen Volkan, a World War II orphan, for allowing me to tell the story of her search for her father, who was killed in Italy fighting Nazi forces when she was only a few months old, and to use her story to demonstrate how memorials, such as the World War II Memorial in Washington, D.C., inform us about large group psychology.

Part I

Georgia on My Mind

1 Massive Trauma in the Republic of Georgia

In November 1991, just one and a half months before the Soviet Union collapsed and Mikhail Gorbachev lost power, I was invited to Moscow as a guest of the Diplomatic Academy of the USSR Foreign Ministry. My wife and I boarded an Aeroflot plane at Dulles Airport in Washington, D.C., and arrived at Sheremetevo Airport in Moscow the next day. We were met there by Yuri Urbanovich, a strong but gentle man in his early forties whom I had met during a previous visit and who was, at that time, a faculty member of the Diplomatic Academy specializing in negotiation theory and techniques. When we were taken to the airport's VIP lounge, I noticed that a polite younger man was accompanying him. Yuri introduced the man as Yalcin Nasirov, a graduate student at the Diplomatic Academy. Yalcin said that he was an Azeri Turk, and since earlier he had been informed that I am a Turkish-American originally from Cyprus, he greeted me in Azeri Turkish, which I could understand fairly well. We were taken in a speeding black car that belonged to the Foreign Ministry to an apartment in a huge building belonging to the Permanent Representation of the Azerbaijan Republic in Moscow.

In the car Yalcin whispered to me, in Azeri Turkish, that our apartment was safe and that it was next door to the world chess champion, Garry Kimovich Kasparov. He added that the Soviet Azerbaijan Permanent Representation had assigned three "bodyguards"—meaning him and two of his friends—to my wife and me to protect us should we leave the apartment unaccompanied by our Soviet hosts. I had been to this city before, but I soon realized that the Moscow I once knew had changed. There was unrest. The comforting sense of personal security I had experienced during my previous visits to Gorbachev's Moscow was gone.

The purpose of my trip to Moscow was to speak—for four full consecutive days at one of the big halls at the Diplomatic Academy—about ethnicity to the representatives of various Soviet republics and autonomous political regions. The invitation for my speaking engagement came from Ambassador Oleg Peressypkin, then rector of the Diplomatic Academy. A better understanding of the underlying forces of ethnicity, it was thought, might be an antidote to growing Soviet anxiety. Many in the Soviet Union perceived that Gorbachev's hold on the country was weakening, and it was feared that various groups would become more and more preoccupied with their own sense of ethnicity rather than with greater unity.

How did I end up in the middle of such intriguing circumstances during one of the most volatile periods of modern history? It all began slowly and innocently, with some tentative steps that pulled an inquisitive psychoanalyst and university administrator into many distant and even dangerous places where few clinicians had ventured before. My work in the Soviet Union had actually started more than two years before my November 1991 trip to Moscow through a contract established between the Soviet Duma and the University of Virginia's Center for the Study of Mind and Human Interaction (CSMHI), an interdisciplinary unit I had founded in 1987. The objective of our collaboration was a better understanding of American-Soviet relations, and included visits to and from the Soviet Union. Through these meetings I had come to know various members of the USSR Foreign Ministry and the USSR Institute of Psychology.

In 1990 four members of our team, including myself and former U.S. assistant secretary of state Harold Saunders, were taken to the headquarters of the Communist Party in Moscow where we met with some of Michael Gorbachev's assistants. They wanted to know if we could shed any light on recent events in the Soviet Baltic Republics and asked us how we thought they should respond to developments there. (It was clear that, despite their initial suspicions, the Soviet authorities did not see us as agents of the U.S. government or spies for the Central Intelligence Agency.) Gorbachev believed, I think, that glasnost ("openness") and perestroika ("restructuring") would help bring together the diverse groups in the Soviet Union. But just the opposite was occurring in the Baltic Republics of Lithuania, Latvia, and Estonia. Their response to the new direction of Soviet Communism was instead an even louder call for complete independence from the Soviet Union. Similar tensions existed in other republics and regions. While at the Communist headquarters, I noted that those working for Gorbachev were sincerely surprised by these developments.

By the time of my November 1991 visit, the rise of independence movements had spread and intensified well beyond the Baltic Republics. These mass movements throughout much of the Soviet Union were shaking the foundation of this once-formidable political entity that Ronald Reagan had called the "evil empire." The Diplomatic Academy hoped that there might be answers to the confusing problems of ethnonationalism that threatened dissolution. But even then I felt their hopes were in vain.

My first glimpse of the power of group identity came through participating in and later facilitating unofficial talks between influential Arabs and Israelis.[1] During these dialogues, held between 1979 and 1986, I came to understand the historical, political, and psychological factors that influenced the behavior of large groups of people who defined themselves according to ethnic, religious, national, or ideological bases. Such large-group psychology—based on large-group identities—involves tens of thousands or millions of people who share certain emotional and ideational sentiments that define them as being different from other large groups.[2]

My work in the Middle East made it all too clear that, when under stress, the forces that define "us" and "them" could quickly regress into the humiliating and killing of "others," and that large groups would respond at times with violence in order to erase the threats, whether real or fantasized, to their sense of "we-ness." Or, they would simply be murderous in order to maintain an illusion of superiority over those who they openly or secretly felt to be inferior or less human. The twentieth century already was one of the bloodiest in history, and the increasing turmoil of the Soviet Union threatened to provide an even more horrible beginning to its final decade.

Yet at the same time, my understanding of individual and group psychological processes led me to believe that the ubiquitous and destructive forces of human aggression did not always have to fall into a downward spiral that ended in misery. My guarded optimism, based in part on my successful treatment of patients as a psychoanalyst, led me to found in 1987 the Center for the Study of Mind and Human Interaction (CSMHI) at the University of Virginia's School of Medicine in Charlottesville. This was the only such center at any medical school in the world. Its faculty was composed of physicians (most of them psychiatrists) and psychologists, as well as prominent retired U.S. diplomats and historians. Our task was to study and understand international relations, especially from a psychoanalytic angle. I thought that by involving a multidisciplinary team in world affairs, we could enlarge the concept of "preventive medicine." I hoped that this concept would include finding new and effective ways to respond to massive human aggression and developing new methods to mitigate its destructive influences on societal and political processes.

Despite some pessimism about human nature, especially as it is manifested in large groups, I believed that we could be successful in certain arenas of international conflict if we were to spend extended periods of time—as a psychoanalyst spends years in treating an analysand—opening dialogues between enemies and providing actual examples of peaceful co-existence on the ground. I knew we could not change human nature in general, but perhaps we could manage to tame massive aggression in certain locations. I believed that, in the long run, large-group psychology was capable of contaminating and influencing every aspect of international relationships, including those involving legal, economic, and military interactions. I considered CSMHI's task to be providing a vaccination against such malignant societal and political developments.

Our center was not set up to compete with official diplomacy—it was set up with the hope that we might suggest new visions that could be utilized by official diplomacy. As the world was changing so rapidly, especially due to technology and the power of the media, the methods of traditional diplomacy certainly needed new input. Traditional diplomacy, in fact, was already being influenced not only by the media and globalization of economic interests, but also by the spread of nongovernmental organizations. At this time some nongovernmental organizations had already brought Americans and Soviets together to improve relations. The faculty of my center simply wanted to add new insights about human nature that might be useful to the diplomatic process, especially about how humans act when they get together under the umbrella of a shared identity.

If novel approaches to diplomacy were not explored, it was easy to imagine that forces at work within the Soviet Union could escalate into increasingly violent protests, deadly attempts to quell dissent, and bloody civil wars in numerous republics and among scores of ethnic groups. But as my visit to Moscow in 1991 indicated, it was hard for the Soviet leadership to understand how or why this could happen. After all, during the heyday of Communist power, it was thought that shared ideology made people from different ethnic groups "brothers and sisters." Ethnic identities of Soviet citizens were clearly indicated in their internal passports. A person was Armenian, Latvian, Uzbek, and so on, but these identities were considered secondary to their primary Communist identity.

Once the huge tent of the Soviet Union began shaking, however, every ethnic group underneath it became concerned with its own smaller tent, and ethnic identity became a preoccupation. It was hoped that my four-day marathon seminars on the concept of ethnicity and large-group psychology would help representatives of the Soviet republics and other autonomous Soviet political entities understand each other, value their togetherness, and not fight among themselves.

The day after my arrival in Moscow, Yuri took me to the Diplomatic Academy building, located near the Krymsky suspension bridge over Moscow River on Ostozhenka Street, where I was met by Ambassador Peressypkin, General Vladimir Illarionov, and others. I took the obligatory walk on the red carpet that covered the long hallway on the first floor. Two years earlier the walls on both sides of the hallway had been filled with posters and pictures gloriously portraying the history of the Soviet Union. Though a red tapestry with the likeness of Lenin woven in the middle still hung on one of the walls, many traditional Communist images had been replaced. New pictures and posters had been chosen to reflect the changes in Moscow, symbolizing glasnost and perestroika and the Soviets' willingness to be friendly with "others," even Americans. In some pictures U.S. and Soviet dignitaries were seen shaking hands.

I spoke for four full days, with "cognac breaks," while Yuri translated my words into Russian for those in attendance. These individuals included Russian, Lithuanian, Kazak, Azeri, Armenian, and Daghestani delegates, as well as representatives and others from different parts of the Soviet Union. Certainly there was interest in what I had to say. But the topics I discussed often induced verbal clashes among representatives from neighboring republics where conflict was already brewing. Ethnic Armenian and ethnic Azeris, for example, got involved in several heated exchanges. On the fourth day an elderly Russian raised his hand and addressed me in perfect English spoken with a heavy Russian accent. "Doctor," he said, "we appreciate your efforts. You have been very informative. But, you and I and, I think, everyone in this hall, know that the cookie will crumble." The cookie of course was the Soviet Union. Without openly verbalizing my agreement with him, I knew that the task assigned to me by the Diplomatic Academy come to an end.

Soon the cookie did crumble.[3] Many Soviet Republics, as well as other autonomous regions, sought independence. Chaos and bloodshed were common. The dream of Soviet brotherhood abruptly evaporated—its "glue" of shared ideology and universal goals quickly dissolved, revealing deep fractures along ethnic, religious, and cultural lines. Hostility against the "russification" of the Soviet era as well as centuries-old tensions between neighboring ethnic groups quickly surfaced. Inflammatory political rhetoric that pitted "us" against "them" became common, and sometimes invoked open violence, "ethnic cleansing," and other atrocities.

What happened? Each former Soviet republic had a different story, but many shared a common problem: how to establish a new nation out of a multiethnic society whose prior amalgamation depended, in varying degrees, upon central Soviet control. The fate of each emerging nation was linked to complex political, historical, economic, military, social, and religious factors. Large-group psychological processes also were simultaneously intertwined with them. To specifically illustrate some of these processes, I will focus on Georgia, the small nation in the Caucasus between Turkey and Russia, where I had opportunities to observe and learn first-hand over the course of more than five years. Although my primary interest is in illuminating the manifestation and impact of psychological factors, a brief description of historical and political factors in Georgia is nonetheless necessary.

Like other countries on the border between Europe and Asia, Georgia has long been a crossroad of civilizations. According to the last Soviet census in 1989, roughly 70 percent of Georgia's population defined themselves as ethnic Georgians, a people of Transcaucasia who trace their history and culture back to ancient times. Ethnic minorities, often with equally rich and ancient cultures, made up about 30 percent of Georgia's 5.4 million people. These groups included a significant number of Armenians, Russians, Azeris, Ossetians, Greeks, and Abkhazians, as well as Kurds, Jews, Meskhetians, and others.

Each of these ethnic groups had lived within the modern political borders of Georgia for centuries and relations among them generally were peaceful. For example, in the old section of Tbilisi, the capital of Georgia, churches, mosques, and synagogues shared the same streets, and intermarriage between groups was not uncommon. Specific provincial identity coexisted with a more general national identity and was not necessarily a basis for being "less Georgian." Nevertheless, while violence between groups was unusual, tensions did in fact exist. Against this backdrop, perestroika and glasnost caused the concepts of nationalism vs. ethnonationalism and independence vs. democracy to become increasingly problematic in Georgia.

In terms of independence, Georgia looked back to previous times of sovereignty, the most recent from 1918 to 1921, and an age-old sense of identity that was uniquely Georgian. The tradition of political dissent and demonstrations against foreign dominance dated back for centuries and continued through both imperial Russian and then Soviet times. Like the Baltic states, Georgia was seen as having been forcibly incorporated into the Soviet Union, meaning its pro-Western and pro-democratic aspirations had been thwarted and Georgian identity had been threatened. While Georgia's political independence existed more in principle than in practice, its modern history suggested that democracy, pluralism, and an inclusive sense of national identity existed in Georgia and would be the basis for the "new" Georgia.

On the other hand, the political rhetoric of independence that followed Gorbachev's reforms became increasingly colored by the slogan that "Georgia is for Georgians." While this slogan at first may have implicitly included those who were not ethnic Georgians, the exclusive component of it became more and more explicit. This rise in ethnonationalism caused anxiety among many of Georgia's ethnic minorities, who could readily cite examples of intolerance and injustice, such as Stalin's deportation of thousands of Meskhetians from their lands along Georgia's border with Turkey and longstanding grievances against policies of "Georgianization," especially in the semiautonomous regions of South Ossetia and Abkhazia.

Nevertheless, an increasing majority in Georgia expressed a desire to break with the Soviet Union and communism in the late 1980s. This consensus was further galvanized on April 9, 1989, when a group of hunger strikers gathered in Tbilisi on the steps of the building known as the Supreme Soviet, to express their desire for independence from the Soviet Union. As crowds of supporters rallied around them, Moscow sent units

of the armed forces to ensure order. However, the Soviet commander, General Radionov, ignored negotiations aimed at resolving the hunger strike and ordered his armored units to drive a wedge between the protestors and the ever-growing crowd of sympathizers, blocking side streets and backing the strikers up against the Supreme Soviet.[4]

The situation quickly escalated, and Soviet troops attacked the strikers with chemical agents and sharpened trenching tools, leaving between sixteen and twenty people dead. The bloody day was especially confusing for many Georgians because Gorbachev's government had seemed committed to reform.[5] Were things really changing, or was the Soviet Union just as oppressive as ever? The killings were experienced as a betrayal and tragic loss, leaving a deep emotional impact on the people. With this psychological fuel added to the fire, it would now be difficult to stop the independence movement.

However, not all of Georgia was united by this rise in nationalism—in fact just the opposite was true. The semiautonomous region of South Ossetia and the autonomous republic of Abkhazia, which were subdivisions of Georgia created by the Soviet Union, both were swept up in their own wave of ethnonationalism and desire for autonomy—not from the Soviet Union but from Georgia itself. While ethnic Georgians felt they were victims of "russification" and Russian hegemony while part of the Soviet Union, many South Ossetians and Abkhazians similarly perceived Georgia as the domineering and unwelcome Big Brother. Both minority groups, which traditionally speak a different language than ethnic Georgians, perceived their culture and homeland—their large-group identity—as being threatened.

The desire for autonomy in South Ossetia and Abkhazia intensified with the rise of Georgian leader Zviad Gamsakhurdia, a prominent dissident whose fervent nationalistic rhetoric had few boundaries. Like many politicians, Gamsakhurdia received popular support by accentuating the "we-ness" of his own ethnic group, which collectively felt in need of a strong leader as it began to chart an uncertain course into the future. This course, under the questionable political skills of Gamsakhurdia, was soon headed for disaster—precipitated by policies such as the declaration of Georgian as the official state language. Anxiety about large-group identities soon increased throughout the Caucasus region and began to taint relations on every level, eventually precipitating a societal regression.

On March 9, 1990, Georgia seceded from the Soviet Union. As a result of growing tensions, in September 1990 nationalists in South Ossetia declared their own independence from Georgia and refused to participate in the first free national elections—the same elections that made Gamsakhurdia Georgia's first president. By the fall of 1990 Gamsakhurdia's autocratic tendencies, virulent anticommunism, and intolerance for opposition of any kind led him to revoke South Ossetia's status as an autonomous region and days later to impose martial law in the South Ossetian capital of Tskhinvali. Group identity and how to protect it became increasingly politicized, and violent armed conflict soon erupted and escalated in South Ossetia. Street battles raged through Tskhinvali. Thousands of South Ossetians fled across the Russian border to North Ossetia, while the many ethnic Georgians in South Ossetia fled to Georgian territories.

Gamsakhurdia's nationalist politics and zealous desire to retain or reassert Georgia's territorial integrity led to a similar rise in tensions with Abkhazia. In response, Abkhazian intellectuals and Communist party leaders channeled growing anxiety and the shrinking proportion of Abkhazians in their own state into a nationalist movement of their own. In 1989, they requested that Gorbachev recreate an independent Abkhazian Soviet republic such as existed between 1921 and 1931 when Abkhazia and Georgia were separate. This was especially problematic for Gamsakhurdia since the population of ethnic Georgians in Abkhazia was more than two times the population of Abkhazians. Violence erupted in the Abkhazian capital of Sukhumi over the establishment of a separate Georgian division within the University of Sukhumi. Political tensions increased further, prompting the Abkhaz Supreme Soviet to reinstate its 1925 constitution, thereby giving it complete autonomy from Georgia. Georgian military forces entered the capital and a violent and protracted armed conflict ensued. Tens of thousands of Georgians, many of whom had lived in Abkhazia for generations, fled with only a handful of possessions as full-scale civil war erupted.

As the conflicts with South Ossetians and Abkhazians were brewing, my own center in Charlottesville, CSMHI, received a visit from Giorgi Khoshtaria, then foreign minister of Georgia in the Gamsakhurdia government, and Tedo Japaridze, a senior officer in the Georgian Foreign Ministry. (Later Tedo Japaridze became a long-term Georgian ambassador to Washington, where he remained until March 2002, when he became national security adviser to President Eduard Shevardnadze.) Khoshtaria and Japaridze had heard about our center's work with the Soviets during the last years of the Soviet Union, as well as our work in the Baltic Republics, especially in Estonia, following the collapse of the Soviet Union, when we tried to help these republics develop democratic institutions and peaceful relationships with Russia.[6] Khoshtaria came to ask for our help with the escalating ethnic conflicts in his own country, but we unfortunately had no funds to begin work in Georgia. I felt helpless but promised to keep lines of communication open.

At the same time, I was fortunate to have an expert on Georgia among my faculty—none other than Yuri Urbanovich, who was the key figure in organizing my seminar on ethnicity at the Diplomatic Academy. In 1992 he had been appointed international scholar at CSMHI, and I soon learned that he was born in Georgia to an ethnic Lithuanian father and an ethnic Armenian mother. When he became the center's international scholar, his mother still lived in Tbilisi, and with his help we were able to keep a close eye on events in Georgia.

But there was little more to do than watch from a distance as the Georgian dream for independence and democracy soon degenerated into complete chaos, fueled by Gamsakhurdia's incendiary political decisions and growing autocratic and even erratic rule. Power outside the Georgian capital of Tbilisi fell into the hands of local warlords and paramilitary commanders, hundreds of thousands of refugees were left homeless, rival factions emerged within the central government, and the economy collapsed. Finally, in early 1992, fighting erupted in the streets of Tbilisi as a coalition of military and government leaders forced Gamsakhurdia from power—though he still maintained an almost cult-like following among many Georgians.

A temporary military ruling body invited the former foreign minister of the Soviet Union and an ethnic Georgian, Eduard Shevardnadze, to lead the struggling country. Later that year he was officially chosen leader of the Georgian parliament in democratic elections, although Gamsakhurdia maintained that he was still the legitimate president and controlled parts of western Georgian through his own faction of armed supporters. (Shevardnadze stayed in power until November 30, 2003, when he resigned following massive protests against the November parliamentary elections; a much younger man, Mikhail Saakashvili became the president of Georgia). When Shevardnadze became president, he stressed that being "Georgian" was a matter of citizenship and not ethnicity, but chaos and warfare continued in Georgia for many years. Though Gamsakhurdia's lingering provocation ended with his apparent suicide in 1993, and ceasefires were eventually negotiated, few conflicts were permanently resolved and relations remained strained over the return of refuges and other issues. The status of South Ossetia and Abkhazia was still unclear during these years, and fighting periodically broke out, but tensions stabilized enough for my colleagues and I to take a closer look.

In the summer of 1995, Joyce Neu, then associate director of the Carter Center's Conflict Resolution Program in Atlanta (and now director of the Joan B. Kroc Institute for Peace & Justice at the University of San Diego), and Yuri traveled to Georgia and Abkhazia to "diagnose" the situation. I had an association with the Carter Center beginning in the early 1990s, when I became a member of its International Negotiation Network (INN) under the directorship of former U.S. president Jimmy Carter. At the time, President Carter was nurturing a kind of "Georgia to Georgia" (state of to republic of) relationship with President Shevardnadze. In the fall of 1995, our two centers brought twelve representatives from U.S. nongovernmental organizations (NGOs) together in Charlottesville, Virginia, to discuss existing initiatives on conflict resolution in Georgia in order to avoid future duplication of efforts. Because we observed that at the time most NGOs were dealing with Georgian-Abkhazian conflicts, CSMHI decided to focus its attention on Georgian-South Ossetian issues. I first traveled to Georgia in May 1998 and continued to do so at least twice a year for the next five years.

My arrival in Georgia in May 1998 coincided with renewed hostilities between Georgians and Abkhazians. About two years earlier, the two sides had reached an agreement that allowed forty thousand Georgian internally displaced persons (IDPs, the policitically correct term for "refugees") to move back to the Gali region of the country. Abkhazians believe that this region belongs to them, and indeed it is under their control. But ethnic Georgians lived there as well. According to the agreement they were allowed to return to their original homes—a sign of hope for lasting peace. But by the time I visited in 1998, renewed fighting between Abkhaz and Georgian forces again uprooted tens of thousands of refugees in the Gali region, and any hope of a settlement was gone.

Some Georgians with whom I spoke blamed the Abkhazians and Russians. The feeling was that Russia, not wanting to lose its influence over Georgia, was keeping conflict alive by maintaining a peacekeeping force in the area. (Only after U.S. president George W. Bush visited Georgia in 2005 would Russia begin to seriously consider—likely due to pressure from the United States—withdrawing its troops from Georgia.) This Russian force, some Georgians felt, was not meant to keep the peace in the country but rather was meant to interfere with Georgian affairs and to keep Georgia dependant upon Russia.

Renewed fighting in the Gali region took place as preparations were being made for a military parade in Tbilisi—where I was staying—to celebrate the eighteeth anniversary of the founding of the first Georgian republic in 1918. Given the resumption of hostilities, the parade and a later reception planned for President Shevardnadze were cancelled. However, I attended an "academic" meeting on the invitation of Redjeb Jordania, grandson of Noe (Noah) Jordania, Georgia's president during its first period of democratic rule in the early nineteenth century.

However, it was difficult to participate in a commemoration of Noe Jordania without first reflecting on the tragic changes that had taken place during the intervening decades. In the 1920s, Tbilisi, a city more than fifteen hundred years old that spans both banks of the Mtkvari River, was known as the "Paris of the Caucasuses." It was filled with intellectuals, artists, and poets. But in 1998, organizers of the anniversary meeting were embarrassed by the lack of toilet tissue in the bathrooms of the building where the meeting took place. The nineteenth-century structure, which once housed the Russian tsars' viceroys in the Caucasus, was not far from the location where General Radionov's soldiers killed the protesting Georgians on April 9, 1989. Some Georgians at the meeting openly referred to these killings as they expressed their pride in being Georgians. I could easily see that the wounds of that day almost ten years earlier remained fresh, while the lack of toiletries and other simple necessities reflected the continuing effects of societal trauma.

I saw these effects elsewhere, however minor they may have been. For example, one day my colleagues and I went to meet a professor at Tbilisi University. Hundreds of students were in the gardens. Almost all wore black clothes. It seemed to me that in Tbilisi almost everyone wore a black or dark-blue garment. I was told that black garments are customary rather than a sign of mourning, and during my later trips to Tbilisi, when the kidnapping of foreigners was taking place, some of my Georgian friends advised me to wear black or dark-blue garments in order to better blend into the crowds. I wondered why these students were not in their classrooms. I found one answer when we entered the main university building. The sewer lines had burst and the first floor of the huge building had been turned into a pool of liquid human waste. We had to walk through it in order to reach a stairway that would take us to the professor's office.

During the armed struggle between the followers of Gamsakhurdia and the opposition in 1991–1992, Tbilisi, especially public buildings on Rustaveli Avenue, were considerably damaged. I could now see first-hand what armed conflict, economic collapse, and the difficult adjustment from communism to democracy had done to the physical appearance of the city. Practically speaking, the city's infrastructure lay in complete disarray. Roads were filled with potholes, and electricity was cut off during the night in certain sectors for hours at a time because of fuel shortages. It seemed that every building in Tbilisi needed repair. I was told that during one winter the citizens did not have regular heat, and this led people to tear down their neighbors' wooden doors and windows and sometimes the trees for heating fuel. Later, in order to discourage further attacks on their property, most people did not repair the exterior of their houses. It was a surprising sight for me when I entered what appeared to be a terribly rundown house, only to find instead that the interior had fine antique furniture and beautiful, very valuable paintings.

When the evening darkness came over the city, Tbilisi looked simply beautiful. But the next morning, with the sun up, once more I could see how much it had been damaged. There were no stores with shining window displays, no neon signs. There was only one advertisement in the center of the city: a huge Coca-Cola display. It was an indication that capitalism was slowly filling the void left by communism. (It took several more years after this first trip for me to notice substantial change in the appearance of Tbilisi. For example, dozens of neon signs ultimately appeared on a street were adult entertainment was being offered.) But the people went about their business. It is amazing how people can adjust to tragedy, at least on the surface.

Signs of the conflict were present in other ways, too. For example, Hotel Iveria, a high-rise building that stands in the center of Tbilisi overlooking a square in which a statue of eighteenth-century leader King Erekle sits, immediately drew my eye. (On the other side of the square stands what I consider one of the ugliest buildings ever erected during the Soviet era. Residents of Tbilisi call it "Andropov's ears" because the building looks like it has two left and two right monumental concrete ears and because the late Soviet leader Yuri Andropov supposedly had large ears.) Countless shirts, pants, and bed sheets of every color hung from each window to be aired or dried. The once-posh hotel was filled to the rooftops with IDPs from Abkhazia—yet the building housed only a small fraction of the roughly three hundred thousand refugees in Georgia. It was like a huge flag of poverty and helplessness; a reminder of what people do to other people in the name of identity. Imagine going to Times Square in New York City, looking up at one of its tall buildings and seeing its gigantic frame wrapped in a flag that symbolized your people's humiliation, a flag of colors so bright that it could not be ignored.

We were interested in understanding the refugee problem from the viewpoint of the Georgian IDPs themselves. I had seen posters and signs saying "Refugees Go Home" hanging at various places in the city. These posters were ultimately removed. But many of the city's citizens feared that these Georgian refugees from Abkhazia would steal local jobs and ruin the city's existing norms. Although we were unable meet any of the refugees from the Hotel Iveria, we heard about another refugee camp that was filled with Georgians from Abkhazia. This was located, we were told, in a former resort area called the "Tbilisi Sea" about half an hour's drive from the center of Tbilisi. Yuri remembered the place. "There is a beautiful man-made lake there," he said. "I used to swim in this lake when I was a kid." Some of our Georgian hosts already had done some work with IDP children at the Tbilisi Sea. One day they took us there, and I met a family whose fascinating story I will begin to describe in the next chapter.

2 Three Generations at the Golden Fleece

Early on the clear Sunday afternoon of May 21, 1998, our Georgian hosts drove Yuri Urbanovich, CSMHI assistant director J. Anderson (Andy) Thomson, and me to the Tbilisi Sea, a huge man-made reservoir north of Tbilisi. We were told that there were three luxury hotels on the shores of the reservoir, establishments dating back to the heyday of Soviet times when it was a popular resort. We were also told that, of the three hundred thousand internally displaced Georgians, three thousand of them lived in these hotels, information that prepared us for the unbelievably crowded conditions we would find there. We would be visiting only one of these hotels, Okros Satsmisi, which in English means Golden Fleece. On one hand, this was an appropriate name since scholars believe that the mythical Greek hero Jason and his Argonauts found the fabled Golden Fleece in what is today Georgia. On the other hand, while Greek legends described Georgia as a fabulously wealthy land where skill in metal working far exceeded those in Europe, modern Georgia and especially the hotels of Tbilisi Sea were a far different place.

After driving from the center of Tbilisi for thirty minutes or so, the car turned a corner and began descending a hill. Then I saw the Tbilisi Sea. The reservoir's water appeared blue and calm, and I could understand why Yuri, as a child, enjoyed swimming in it. Then I saw a building that looked from a distance like a resort hotel. As we came closer to it, it became clear that it was a rundown place, exhibiting poverty and neglect. A huge metal circular sign attached to its eastern wall, which read "Okros Satsmisi" in the Georgian alphabet, looked completely out of place on this eight-story building, an incongruous symbol of affluence and comfort on a structure whose glory was now gone. We passed the eastern wall and parked in a parking lot in front of the building. The front door was gone, replaced by a huge hole in the wall. Windows were broken and the entire

35

place lacked paint. A big hall beyond the entrance was empty except for a few children playing. On the left side of the hall a stairway to the upper floors had a loose railing and damaged steps.

Between 1989 and 1994 in the Republic of Georgia, net material production fell between 70 and 80 percent, one of the sharpest declines among the former Soviet republics. In the early 1990s, employment declined almost 30 percent, and in the spring of 1993 the open unemployment figure was 8.4 percent. Prices, however, kept rising. In 1992 they rose, on the average, 900 percent. In 1994 monthly inflation reached 60 percent. At the same time, a state university professor earned the equivalent of about $5 a month, though a secretary in a private firm could earn even more—about $30 a month. With a vast majority of the population struggling to survive, Georgians perceived the refugees as a burden on the economy. The refugees, in turn, held onto the illusion that they would return to their considerably more comfortable lives in Abkhazia.

After the 1994 ceasefire in Abkhazia, Georgia's economy began to improve. A new stabilization program reduced the budget deficit from 26 percent of the GDP in 1993 to an impressive four percent in 1997. With this, "Refugee Go Home" signs practically disappeared, but the economy was still fragile, and on-and-off bloody skirmishes still took place at the border between Georgia and Abkhazia. Few gave up hope of returning to Gali. The refugees from Abkhazia had organized themselves, with the approval of the Shevardnadze government, into a paramilitary force. When new conflicts broke out they would fight Abkhazians for several days or weeks, with each mini war resulting in casualties. These skirmishes would not be reported in the *New York Times* or *Washington Post*, but they were certainly keeping open the wounds of Georgians—especially Georgian IDPs—and Abkhazians. By 1998 the renewed fighting had obviously retraumatized the IDPs, and on Sunday, May 21 of that year, activities we witnessed in the Golden Fleece parking lot reflected these reopened wounds.

Two military vehicles were parked in front of the rundown entrance of the hotel. Some eight men, dressed in clean paramilitary uniforms, stood beside their vehicles. The leader of this combat group was a serious man about five-feet tall, well-built, and strong. His wrinkled face reflected a certain wisdom and determination. He was introduced to us as Mamuka Kachavara. With the help of our interpreters he told us that he was very busy, but he would take time to talk with us, so we went to a small room on the right side of the hall behind the entrance. Mamuka told us that he was forty-five years old and from Gagra, a city in Abkhazia near the Russian border, north of the Gali region. Besides being a well-known soccer player, he had been a major in the Abkhazian "police force," a kind of internal security force during the Soviet era. He and some younger men in the parking lot, as well as many other IDPs from the other hotels at the Tbilisi Sea and elsewhere, were preparing to go to the border and fight, as they had done in the past whenever there were hot conflicts at the border. Even though he did not personally know Georgians who were under attack in the Gali region—a seven- or eight-hour drive away—this did not matter. Mamuka was ready to give his life for the cause.

Mamuka told us that before he became an IDP he and his family had a house in a section of Gagra where both ethnic Georgians and ethnic Armenians had lived. He had gotten along with ethnic Abkhazians in Gagra and had many Abkhazian friends. He nostalgically recalled how in 1981 the Tbilisi soccer team won the Cup Winners' Cup in Europe. He had watched the game at an Abkhazian friend's house where they all drank wine and sang Georgian songs. But things were different now. Abkhazians had forced him and his family to flee from their home in order to give Abkhazia a purer Abkhazian identity. He knew that in the name of identity Abkhazians would kill him and in the name of identity he, in turn, could kill them, even though he did not wish to do so.

He explained to us that during Soviet times, there were three languages in Abkhazia: Russian, Abkhazian, and Georgian. As a young man Mamuka had gone to a Georgian-Russian school. As an adult, Mamuka had noticed discrimination by Abkhazians in Gagra toward Georgians who worked at the police department. He said that it was difficult to get a promotion if one was not Abkhazian. As the end of the Soviet Union neared and as ethnic tensions escalated, he heard Abkhazians say, "The time will come when we'll force you to leave this place." He had "smelled" war before it began.

In 1992, after the eruption of ethnic conflict, Abkhazians burned the home that had taken Mamuka twenty years to build. The house had been built in Gagra on the same lot where his father's house had stood. His father was a police officer and had died when Mamuka was only nine. His mother, left with little, worked hard during Mamuka's childhood in order to provide for him. After fleeing Gagra, what pained him most was the fact that his mother was still there. Eventually, she would also become a refugee and later die in Tbilisi. I got the impression that Mamuka held Abkhazians responsible for his mother's death. He had asked for their help in protecting her and had been betrayed.

Mamuka informed us that his family—his wife Dali, their three children, and his wife's parents—like others at the three hotels in the Tbilisi Sea area, were IDPs well before the fury of the war descended on the Gali region. Because of this, some considered them less traumatized than the refugees who left Abkhazia in the middle of the real war. Nevertheless, Mamuka took part in the war and saw unimaginable things, such as corpses dismembered by the enemy. "Seventy years of Soviet rule disconnected me from any deep belief in religion," he said, adding, "I can't find answers in religion. I don't have nightmares, but I am very surprised that I don't have them. I just don't speak about the terrible things I've seen." In 1993 he suffered a severe chest wound and head injury from which he recovered. After this he joined his family at the Golden Fleece. Having been given a job in Tbilisi's police force, he considered himself and his family luckier than other refugees who were mostly without jobs. I understood that government funds given to the IDPs totaled $5 per person per month.

Though he was hesitant to open up to us further, Mamuka's hand gestures indicated that he was full of emotion. What else could I expect from a man who was preparing to go to war? Maintaining control of himself and those he would lead was paramount. Looking back I am still amazed that Mamuka agreed to talk to strangers on his way to "protect Georgians in the Gali region." He was in a hurry to leave and, given the external circumstances, we could not expect this dignified man to let us delve further into his internal world. We thanked him, and he quickly joined the other men who gathered in front of Okros Satsmisi on their way to the Gali region. The men, all younger than Mamuka, looked to him for guidance and direction. Mamuka was their leader.

Some women in the parking lot watched as Mamuka and his men departed. I noticed a thin woman with fair skin and reddish hair cut in a short bob. (I learned later that she was a Mengrelian, a tribe of Georgians from the Gagra area whose members often have red hair). She was beautiful, but she appeared to be carrying an invisible load. I was told that she was Dali, Mamuka's wife. When she was introduced to us she was able to smile and maintain a kind disposition. But I sensed that she was very anxious. She kept saying, "What can I do? My oldest son also wants to go to fight!" She then added that she too wanted to go to the Gali region and that she wished they would allow her to. It was not clear to me why she would want to go to a war zone. Was it her patriotism, her worry about her husband and son being in harm's way, her separation anxiety, or all of the above that motivated her to express such a wish?[7] Dali accompanied us to the room where we had talked to her husband earlier and told us her own story.

Dali, like her husband Mamuka, was born in Gagra to an intellectual family. She was the oldest of three siblings, and her father, Nodar Khundadze, was a well-known journalist who had published many books. Dali was born in a Georgian neighborhood in Gagra and attended a Georgian school there.[8] Since her parents were strict, she was never allowed to wander from her neighborhood and therefore had no lasting or psychologically meaningful experiences with ethnic Abkhazians while growing up. She would later become a teacher and, after a short first marriage, she married the popular soccer hero, Mamuka. She was very aware of Mamuka's emotional investment in building their home in Gagra, a house she loved.

In the 1970s, Dali sensed the existence of ethnic tensions. Shevardnadze, then a Soviet official, even came to Abkhazia to help calm things, promising to punish individuals who were actively suppressing others. Tensions continued nonetheless. The Writer's Union, of which Dali's father was a member, was divided into Georgian and Abkhazian groups, and a new Abkhazian university and Abkhazian television station were opened. Abkhazians were able to demonstrate their alliance to their own large-group identity more openly within the Soviet Union. In 1979, Dali was working as a teacher when the school principal, an Abkhazian, ordered all books written in Georgian be collected and, according to Dali, burned. She said that the principal was acting according to the wishes of ethnic Abkhazians who held all the top governmental positions in that part of the Soviet Union.

Dali recalled the day she and her children became IDPs. It was September 20, 1992, five years and nine months before I met her for the first time. Gagra was lost in October 1992. Mamuka, who had gone to fight, urged Dali and the children to flee Gagra before the war got even worse. A Georgian helicopter flown by a Ukrainian pilot was already evacuating other Georgians from the city. Since he knew Mamuka, the pilot agreed to fly Dali and the children to safety. She recalled that they only had fifteen minutes to prepare for their departure. She did not even have time to take her jewelry. The rush with her children—the youngest one was eleven at the time—to the soccer field where the helicopter had landed, and the flight to Sukhumi, remained vivid in Dali's mind. While running to the soccer field they saw burned cars and dead bodies. "So many people got killed, thank God we were able to stay alive," Dali said. In Sukhumi, the capital of Abkhazia, help was available to take the fleeing

Georgians to the safety of the Tbilisi Sea. Left behind in Gagra, Mamuka fought alongside fellow Georgians before rejoining his family.

After having carried Dali and her children to safety, on a return flight to Gagra, the helicopter was shot down and the Ukrainian pilot was killed. I would later learn about the impact of this incident on Dali's psyche, as I will describe in the next chapter. During my first talk with Dali, she mentioned that the most significant event of their escape was her conscious decision not to take her internal passport with her. As I reported earlier, during Soviet times everyone had an internal passport on which one's ethnicity was written. Dali feared that, in case of trouble or capture by Abkhazians, her passport would identify her as the daughter of Nodar Khundadze. Dali's father had been involved in protesting the treatment of Georgians in Abkhazia and in promoting nationalistic feelings among Georgians living there. Khundadze was in fact hiding out and Dali believed Abkhazians were actively searching for him before they fled. At one point the Abkhazians apparently captured at gunpoint an old Georgian man who they mistook to be her father, but released him when they discovered their mistake. Although Dali's married surname of Kachavara was listed on her passport, she said that in Gagra everyone knew that she, the wife of Mamuka the popular soccer player, was Khundadze's daughter.

I wondered why during our first meeting Dali told me so much about the internal passport that she had left behind. Then I suddenly realized that leaving behind her passport symbolically came to mean leaving her identity behind—her identity as a Georgian woman who had grown up in Gagra with her family, married a popular soccer star, and lived in the home that her husband had spend half his life building on land left to him by his father. She said that she felt she had no identity as a refugee, and this induced in her a sense of shame. "When I go to a bank in Tbilisi, they ask for my identity. I tell them my name and they do not believe me," she added. She informed me that if she had an "identity," she would be eligible for financial help from the IDP funds. In order to prove who she was and to get a temporary identification card, Dali would have to go to court in Tbilisi—but so far, Dali had refused to do so. She said that she was ashamed of telling people she had no identity. I suddenly realized that her internal psychological process prohibited her from going to court. As an IDP she certainly needed any money she could get. But economic gains were strikingly secondary to her wish to hold on to her lost identity. It was because of her identity that she and her family were banished from Gagra by Abkhazians.

Instead of degrading her "Gagra identity," one that caused her so much trouble, Dali was firmly holding on to it. I have seen this phenomenon elsewhere in the world, such as in Palestine, where ethnic groups are humiliated and under stress. To be subjected to humiliation and other hardships paradoxically increases victims' investments in their societal or large-group identities. I learned from Dali that there were many others in the Tbilisi Sea area lacking their internal passports and therefore their identities. All, according to Dali, found it "very humiliating" to go to court and receive "new" identities.[9]

When I first met Mamuka and Dali, their oldest son at home, Valery, was twenty-two. Another son, Aleco, was eighteen, and their daughter, Tamuna, was seventeen. I did not see the children in the parking lot or inside the Golden Fleece, but Dali did share the fact that she spent some of her time watching the refugee kids playing war. I was not surprised to hear this since I had seen such a phenomenon elsewhere—in the Turkish enclave of Nicosia, Cyprus, for example, when a war-like situation existed in 1968.[10] During and soon after wars children create their own symbolic weapons and play war. This is one way they try to control their feelings of helplessness; by becoming "soldiers" themselves they attempt to turn passivity to assertion and to control their anxieties. Dali said she did not like to watch kids playing war. She did not wish to be reminded of people killing other people. As is typical for many traumatized adults, she and Mamuka did not speak about their own emotions concerning events in Abkhazia and were silent about their personal trauma in front of their own children. But one day Dali was watching Russian television and witnessed her family house in Gagra being burned to the ground by Abkhazians. Then she saw their family's black dog, Charlie, wandering around the ruins. She broke down and sobbed until she was exhausted.

Unlike her husband, Dali said that she had frequent nightmares about what had happened to them in Abkhazia. Then she proceeded to report a vivid dream she had two nights previously, when Mamuka told her he would once more go to war. In the dream she was in Gagra visiting a woman who lived in their old neighborhood, a section of the city where both ethnic Georgians and ethnic Armenians had lived. The woman in the dream was an Armenian. In the dream this woman was crying because her husband—an Armenian dentist—had been shot to death.

Then Dali told me the story of this dentist. He was one of Mamuka's best friends. After ethnic tensions started to become hot in Gagra, one day Abkhazians kidnapped the Armenian dentist while he was walking in the neighborhood, forced him into a car, and took him away. Many people witnessed this event. Dali and Mamuka later learned that Abkhazians forced the dentist to fight for them and kill Georgians. In her dream, Dali did not know how to react to the news of the dentist's death. She felt sad that an old friend of her husband was dead, but she also thought that she should not care about the news, because the dentist, after all, was killing Georgians. She woke up from her sleep puzzled.

As a psychoanalyst I am accustomed to hearing my analysands' dreams. But people on my analytic couch give "free associations" to their dreams. This helps me to understand hidden meanings these dreams express. I am careful not to pay too much attention to the surface—what psychoanalysts call "manifest"—content of dreams. But an experienced psychoanalyst sometimes can guess what the manifest content of a dream stands for. When she reported this dream to me, I thought that she was superimposing her own expected predicament onto others. Dali dreamt that someone else was grieving over a dead husband, but in reality she was the one who feared Mamuka might soon die in war. She was also unconsciously angry at Mamuka for making her anxious by taking up arms. I was not going to tell Dali what had come to my mind, but I was delightfully surprised when she interpreted her dream herself and told me things that were very similar to my own thoughts. I was dealing with a very intelligent and psychologically minded woman.

Two days later we were at Okros Satsmisi again. Dali met us at the entrance and took us to her apartment on the sixth floor on the far west side of the building. We carefully climbed up the broken stairway. Inside, the floor plan of the Golden Fleece was like any typical hotel—long hallways lined on both sides by doors. But that is where the similarity ended. The hallways on each floor were cluttered with countless items—old pots and pans, stoves, jars of various sizes, wooden beams, metal containers, and so on.

Having visited other refugee sites, I was not surprised. Refugees regress to and create what psychoanalysts call an "oral and/or anal" world. They collect things as if they want to be sure that they will have enough "milk" for a future rainy day, and they pile up things as if they were piling up human waste material to express their helpless rage for the world to see. Although there may have been an intended use for some of the collected things, and the residents of the Golden Fleece certainly did not have enough money to clean up their environment, I believed that they were also angry and that they spoiled the place they lived in as if to send a message to "mother earth," who no longer took care of them.[11]

The apartment that Dali, Mamuka, and their children lived in was once a typical hotel suite with a kitchenette, bathroom, and some hotel furniture. A small area served as both a living room and dining room. It contained an old wooden table, a closet, and three chairs, but otherwise looked bare. A picture of Jesus was nailed on the wall. An old blanket hanging from the ceiling separated this room from the couple's bedroom, in which stood their single bed—in fact, it was a cot. On the opposite side of the living room a door opened onto a very small kitchen and a balcony, which was cluttered with various items. From a big window in the living room, behind the items on the balcony, I could see the Tbilisi Sea. In the hotel's heyday this might have been a preferred suite, but there was obviously not enough space for five persons to sleep comfortably here. Later I learned that Dali's father and mother lived in an apartment on the seventh floor just above the one we were visiting, and I understood that the children often slept upstairs.

What was so unique about this apartment was the existence of a most precious object: an old, pale-yellow telephone standing alone on the wooden table. Dali told us that this was the only telephone for the three thousand IDPs at the three hotels in the Tbilisi Sea area. I knew at once that, indeed, Mamuka and Dali were the leaders of this refugee community. Their living room was a kind of command center. When Mamuka and other partisans from the Tbilisi Sea area were involved in miniwars, the wives would come to Mamuka and Dali's apartment and make calls to learn news of their husbands. Dali said that she had been extremely busy with other wives since we had last seen her and that she had not slept the night before. She looked very tired, but insisted on making Turkish coffee for us, which she served with some biscuits. It is a tradition for Georgian families to indulge their guests with coffee and food. Even under these stressful conditions, Dali made no exception, but we kept our visit short.

The miniwar lasted less than a week, but had disastrous consequences for many Georgians. We learned of them from a couple of our Georgians hosts, both psychologists, who had gone to Zugdidi, on the Georgian side of the Gali region, to offer help to a new wave of refugees. For many of them it was their second traumatization. They had earlier been forced to leave the Gali region, but then were allowed to return to their homes, and now were refugees again. The chance of returning again was grim, and the whole city of Zugdidi was once more turned upside-down. Returning refugees were housed in the city's main school building at a time when children were scheduled to take exams. Despite their own losses, many refugees had a renewed sense of guilt for being a burden on the residents of Zugdidi. The Georgian government was helpless. They did not want to start or, for political or military reasons, could not start a new, full-scale war. Shevardnadze's government ordered paramilitary forces, including Mamuka and his men, to return to their homes at refugee camps or places like the Tbilisi Sea.

I went back to the Golden Fleece once more during our first visit to Tbilisi in 1998. My interpreter, a Georgian psychologist named Manana Gabashvili, and I entered the Kachavara apartment to find Mamuka, now wearing civilian clothes, sitting in the living room. I was shocked to see an expression of dejection and depression on his face. His body posture suggested a man resigned to a fate he did not desire. He said that he wanted to take Gali back but was ordered to return to Tbilisi without a fight. "I did not want to kill Abkhazians," he said, "but we should and can put Gali under Georgian control again." He felt betrayed. I was moved by his despair and depression.

Mamuka reported that he was getting ready to drive for seven hours to attend the funeral of a young IDP who had been killed by Abkhazians during this most recent miniwar. Mamuka told us the name of the young man and said that he had not known him personally. Yet Mamuka felt compelled to attend the funeral. Dali was in the room, too, sitting in silence and looking at Mamuka as he talked with us. When Mamuka had nothing more to say, Dali began speaking about the shame and humiliation felt among the IDPs at the Tbilisi Sea hotels. "I am, of course, happy to have my husband back," she said, "but not having secured the Gali region under Georgian control has induced in me an unbearable feeling of hopelessness." It was clear that Dali and Mamuka, like the second-wave refugees in Zugdidi, had been retraumatized. Dali expressed it in this way, "This is a wound that will remain open forever."

As Mamuka bade us farewell and left for the funeral, a distinguished man in his late seventies with white hair and moustache and bright blue eyes entered the apartment. He was dressed neatly and walked erect with pride. Dali told us that this man was her father, Nodar Khundadze, who lived above them on the seventh floor. It was obvious to us that Dali was very proud of her father. She informed us that Khundadze was a well-known writer. He had written thirty-five books, including six novels, and after he and his wife became refugees, he had taken up poetry. Khundadze wanted to know who Manana and I were and why we were visiting his daughter and son-in-law. He seemed to be satisfied by our explanation that Manana and I were interested in knowing about the lives of IDPs, but he appeared very uncomfortable speaking to us in such a physically run-down environment. I sensed that it hurt his pride. In turn, I felt very uncomfortable for making this dignified man feel this way. As I was wondering what to say or do to improve the atmosphere, Khundadze said, "I am ashamed of the newly created culture of beggars." I knew he was referring to the refugee children in Tbilisi who had become beggars, and I also suspected that they represented a solution for dealing with his own sense of humiliation. Instead of exposing himself further to such a horrible feeling, he was displacing his hurt self onto the beggars. Then I witnessed how this displacement also gave direction to his creative mind. Khundadze began reciting a poem he had written recently about child beggars. Manana translated it line by line:

> When I see your hand begging
> My dignity suffers.
> I cannot give you my soul (*suli*)
> Since it is impossible to give one's soul to someone.
> But, I have nothing left except my soul.
> I am pressing against prison bars.
> If you need my life,
> I can give it to you.

When Manana and I showed a genuine interest in his poem, Khundadze's mood changed. He seemed to be pleased. He informed us that soon after he became a refugee he began writing a poem each day about his and other IDPs' lives. It seemed that writing poetry was a lifeline to the dignity he had lost since becoming a refugee. He asked Dali to go upstairs and fetch his poems. Dali returned with a thick and neat folder that she held as if it were a precious and breakable heirloom. I sensed that her father's poems spoke for the whole family. As Khundadze took the folder from his daughter's hands he told us with sadness in his voice about the rich personal library he had left in Abkhazia. He believed that, like his life, it had been destroyed.

Khundadze opened the folder and took out the first sheet of paper. It was a poem that he had written and neatly typed the night before. He asked that Manana not translate it line by line. He wanted to read the poem in its entirety. I understood the reason for this; Khundadze wanted to express his full emotions. If the poem were translated line by line, and his reading of it interrupted, its emotional impact would be destroyed. Manana later translated the following:

I feel there is a betrayal in my motherland
Dishonesty wins
I am leaving all that I have here
I am coming to you, the sun.
Everything around me is in darkness
I do not see a thing
A snake is biting me bitterly
And, is achieving its betraying aim
We could not realize what was happening
Everything appeared to be confused
But, I know the enemy is in Tbilisi
Oh! Oh! Let my enemy's life to be short
I see my motherland's suffering from betrayal
Oh, the devil wins
Depression conquers my soul
I pray you, the sun, help us.

What Mamuka and Dali felt about the loss of the Gali region and their inability to take it back during the last miniwar came alive in Khundadze's poem and in the way he read it with such sadness. There was a silence in the room after the poem was read. I sensed that Manana and I were no longer strangers to Khundadze. Dali brought us Turkish coffee and Khundadze, now sitting on a chair, proceeded to give us his version of events in Abkhazia. He believed that the present Georgian government had betrayed them by turning the partisan fighters back at the border. Dali, who had campaigned for Shevardnadze during the presidential election, joined her father in once more voicing her disappointment, helplessness, and feeling of betrayal.

I also learned more about the family. Khundadze had three children and eight grandchildren. His son's family had left Abkhazia long ago and were not refugees, but his youngest daughter and her family were also IDPs living at Okros Satsmisi. That day I briefly met three of his grandchildren. Valery and Aleco, two handsome young men, had to leave right away for some school activity. They told me that they were attending college in Tbilisi and were majoring in business. I also met Dali's daughter, Tamuna, who had recently turned seventeen.

Tamuna was a little overweight and looked depressed. I asked if Manana and I could speak to her privately. After the others left the apartment, Tamuna told us that she was going to a nearby high school. Her classmates included refugee children as well as long-time local residents.

Tamuna clearly described how, between the two groups of students, there was a palpable sense of "us" and "them." Tamuna was well aware of her refugee status and the sense of shame that went along with it. As she spoke, I realized that her way of dealing with the situation was to apply herself to her studies.

In a low voice Tamuna told us that her father's most recent visit to the war zone had produced "familiar feelings" in her. For Tamuna, past events were very vivid. She spoke to us about their helicopter escape from Gagra. She had been terrified. She recalled crying and hearing the cries of a fellow passenger, a man whose son had just been killed. After we finished talking with Tamuna, Dali joined us. I thanked her and Tamuna for sharing their stories with me.

While we had gone to Tbilisi to try to develop a project that would open meaningful communications between Georgians and South Ossetian, the eruption of the miniwar in Gali made access to some government officials difficult. Everyone was busy and preoccupied with the recent events and feelings concerning them. But in coming to the Tbilisi Sea to learn about the problems of the IDPs, we had met a remarkable family. It dawned on me that my team and I would not be of any help to the three thousand refugees on the Tbilisi Sea if we tried to respond to their needs and wishes in general ways. But I thought that if we continued to develop a relationship with the Kachavara family, as well as with Nodar Khundadze, we might be able to provide some psychological support for them. I told Dali and Tamuna that I would most likely visit Georgia two or three times per year for some years to come. "Would you permit me," I asked them, "to come to see you during my future visits and spend some hours with you each time?" They said that they would like this very much and that they found me to be a kind person. After all, they said, no one from the outside world, from a far away place like the United States, had ever come to see them before.

I had a vague idea at the time that if I could play a role in changing this family's life for the better, they, in turn, might provide a model for positive change for other IDP families at the Tbilisi Sea. After all, I thought, the Kachavaras were the leaders of their community. The biggest proof of this was the pale-yellow telephone on the old wooden table in their bare living room.

3 Waiting Ten Years to Mourn or Not Mourn

After May 1998, I visited the Kachavara family roughly once every five
months until 2002. Manana Gabashvili usually accompanied me as a
professional coworker as well as an interpreter. On occasions when
Manana was not available, Jana Javakhishvili, another Georgian psychologist, joined me. Each time we spent at least half a day at the Kachavara
apartment, speaking mainly with Dali. If Mamuka or the children or
Nodar were around, we would also speak with them. I either conducted
separate "therapeutic interviews" with family members or talked with
them collectively. We also just sat around as guests and observed the family members interacting among themselves. Tamuna, who learned
English when she went to college, continued to communicate with me
after 2002 through e-mail.

During my second visit to the Golden Fleece, I met another important
member of the Kachavara family, Charlie, a black dog. Perhaps it would
be better to call him, "Charlie, the Second," since he was a "replacement
dog,"[12] the other Charlie having been left behind in Gagra when Dali and
her children rushed to the helicopter that took them to safety. The first
Charlie was the dog Dali glimpsed when she saw the burning of their
home on Russian television. Dali told me how she had become preoccupied with the fate of the first Charlie. Though it was very difficult to send
a message to a former neighbor in Gagra asking about the dog, after
Mamuka joined the family at the Tbilisi Sea he managed to do so. I think
that this neighbor, like the dentist and his wife, was an ethnic Armenian.
She informed the Kachavaras that Charlie had been hit by a car and killed.

The death of the first Charlie was a blow to Dali, as she explained to
me. During the initial months as IDPs, Mamuka and Dali used to talk
about their "one-year plan." They believed that ethnic problems in
Abkhazia would be resolved in a year, they would return to their homes,

and Mamuka would start rebuilding their house. At night they would lie in their bed whispering to each other, making plans to return to Gagra. As long as they had their family dog in Gagra they could easily keep their link to their home alive, even though their house had burned down. The first Charlie's death was a blow to their "one-year plan." Dali told me how she and Mamuka remained depressed until one day, early in their second year as IDPs, she saw a black street dog that looked exactly Charlie wandering around Golden Fleece. She knew at once that she had to have this dog as the family's new pet. Everyone in the family agreed with her and they brought the dog to their apartment, naming him Charlie.

I like dogs. When I first met the second Charlie I petted him, but I noticed that it was strange to have him in the Kachavaras' apartment. He was a medium-size dog and there didn't seem to be enough space in the living room when family members and guests such as Manana or Jana and me were around. Charlie was clean and he liked to lie down at Dali's feet. Dali's emotional attachment to the dog was very visible. I realized that Charlie's presence in the Kachavara apartment and the way he was treated by the family were important clues indicating that Dali and her family were perennial mourners and the dog himself was a living linking object.

To understand the Kachavara family members' internal psychological processes, one must first understand what mental health professionals mean by the terms trauma, perennial mourners, and linking objects. Personal trauma occurs when an external event or an accumulation of a series of events crowd and burden an individual's mind. In effect, the quantity of stimulus encountered is too great to be dealt with or assimilated in usual ways. During such trauma(s), the individual's mind is either flooded with intense anxiety; or just the opposite occurs, and the person senses the mind as paralyzed. Either way the person, while he or she may continue to perform certain tasks, experiences helplessness.[13] For example, even though Dali and her children were able to reach the helicopter, Dali was traumatized by the experience. Still, she was able to have logical thoughts about her internal passport (her identity card). After the traumatic event(s) is over, traumatized individuals often recall the traumatic event(s) in flashbacks, in dreams, and in perceptions of current life experiences. Or, they repeat the traumatic event in symbolic actions. They relive it again and again with a presumed—but unconscious—wish that one day they will master and assimilate the original overwhelming stimuli. Usually they do not succeed. Both Dali and Tamuna described to me how they often had flashbacks of the helicopter ride.

However, the concept of trauma, in reality, is more complicated than the above brief description. To simply label people as suffering from Posttraumatic Stress Disorder (PTSD) takes our attention away from an examination of individualized and specific responses to traumatic events. (See chapter 6 for a more detailed examination of PTSD.) Each individual's inborn potentials and previous experiences prepare or sensitize the person, and therefore every reaction to drastic events is different. Also, individuals' memories of other events, fantasies, wishes, and mental defenses against such wishes that become connected with the actual trauma change from individual to individual. In the long run, some people show more resilience[14] than others. For example, some people deal with trauma through creativity,[15] while others are doomed to repeat it in symbolic fashions or develop symptoms or new character traits. Still others separate and put their traumatized selves, in a sense, in an envelope (this is called dissociation) and go about behaving as if nothing has happened. But sometimes the traumatized self slips out of its envelope and dominates the rest of the individual's personality, asserting itself as if the individual has a new personality. So-called double or multiple personalities stem from childhood traumatic experiences that remained active despite attempts to psychologically encapsulate them.[16]

Traumatic events that IDPs such as Dali experienced come under the umbrella of shared trauma that are connected with ethnic sentiments and that activate large-group identity issues. Dali and her family members were not traumatized because of who they were as individuals; they were traumatized because they belonged to a certain specific ethnic group. Shared traumatic events, which are connected with large-group identity issues, are always contaminated with shame and humiliation.[17] When people are attacked by an enemy group and suffer, they also feel shame and humiliation. Such traumas are also accompanied by a combination of great emotional (abstract) and concrete losses. Sometimes these people only lose their sense of security and dignity, but other times such emotional losses are accompanied by concrete losses, such as the loss of relatives or friends, homes, dogs, and even gardens. In the case of shared trauma, reactions to being hurt by the enemy at individual, familial, and regional levels spread over the entire large group. If the shared trauma creates a refugee problem, those who are not directly affected show empathy for the refugees from their own side. But when refugees, such as the Georgian IDPs, become a burden or are perceived to be a burden to other people of the same group, we may see splits in the large group. Renewed hostility with the outside enemy, however, can easily erase such splits.

Refugees who are forced to leave their usual environments are too help-less and at the same time too angry to mourn what they have lost because their trauma complicates the typical mourning process.

The loss of a psychologically important person or thing initiates grief and mourning. We know the stages a physical wound goes through as it heals if it does not become infected. Similarly, we know the stages of a psychological wound following a significant loss if it does not become complicated. In psychology literature grief and mourning are often not differentiated. The initial reactions to a loss are considered grief. A mourner, in a sense, keeps hitting his or her head against a wall—one that never opens up to allow the dead person or lost thing to return. The grief reaction includes, at one time or another, some or all the following signs: shortness of breath, tightness in the throat, a need to sigh, muscular limp-ness, loss of appetite, a sense of being in shock or pain, crying spells, denial of the loss, bargaining with God or fate to bring back what is lost, and splitting of ego function so that opposing perceptions and experi-ences can take place simultaneously. The last sign explains, for example, how even though a woman knows that her dead husband is lying in a coffin at a funeral home, she "hears" his car as it crunches the gravel in the driveway. In the end grief induces anger, which is a "healthy" indica-tion that the mourner is beginning to accept the fact that what is lost will not return. A typical grief reaction takes some months to disappear. In truth, there is no typical grief reaction, because the circumstances of a loss are varied, and because each individual has his or her own degree of internal preparedness to face significant losses.

To help explain Dali and her family's story of being refugees and expe-riencing many emotional and concrete losses, I will focus more on the mourning process rather than examine in detail various expressions of a grief reaction. Mourning is a more silent and internal phenomenon. It begins while an individual still exhibits grief, and then continues for years. The physical loss of a person or thing (a concrete thing such as a house or an emotional thing such as one's dignity) does not parallel the mental "burial" of the mental representation (a collection of many imag-es) of what had been lost. In fact, the physical loss (or even the threat of a physical loss) turns the adult mourner's attention to the mental images of the lost person or thing.[18] The adult's mourning process refers to the sum of the mental activities the mourner performs in reviewing and deal-ing with the mental representation of the lost person or thing. This includes an experience of anger during the mourning process. This anger is different than the anger of the acute grieving process. During the latter, the mourner is angry because the loss, which the mourner strongly wishes to reverse, is not reversed. During the mourning process, as the acceptance of the loss grows stronger and stronger, the mourner experiences a narcissistic wound inflicted by the lost person or thing. By dying or disappearing, the lost person or thing has caused a painful process that the mourner has to go through. Usually, the mourner is not aware of this anger directed toward the lost person or thing; their anger is directed toward someone or something else. For example, the Kachavaras and other IDPs were angry with Shevardnadze every time a new miniwar retraumatized them and they reexperienced their losses.

As long as we live we never lose the mental representation of significant others or things, even when they are lost in the physical world. If a mourning process is completed, for all practical purposes, we make the mental representation of the lost person or thing "futureless."[19] Such a mental representation is no longer utilized to respond to our wishes; it has no future, no ongoing or perpetuating influence. A young man stops fantasizing that a wife who has been dead for some time will give him sexual pleasure, for example. Or a woman stops wishing to boss her underlings at a job from which she had been fired years before. We "bury" the mental images of a lost person or thing when we manage to make them futureless. During the mourning process the mourner reviews, in piecemeal fashion, the images of what has been lost, and in doing so is able to keep aspects of the lost person or thing's images within his or her own self. In psychoanalysis we refer to this as the mourner's identification with characteristics or functions of the lost person or thing. For example, a year or so after his father's death, a footloose young man becomes a serious industrialist just as his dead father used to be. Similarly, an immigrant who has lost his country may create a symbolic representation of his homeland in a painting or a song, indicating that this mourner has internalized and maintained certain images of the land he lost.

However, complications may occur during the mourning process. One of the common reasons for complications is the contamination of the mourning process with reactions to a trauma. When a loss is associated with experiences of helplessness, passive and therefore ineffective rage, shame, and humiliation, the mourning process is accompanied by other psychological tasks, such as turning helplessness into activity, transforming passive rage into assertion, reversing shame and humiliation, and even idealizing victimhood if circumstances do not allow the person to carry out the other tasks. A loss itself may be traumatic in its own right, especially when it is sudden, unexpected, or associated with violence, such as murder or suicide. But above and beyond the loss itself, the combination of a meaningful loss with actual trauma accompanied by experiences of helplessness will complicate the mourning process in a serious way.

Complications in a mourning process lead to various outcomes. Mourners may become depressed[20] or may become perennial mourners, doomed to carry their preoccupation with the mental images of what had been lost for decades to come and even until the end of their lives.[21] Perennial mourners experience their mourning without bringing it to a practical conclusion. There are degrees of severity with such a condition. Some perennial mourners live miserable lives. Others express their unending mourning in more creative ways, but even these people, when not obsessed with creativity, usually feel uncomfortable because they spend their energies on things that are gone and have less energy for actual and current life activities. Every day the perennial mourner is concerned with "bringing back to life" or "getting rid of once and for all" the lost person or thing. In one way of dealing with this unending preoccupation and avoiding the uncomfortable feelings associated with it, the perennial mourner utilizes certain inanimate objects or living beings to symbolize a meeting ground between the mental image of what had been lost and the mourner's corresponding self-image. I call such inanimate objects linking objects and such living beings living linking objects.[22]

A linking object may be a personal possession of the deceased, often something the deceased wore or used routinely, such as a watch. A letter written by a soldier in the battlefield before being killed may evolve into a linking object. Or, as happened in the Kachavara family, a pet may become a living linking object. Once an item or a pet truly evolves into a linking object or a living linking object, the perennial mourner experiences it as "magical."[23] The work of mourning is to examine, again and again, the mourner's relationship with the lost person or thing until such examinations are no longer urgent and no longer accompanied by hot feelings. It is an internal process. A perennial mourner, by having a linking object, removes the mourning process, to one degree or another, from an internal process and puts it "out there." By controlling the linking object or a living linking object, which is "out there," perennial mourners externalize their complicated mourning. Without being aware of it fully, they postpone the mourning process by giving the image of what was lost a new life in the linking object. But as I indicated, while having a linking object postpones the internal work of the mourning process, it also keeps hope alive for restarting and completing the mourning process at a future time.[24] Some mourners hide their linking objects in locked drawers or closets. What is important is the perennial mourner's need to know the linking object's whereabouts; it must be protected and controlled. I must add here that not every keepsake or memento that emotionally connects us to persons or things is a linking object. In fact, to have such mementoes and keepsakes gives our life experiences a sense of continuity and helps us maintain our sense of self.

As I mentioned, I sensed that the second Charlie was a living linking object for the Kachavara family, especially for Dali. (As I will explain later in this chapter, the real proof that the second Charlie actually was utilized as a living linking object would come when I witnessed Dali's reaction to this dog's death.) Other visible linking objects shared in the Kachavara family were Dali's father's poems, written daily, which were linking objects created by a mourner. Every morning family members would gather in Dali and Mamuka's apartment so that Nodar could read the poem he had written the day before. While he read his poem no one would speak. After he finished, other members of the family would make comments about the poem, the content of which, directly or indirectly, linked the family to their past in Abkhazia and to their emotional struggle to give up what they had lost physically or to keep the wish of regaining what was lost alive.

I noticed other phenomena (linking phenomena) that constantly connected the members of the Kachavara family to the images of their lives in Abkhazia. A linking phenomenon, unlike an inanimate or animate linking object, is not visible like Charlie the dog was, but functions in the same way. Tamuna brought an example of a linking phenomenon to my attention during my visit to Georgia in the fall of 1998. When I visited the Kachavara family Dali took Manana and me aside and asked me, as a psychiatrist, to help her daughter lose some weight. She pointed to the reservoir, the Tbilisi Sea, through the window over their cluttered balcony and said, "Many people swim there during the summer and even now. I push Tamuna to go and swim there, too. She always refuses. If she swims regularly she will keep her weight down. What should I do?" Later, when Manana and I were alone with Tamuna, I told Tamuna about her mother's concern. She gave me a look as if she were surprised that I could not already know her reason for not swimming in the Tbilisi Sea. She said, "When we were in Gagra I loved to go to the Black Sea and swim. If I swim in the Tbilisi Sea I will hurt my memory of the Black Sea. By not swimming in the Tbilisi Sea, I keep alive my idea that one day I will return to Gagra."

I found Tamuna to be a remarkable young lady. Like her mother she was intelligent and had an uncanny understanding of her own psychology. Unlike her mother, Tamuna preferred to remain silent most of the time, and she appeared to be somewhat withdrawn and depressed. But, whenever I spoke to her alone (of course, in the presence of Manana or Jana) she would come alive. She informed me that her refusal to swim in the Tbilisi Sea and in fact her avoidance of any other physical exercise had another meaning. Whenever she slept in the living room, which was separated from her parental "bedroom" only by a curtain, she would hear Mamuka and Dali whispering about not having enough money to buy food. They were worried about not being able to feed their children properly. They did not express their worries openly. But Tamuna knew their secret fears. She told me, "By staying a little overweight, every day I tell my mother, 'Look Mom! I am not hungry; in fact I am overfed!'" I was moved to hear this. Tamuna was communicating with her mother through the appearance of her body and not through verbalizing her wish to ease her parents' pain. With Tamuna's permission I told Dali why Tamuna insisted on being a little overweight. I suggested that it would be better if they spoke about their family concerns openly. Dali still perceived Tamuna as a scared little girl running to the helicopter to escape possible death. I told Dali that Tamuna now was seventeen, that she wanted to be seen as a grown up, and that she could tolerate hearing about money matters.

Some months later I was in Georgia again. Part of me wanted to bring the Kachavara family gifts, such as food items, that they could not afford to buy. I decided against doing so. I thought that such gifts would embarrass them. I wanted to respect their cultural expectation that a visitor brings gifts, but at the same time I did not wish to appear as someone richer and superior to them. Finally I came up with a compromise: I would bring gifts that they could give to the IDP children at the three former hotels. Thus, I arrived with a bag full of pens, pencils, writing pads, and other school items to give to Dali. She, in turn, could pass around these items to children. During this visit Dali told me how she and Tamuna were communicating verbally and sharing their family concerns. Tamuna already had lost some weight and she was smiling. When they addressed me they called me "our Vamık."

Manana or Jana always knew when my team and I would arrive in Georgia and they would call Dali and inform her of the date. Thus, Dali and other members of her family would be waiting for me to visit them. When I went to their apartment and began my individual therapeutic interviews, I usually opened the conversation by saying something like this: "Well, you were aware that I would be visiting you today. What dream did you have last night to report to me today?" My aim was to remind them that I was always interested in their internal worlds. They always had a dream or two to report. During the first year or so the "manifest" content of their dreams was similar to that in Khundadze's poems about beggars and people in Tbilisi (meaning the father figure Shevardnadze) keeping them helpless and provoking them to remain angry. As a psychoanalyst I could hear a reflection of typical refugee oral and anal concerns. By oral I am referring to symbols and references in their dreams that reflected a dread of remaining hungry, a wish to be fed, the displacement of their own neediness onto others, and the "chewing up" of the enemy. By anal I am referring to symbols and references I noticed in their dreams that reflected a wish to collect many items (psychoanalytically speaking, reflecting the mental image of constipation) and to make a messy pile or to explode and blow up things (reflecting an aggressive bowel movement). In the dreams that they "had for me" the night before my visiting them, sometimes I appeared in an undisguised fashion and sometimes as a visitor from outside their oral and anal worlds, a visitor who gave them nutrition or helped them blow up things without inducing guilt. No wonder, I thought, I became "our Vamık" to them.

I was aware that someone coming from a faraway place and showing genuine interest in them was important in mobilizing the Kachavara family members' internal orientation and in changing their interpersonal relationships. Dali informed me that she now had a group of Tbilisi Sea IDP ladies visiting her regularly. By identifying with me she would conduct "therapeutic" talks with them, tell them not to be so silent about their worries and to not keep secrets from their grown children. I was amused to hear that Dali would even ask these ladies about their dreams!

Within a year or so after I first met the Kachavara family, there was a significant change in the dreams Dali and Tamuna had the night before I visited them. It would have been very interesting to hear Mamuka's dreams, too. Unfortunately his work schedule at this time kept him away from the Tbilisi Sea and I could not talk with him. In Dali and Tamuna's new type of dreams I no longer brought goods to satisfy their oral and anal needy and aggressive wishes. The new dreams suggested what I called a re-oedipalization of their internal worlds. Oedipal concerns for girls involve a father figure giving them love and babies (of course in fantasy) and helping them feel good about their developing femininity.

Tamuna's dreams clearly changed from my (or my symbolic representation's) bringing her food to my bringing her a baby. In one dream she was putting a new dress on a baby girl, playing with her and making her laugh. Dali began dreaming that I would be sleeping in their apartment. As children we normally go through developmental stages as we grow. The classic psychoanalytic classification of these stages refers to a child moving from oral to anal and then genital and oedipal concerns that express struggles and solutions for internal issues. Trauma pushes refuges to pregenital fixations. My coming from outside and paying attention to them, I sensed, mobilized Dali and Tamuna's attempts to move up and relibidinalize their internal worlds. They would love themselves and have more self-esteem. This would initiate, I thought, a new and less frustrating adjustment to their still-miserable external conditions.

Dali had a dream and wish that when I visited Georgia I would sleep in their apartment, and she informed me that they should find a solution so that I could have a proper place to sleep since my sleeping next to her and Mamuka would not be proper. So, the Kachavara family, in late 1999, began to build a room for me. They called it "our Vamık's room." I said nothing to stop this because, psychologically speaking, I realized that building this room was related to libidinalization of their internal world—it was an outward expression of their desire to make the miserable more lovable. Since the Kachavara family's apartment was at the far end of the west side of Okros Satsmisi, they could wall off a section of the hallway and turn it into a ten-by-ten foot living space.

The building of "our Vamık's room" took a year. During my visits I noticed that the family was involved in a kind of "therapeutic play," repairing their external world and their corresponding inner worlds. The Kachavara family members were like Tamuna who, in one of her dreams, was putting a new dress on the baby I had "brought" her from America. "Our Vamık's room" was the Kachavara family's shared new baby, representing their sense of being "reborn" out of complicated mourning and depression. Psychoanalysts, especially those who work with children, have suggested that "play" is best described by its functions, and they consider the many ways children play to be attempts at finding solutions for conflicts, the establishment of ego mastery and creativity.[25] By naming the room after me, they kept my "therapeutic" image with them as they were involved in a year-long play. When I was at Okros Satsmisi they would not allow me to see their work on the room. They wanted me to wait and see the finished product. The door of the room that they were building was covered with a hanging cloth. They told me that they would add a fireplace to the room, and Mamuka spoke of how he would finish the floors with beautiful wood. Dali had a new dream in which she saw me sleeping in this room. I began imagining that "our Vamık's room" was going to be like a jewel in the middle of a garbage pile—an external expression of the relibidinalization of their internal worlds. I very much enjoyed listening to their description of the future room and seeing their excitement.

I also wondered why I invested so much in this family. Was I spending time with them only for my own academic interests and to collect data about the long internal adjustment to forced exile? From the beginning I was aware that there was more to my desire than simply the pleasure of being some help to the Kachavara family. Two stories they told me had connected me to them emotionally and made me identify with them. I did not tell them how these two stories were similar to things I had experienced in my own life. Sharing my past, I thought, might be a burden, since they certainly would wish to help me with my own old wounds and this might entail extra psychological work for them.

I was born on the Mediterranean island of Cyprus and left that part of the world just as an ethnic conflict between the Greeks and Turks on the island became nasty. Before I came to the United States in 1957, I shared an apartment in Ankara, Turkey, for more than two years with another Cypriot Turk. Both of us were attending medical school there. Three months after I arrived safely in the United States, my former apartment companion was shot to death by Cypriot Greek terrorists while he was visiting his family in Cyprus. He was not killed because of a personal vendetta. He was killed in the name of identity. He was an up-and-coming young man in the Turkish community in Cyprus, and he was killed because he belonged to that community, and because the enemy wanted to hurt and humiliate the opposing large group and inflict a wound in a collective sense—that is, in the name of their own large group. When I learned of my friend's death while I was an intern at Lutheran Deaconess Hospital in Chicago, I experienced survivor guilt.[26] Also, on many occasions, and for months at a time over a period of many years, I could not get in touch with my own family members who were forced to live in a Turkish enclave on Cyprus that was surrounded by their enemies. Finally, in 1968, I was able to go back to Cyprus after the political-military situation improved. While there, I visited my poet friend, Özker Yashın.

On December 25, 1963, a day that the Cypriot Turks came to call "Bloody Christmas," Özker's wife and mother were captured by the Cypriot Greeks, as were most of the other Turks living in their mixed village near the capital city, Nicosia. Özker escaped capture himself because on the day of the seizure he had gone to the Turkish section of the capital. On the night of his wife's captivity she gave birth to a son in the Nicosia General Hospital, which was then under Cypriot Greek control. The newborn child was left in a crib with other Turkish infants who happened to be there at the time and placed in a room that also served as a morgue for Turkish casualties. Finally, a British nurse, shocked at this situation, managed to separate the living infants from the dead Turks. Özker did not know for some time if his wife and his mother had survived their capture, but they were reunited on January 10, along with the newborn child, who was named "Savash" (meaning "war" in English) because of the circumstances of his birth.

On January 13 my poet friend wrote a poem addressed to his son:

With a bullet from a lowly person
You could have died, Savash,
Before you were born:
You would die in your mother's belly
Without getting to know
The miracle called life
Thanks to which you were saved
You were born. . .
You might not have been born.[27]

Between January 13 and March 10, 1963, the poet wrote a series of additional poems addressed to his son. They were published under the title *Letters to my Son Savash*. Along with Özker's two previously published volumes,[28] these letters constituted a poetic history of the Cyprus struggle seen from the point of view of a Cypriot Turk. In fact, for all practical purposes, my friend had written a poem a day for some years. When I visited him he gave me copies of all three volumes. Some days later as I read them I was moved.

Eleven years later, in the spring of 1975, I spent some time with young Savash when, once more, I was visiting Cyprus. After seeing a corpse in a nearby orchard, another victim of the on-and-off Cypriot Turkish-Cypriot Greek struggle, eleven-year-old Savash developed an odd sensation in the skin of his face. His skin felt dry, and he thought that if he scratched it, parts of his countenance would chip off as though it were the face of a stone statue. Talking with him, I realized that he had carried the burden of being a special symbol of the Cyprus struggle for as long as he could remember. At this time, I thought, he had turned into a "living statue," a kind of living linking object. I was able to help Savash and his symptom disappeared.

When I heard that Nodar was writing a poem a day just as my friend Özker had done, I quickly identified the world of the Georgian IDPs with "my people's" world in Cyprus in the 1960s and 1970s. This was my first observable emotional link to the Kachavara family. The other story that intensely connected me to the Kachavara family and made me identify with them further had come from Dali when she told me about her seeing, by accident, the burning of their house and the first Charlie on a Russian television broadcast. In summer 1974, the Cypriot Turks once more faced an uncertain fate at the hands of the Greeks on the island. This time, however, the Turkish military intervened and controlled the northern part of the island, dividing it into de facto northern Turkish and southern Greek sectors. Of course, this war resulted in new tragedies and many people perished on both sides. But as I was living in the United States, I could not communicate with my family on the island. I had no idea what might be happening to them and I worried they might be killed during the war.

Then one late night I was watching television in my home in Charlottesville, Virginia, and suddenly, my mother's face, full of fear, appeared on screen. Next I saw one of my sisters and some of her neighbors. A reporter spoke and said that the television images were showing Cypriot Turks evacuating their homes because they were expecting to be attacked by Cypriot Greeks. My sister's house was (and still is) at the very border between the Turkish and Greek sections of Nicosia. I could not believe what I was seeing and hearing. I was shocked and felt guilty for being in a safe place, unable to help my mother, my sister, and "my people." I was also scared. After a while I thought that I had hallucinated the whole thing. The next morning the same television station repeated the news of the night before and showed the same pictures, and this time my wife also saw it. My defense—my belief that I had hallucinated—against my troublesome ideas and feelings crumbled, and I was left at the mercy of my fears. When I heard Dali talk about seeing her home burning and the first Charlie running around on the television screen, I felt very close to her. Obviously, my wish to be helpful to Dali and her family included aspects of my wish to work through my own unfinished issues that were related to traumas from my past.

The next time I went to Georgia, I was expecting to see the finished "our Vamık's room." The morning after my arrival in Tbilisi I met Jana who gave me the bad news. She informed me that some weeks before my coming to Georgia Dali had a stroke and that she was in very poor health. Jana added, "I am sorry!" This had happened after the Kachavara family had finished structurally completing "our Vamık's room." Jana had seen Dali. Apparently she had lost weight and she did not look good. She also told me that a Georgian doctor was called to Okros Satsmisi to examine Dali and it was he who had diagnosed her condition as a manifestation of a cerebral stroke. I was dumbfounded and insisted on changing my schedule to go to Okros Satsmisi right away. Jana and my other Georgian friends told me that there would be not much that I could do since Dali was having difficulty speaking. But at my continued insistence they gave up and drove me to the Tbilisi Sea.

Dali was lying on a cot that was placed in the living room area. She looked pale and sick, like a ghost wasting away. I pulled a chair next to her and she gave me a faint smile and told me that some weeks ago the second Charlie had died from natural causes. From what I could tell, her mind was working fine. Even though I had not performed any neurological examinations in my psychoanalytic practice for decades, I quickly realized that Dali had not had a cerebral stroke. Instead, she suffered from a very severe depression. I recalled that during nearly every one of my visits to the Tbilisi Sea there seemed to be a funeral ceremony in front of one of the three former hotels. I was told that in this community of IDPs, some men and women, "for no apparent reason," suddenly dropped dead. I had come to the conclusion that being a refugee and having depression was a deadly combination. I did not know what physiological or biological changes had begun in this place or how they had progressed to be fatal to its residents. Now Dali looked like she would soon be dead, too. But I was also pleased to recognize that she had not had a stroke and that she was able to tell me the reason for her severe depression—Charlie's death.

I asked all the others to leave Jana and me alone with Dali. They all left and Dali and I spent many hours talking (of course through Jana's help) without taking time to do anything else. I "interpreted" the meaning of Charlie's death to Dali. I explained that, without her living linking object, she could no longer postpone or control her mourning. She was forced to fully face her sadness and guilt over losing her beloved home in Gagra, the death of the pilot who had saved her and her children, and the loss of the first and second Charlie—in short, her previous life and identity. Slowly Dali told me of recent events and both of us could understand how she had replaced Charlie and how she and not the pet had become a living linking object for the rest of the Kachavara family. The weight of being a living linking object was killing her. She was performing all alone the task that a linking object or phenomenon provides.

The completion of "our Vamık's room" took place, by coincidence, just before the second Charlie died. Also at this time, Dali's yonger children were expanding their environment by leaving the settlement during the day to attend college. Before Charlie's death, Valerey married his girlfriend from the Tbilisi Sea area and Aleco was in love with another girl who was also an IDP. Dali felt that she was left outside these changes. As I will describe, the family had "assigned" her to carry their refugee identity burden. At this time the family had changed their one-year plan to return to Abkhazia to a five-year plan.

The completion of the room and the death of the dog also became connected with other identity-related events. The process that I call the "verification" of refugees' new identities as a continuation of their previous identities through psychologically significant others is crucial for a refugee's adaptation to his or her new environment. The members of the Kachavara family saw me as a significant other who had been performing such a verification process. Psychoanalysts would say that the members of the Kachavara family had developed a "positive transference" toward me. Two recent events further "verified" Nodar and Mamuka's identities as a continuation of their identities in Abkhazia.

Nodar, a prominent writer and journalist in Abkhazia before the war, received verification when the poems that he began writing at Tbilisi Sea were published in book form and were recognized as an important piece of literature. Dali also told me that Nodar was given an award for his book and that he was transformed by the experience. Dali knew that previously her father had been an angry man, but now she frequently saw him smiling.

Dali told me about a very significant event in her husband's life, too. Soon after the second Charlie's death, the Georgian Ministry of Internal Affairs organized a soccer match between local soccer players from Tbilisi and the Georgian IDP soccer players from Abkhazia to honor the memory of a Georgian player from Abkhazia who had been tortured and killed by Abkhazians. Dali explained how Mamuka took part in this soccer match and scored two goals, establishing himself as a hero among the spectators. More important, the authorities gave him a trophy inscribed with his name and the date of the match.

At this point, Dali managed to get up and escorted Jana and me to "our Vamık's room," which clearly had been built with care and love. The wood floor was polished; the room had a fireplace and a window. However, it was empty except for Mamuka's trophy, which stood on the wooden mantle and Dali wanted us to see. When we returned to the living room, all of us sat on chairs and Dali talked about Mamuka's work. Mamuka was still a policeman in Tbilisi, in command of lower-ranking policemen, all of whom were IDPs living in the Tbilisi Sea. Dali knew that Mamuka's local boss was a good man who treated Mamuka with respect. Dali told me that recently Mamuka had begun talking about changing their five-year plan to a ten-year plan. I sensed that Dali was not yet ready for such a change. Through our talk that afternoon, she saw proof that she was becoming the living linking object for everyone in the family since Charlie's death. An old family ritual was again being conducted.

Dali told me that, even after her father received his award, he continued to write a poem a day. He would still ritualistically bring his poems to the breakfast table each morning, but now no one but Dali would sit down and listen to him recite them. According to her, they still included references to the refugees' lamentable situations. Then Nodar would give them to Dali, smile, and leave the room. It became clear to us that Dali had become the only person who functioned as a "reservoir" for his daily sadness, frustration, and guilt. I told her that her replacement of Charlie might cause her to feel responsible for breaking or maintaining the family's ties to the past. As long as she thought of such tasks as obligations, she would find herself under stress. Her "power" to cut off this bond—in other words to "kill" the family's prerefugee identity—was causing her guilt. Dali said that she understood my explanation.

Yet another factor was intruding into Dali's inner world and contributing to her severe depression. She told me that "our Vamık's room" was structurally complete, as I had seen. Soon they would start decorating it. Dali told me that as the room was approaching completion she came to a realization: I would not sleep there. She had to give up her previous illusion. She said that she came face to face with the reality that I was not a family member. Listening to Dali in my role as a psychoanalyst, I heard how she was getting ready to give me up as an idealized "libidinalizing" (transference) figure, perhaps representing an oedipal father. I told her in nontechnical terms that she had to give me up and mourn this "loss" much in the same way that an oedipal girl "mourns" the loss of her oedipal father as she resolves the Oedipus complex. She listened carefully. I also told her that I could still care for her even though I would not sleep in "our Vamık's room" and that this room really belonged to her and her family. As our long conversation that day was coming to an end, I reminded Dali that people Dali's age and even younger were dying at the

Tbilisi Sea, often for no apparent reasons. Knowing her positive feelings for me (transference), I then raised my voice and told her that I would not give her permission to die and added that, if she did not die, she could be a model for other depressed IDPs, someone who could survive and adjust.

When I returned about five months later, I noticed something on the west side of Okros Satsmisi, on the wall facing the parking lot—a very tall chimney pipe that started at the sixth floor and rose almost to the roof. As the only such structure on the outside wall, it looked very out of place, but I knew right away that the fireplace in "our Vamık's room" was now functional. As I climbed the stairways to the Kachavara family, I noticed how clean the hallways were. My Georgian companions told me that recently some money had come from Norway and the IDPs at the Tbilisi Sea were now better able to take care of their physical surroundings.

When I met Dali I hardly recognized her. She had gained weight and was smiling and for the first time I saw her wearing make-up. A midsized dog with a black-patched golden coat was standing beside her. Dali, with excitement in her voice, told Jana who was accompanying me to translate her words right away while pointing at the dog. "This is Linda," she said. "You see she is a female dog and not a black one. She is not a continuation of the first and second Charlie. She is just a dog. Besides, we fixed a fenced area outside Okros Satsmisi for her and she spends a lot of time outdoors. I am not depending on her company all the time. And, I am not using this dog to struggle about going back to Gagra or staying here at the Tbilisi Sea."

During this visit, Mamuka, who was dressed in his best civilian clothes, was waiting for us. Right away I understood that this was a special day. The Kachavaras would introduce us to "our Vamık's room" rather "officially." Mamuka wanted Dali to set up a table for us with cookies and coffee in the new room as he informed us that it was now completely finished and furnished. However, Dali said that she did not wish to break our tradition of meeting in the original living room of the apartment, which had also been renovated. Dali was quick to inform me that the new room was no longer called "our Vamık's room"; it was theirs. While we were having our coffee Mamuka described how their lives had changed after Dali recovered from her illness. "We now have no one-year or ten-year plans," he added. "How foolish it was for me and my men to go to the border and fight. Abkhazia is gone. We will need to wait for a long time to see how things will work out politically. Meanwhile, we are here at the Tbilisi Sea, and we have to make this place our home. Of course, it will never be like our home in Gagra. But right now we cannot afford to buy a better place in Tbilisi." Mamuka continued to evaluate his situation. He was much calmer now, but he was having some occasional headaches and was unable to stop smoking a lot. "I guess this is the best adjustment I can make. I am all right during the day but have some difficulty falling asleep," he murmured. Nodar came down, also dressed up for the occasion, with a signed copy of his collected poems. In a rather formal way he presented the copy to me and left. I had never seen him this happy. Then Dali and Mamuka took Jana and me into their new room.

The room was furnished with care. Besides a sitting area with an ottoman, there was a display cabinet facing it. In the cabinet stood framed pictures I had taken of them during my previous visits and mementos of Charlottesville that I had brought them, such as a coffee cup with the University of Virginia emblem on it. Next to the cabinet an oil painting of a fancy building surrounded by trees was hanging on the wall. The soccer trophy was still on the wooden mantle. Mamuka wanted me to hold it to feel how solid and heavy it was. I thought that it was like a monument of his identity, verified as a continuation of his identity as a popular soccer player from Gagra. Then Mamuka told me the story of the oil painting.

When he received his soccer trophy, another IDP player was given a painting of Hotel Gagribsh. According to Mamuka, Hotel Gagribsh was the best-known location in Gagra when the Kachavara family lived there. After the soccer game, Mamuka thought he also would like to have a painting of Hotel Gagribsh. He did not volunteer to tell us whether or not he had a personal memory involving this hotel and I did not ask. He found out who had painted the picture given to the other soccer player and made arrangements for the artist to paint another one for the Kachavara family. When I asked them to tell me more about what the painting meant to them, Mamuka and Dali told me that they were fully aware that the painting was a memorial to their pre-refugee identities. Now it was in the former "our Vamık's room," like a tombstone that helps mourners complete their mourning. Since she knew a great deal about linking objects due to our previous conversations, Dali was ready to inform me that the painting was not a linking object because, she and Mamuka told me, it symbolized that there would be no return to Gagra. Now they had no plans to return. I realized that the painting was a "futureless memory."[29]

Soon Tamuna and Aleco, Valerey, and their wives appeared. I thought that Valerey's wife looked like a young Dali. Aleco's wedding had taken place a week prior to my coming to see the former "our Vamık's room." There was an atmosphere of festivity in the family's home. Mamuka had to go to work and the children also had to leave, but before they left, the Kachavara family presented me with a gift. It was a typical Georgian sword with an ornate case. After the other members of her family departed, Dali asked Jana and me to join her in the original living room. She wanted to have a conversation with me like the one we had during her illness some five months earlier. "I noticed a problem" she said, "and I would like to understand it. I did not share it with Mamuka and others." I sat on a chair in front of her and she began talking. She explained how happy she was with her youngest son's marriage. She had, however, an anxiety attack the day after her son got married, and now she wanted to understand why. As I stated earlier, Dali and Mamuka had separated the main room in their apartment into two sections with a curtain; the space behind the curtain served as their bedroom. The night before his marriage Aleco slept on a cot in the other section, where I usually conducted my interviews with them. The son and his new wife were to move elsewhere in the Tbilisi Sea after their marriage.

Dali woke up on the day after her son's marriage and came out from her bedroom to find her son's cot empty. Aleco apparently had gotten up early and left the apartment. Upon seeing the empty cot, Dali was immediately filled with anxiety. She said that she anticipated that separation from her son would be difficult but sensed that her anxiety was connected with something else. She also had a feeling that someone was about to die. She was very puzzled. Her anxiety attack did not return, but since I was there now she thought it would be a good idea to try to understand the reason it had occurred. She remembered her fear that her children might die during their escape from Gagra. She said that she was seeing in her mind's eye her children huddled around her in the helicopter that had flown them to safety. Then she recalled the event in great detail and visualized herself crying. She remembered feeling that she would die if she lost one of her children. She realized that seeing Aleco's empty cot had rekindled the old fear that had overwhelmed her on that trip. Separation and a sense of actual death were connected in her mind.

At this point Dali told me something that I had not known before: the Ukrainian helicopter pilot who was killed had the same name as her oldest son. She began describing in detail the physical characteristics of this pilot. He was young and handsome, like her two sons were now. She realized that not finding her youngest son lying in his cot symbolized her guilt over "killing" the young pilot. Dali told me that when she and other

IDP ladies at the Tbilisi Sea got together, the pilot's name would on occasion come up but that the ladies would quickly change the subject. I learned that before his death the young pilot had saved many others who now lived at the Tbilisi Sea. The flight that carried Dali, her children, the man whose son had just been killed, and a few others to safety was his last one. On his way back to Gagra to save still others, his helicopter was shot down and he died. Dali, with tears in her eyes, told me that there was no memorial or public mourning for the dead pilot. She added, "As we [the Kachavara family] are completing our mourning ten years after leaving Gagra and putting our lives on a better tract, and as I see my sons with their wives, I am now more aware of feeling guilty over the pilot's death. There are others here who also feel guilty and we do not even talk about him and we do not openly say how much we owe him."

I suggested that perhaps she could attend church and perform a funeral rite for the dead pilot and that doing so could decrease her feeling of guilt and help her emotionally separate her son(s) from the image of the dead pilot. She agreed. A week later, when I returned to the United States, Dali sent me a message through Jana. She wanted me to know that she had indeed gone to church, lit candles for the pilot, prayed for his soul, and was feeling much better.

After the "festivities" in the former "our Vamık's room" and after accepting their gift of a traditional Georgian sword (a gift that perhaps, in their eyes, symbolically supported my manhood), I knew that my "therapeutic" visits to the Kachavara family had come to an end. Ten years after becoming refugees they had mourned their losses as much as they could and were now beginning to give adaptive responses to their shared trauma. My team's other programs in Georgia also had come to an end, and following this last visit I had no chance to return to Georgia. I did continue to work with Georgian and South Ossetian colleagues for one more year, but during this time they came to Turkey for our meetings. A year or so later I was delighted to receive an e-mail from Tamuna. She told me that she had waited to write to me until she learned better English. According to her, the family was doing well. She said that Dali's life had changed greatly; Valerey and his wife had a little boy and she had become a grandmother. Tamuna even sent me copies of Nodar's new poems, but they were in the Georgian alphabet and I could not read them. Tamuna wrote that his poems still principally centered on the Georgian-Abkhazian conflict. Tamuna also included a poem that Nodar had written for his daughter Dali, which she translated line by line. I wondered why Tamuna had sent this poem to me. I also wondered if Dali had told her to do so. I thought that her father's poem "verified" Dali's identity just as the trophy had verified Mamuka's. The poem, titled "A Little Girl," read:

To My Oldest Daughter Dali
I'm not the same as I was in those old days,
But I still stumble on the language of children.
Your childhood is still a part of me,
And makes me do what it wants.
I kept you warm in the cold,
Even as I was suffering.
You're my loveliest child,
As you are a little girl.
You're already a mother,
And you have a daughter and two sons.
I can't lie—I believe in God—
I can't live without you even a moment.

4 More on Refugees and Their Linking Objects

After the collapse of the Soviet Union and the end of the Cold War, U.S. president George H.W. Bush introduced the idea of a "New World Order" that envisioned "kinder and gentler" times. This vision, as we all well know, has by no means materialized. Massive human tragedies deliberately caused by "others"—people usually known as "enemies"—have occurred at various locations in the world during and after his presidency, resulting in, among other disasters, countless refugees and asylum seekers. Later, the former president's son, George W. Bush—and of course all of us—became more aware than ever of a new kind of international aggression in the form radical Islamist terrorism, as well as a new kind of ruthless response to it, one that is supported by a new kind of American political doctrine that allows striking at a potential enemy first and asking questions later.

Why have kinder and gentler times and a New World Order remained so elusive? The fact is that human psychology, whether of individuals or large groups, has not changed. On one hand we embrace the modern trappings of technology and commend our own "civilized" sophistication. But on the other, as members of large groups, such as ethnic or religious groups, we continue to follow this or that leader and various ideologies and belief systems, and when our shared identity is threatened, we have a tendency to humiliate, cripple, burn, and kill "others" for the enhancement, protection, or survival of our own large-group identity, even in cases when our own physical survival is not threatened.

In my book *Blind Trust: Leaders and Their Followers in Times of Crises and Terror*, I explain the violent potential of large groups through the use of a tent analogy.[30] We all wear, from childhood on, two layers of clothing. The first garment, which belongs just to the individual who is wearing it, fits snugly and represents personal identity. The second set of looser outer clothes is made from the fabric of the large group's ethnic (or religious or ideological) tent. Each member of the large group is cloaked by a piece of this same cloth, and it protects the person like a parent or other caregiver. The canvas of the tent thereby shelters thousands or millions of individuals under it as though it were a gigantic single piece, and represents the large-group identity.

As long as the tent remains stable and strong, the members of the large group can go about their lives without being obsessed with the nature of their tent's canvas. However, if the canvas of the tent is shaken or torn, such as during situations of shared helplessness and humiliation caused by "others," shared emotions such as anxiety and rage peak and practically all individuals under the tent become preoccupied with trying to make the tent stable again. They also seek to support leaders whom they perceive as saviors and, therefore, easily become responsive to political propaganda and manipulation. At such times, wearing one's own personal garment becomes less important than being collectively covered by the second canvas garment. For example, in refugee camps, people are naturally concerned with their own or their family members' survival and adaptations. But the sense of "we-ness" quickly expands from the family and the clan and includes a renewed investment in the whole ethnic, national, or religious large group. This happens because the people experience their own victimization not just as a result of an attack on themselves by "others," but also as a result of their mutual identification as members of a shared large group.

As far as ethnicity, nationality, or religion is concerned, all individuals under this tent share a subjective sense of sameness, even though most of them will never meet during their lifetimes. Thousands or even millions of people feel equal in relation to this shared sense of sameness, whether they are men or women, rich or poor. If the individuals are Georgians, for example, their sense of being Georgian is not affected by such factors as social status or degree of wealth. Especially under stressful conditions, all members of the group identify with their shared ethnic identity, even though Georgians are made up of individuals who also strongly associate themselves with different regions of Georgia, such as Kaheti, Imereta, Mteuleti, Guria, and so on, and even though some of them primarily speak their own language, such as in Megrelia, and may be Muslims, such as in Adjara.

I must make clear that when I speak of a large group I am focusing on its shared general psychological processes. Although some members of the group do not go along, to one degree or another, with these processes,

I am not focusing on them. Within each large group there will always be dissenters. Some time after a trauma, if the political leader can not remain as a "savior" in the eyes of the followers, a severe split may occur in a large group between those who still follow the leader and those who oppose the leader. Here I am focusing on situations where there is an acute sense that the large-group tent is shaken. Furthermore, within each large group, there will be people who may have one parent or ancestor from another ethnicity, nationality, or religion. For example, the son or daughter of a Georgian-South Ossetian couple living in Tbilisi would most likely have difficulty choosing between the two ethnic groups when finding themselves involved in a hot conflict. But in a refugee settlement, this generalized large-group togetherness becomes palpable. It was because of this close connection among refugees that I considered the possibility that working with the Kachavara family would, in fact, help many other people in the Tbilisi Sea, even if I never met them.

When I first met Mamuka and Dali I noticed that they were influential people in their IDP community. By getting to know them and other members of the Kachavara family and therapeutically dealing with their mourning and adaptation processes, I hoped to develop a methodology for reaching many IDP families without actually working with them. The day the Kachavara family, Jana, and I had a kind of ceremony celebrating the completion of what had once been called "our Vamık's room," I learned that at least a dozen other IDP families at the Tbilisi Sea had completed or had begun adding rooms to their own apartments. I also learned that the Kachavaras had built a garage and that about forty more garages were now in existence. When I went to see the fenced area for Linda near the parking lot in front of Okros Satsmisi, I noticed other fenced areas for other families' pets. I was pleased that the "methodology" I had envisioned for reaching other refugees by working intensively with the leaders of their settlement seemed to be working.

I also knew that I was very lucky to find a person like Dali. As she began to observe and understand her own psychological issues as a refugee, she became a kind of consultant to others in this community. I believe that when Dali survived her "stroke,"—I understood that many at the Tbilisi Sea closely followed her illness and her remarkable recovery— she emerged as a model for defeating depression. I did not carry out a scientific study at the Tbilisi Sea—and I cannot provide any statistical findings, for to carry out a scientific study there would have been extremely difficult—but by the time I stopped going to Okros Satsmisi, Jana reported to me that the general consensus was that the number of people who dropped dead for "no apparent reason" there had decreased considerably after Dali's recovery from her "stroke."

Before we first went to this area, Jana and others, using funds from Norway, had worked with the IDP children at the three former hotels, dealing with the children's attachment problems. After shared massive traumas, most refugee children lose much of their ability to "attach" properly to one another as well as to adults. Such difficulties may cause huge problems for such children as they grow older. Even after funding for this project dried up, our Georgian friends continued to be interested in the welfare of the Tbilisi Sea children and adults. This was, I believe, a significant factor in the apparent success of our "methodology." By the time I finished working at Okros Satsmisi, the place had become considerably cleaner. The money that had come from Norway was certainly helpful. However, I cannot help thinking that without improved adaptation to their new environment, without needing to express their shared "anal sadism" against "mother earth," so to speak, and without working on their mourning processes, these refugees would have been less successful in taking care of their environment.

When the Kachavaras finished the addition to their apartment, they also created a very small hallway behind their entryway, where they placed the yellow telephone on a stand, moving it from its original location. As a decoration above the telephone, they hung a ten-inch stuffed elephant made of grey cloth wearing a green coat. I wondered about this stuffed animal, but I had no opportunity to investigate where it came from. As a psychoanalyst I had studied the meaning of children's stuffed animals, specifically teddy bears. In 1953, Donald Winnicott, a British pediatrician who later became a very well-known psychoanalyst, called such toys and things such as the cartoon character Linus's blanket, "transitional objects." A transitional object, in a child's mind, becomes their first "not-me" possession, something that actually exists in the external world. But a transitional object is not entirely a "not-me" item, because it also represents the child's image of mother who is under the child's absolute control (an illusion, of course).[31] Later other psychoanalysts studied further what is called "transitional relatedness": by placing the teddy bear or another stuffed animal between his or her self and adults in the environment, the child begins to get to know the surrounding world. The child relates to the environment by using the transitional object as if it were a spotlight that illuminates pathways of reality. If the environment becomes frustrating, the child relates only to the toy itself and, in a sense, wipes out what is beyond the toy. From our clinical work we are aware that some adults who are in a regressed state continue to utilize adult versions of transitional objects and/or transitional relatedness.

I often thought that the yellow telephone functioned like a transitional object for the Kachavara family, as well as for the three thousand other IDPs at the Tbilisi Sea. By using it they could "know" what was beyond their settlement, and by disconnecting it they could wipe out the frustrating external world. It occurred to me that by hanging a stuffed elephant above this telephone, the Kachavaras symbolically informed visitors of the function of this telephone. Although it still remained one of the most important items at the Tbilisi Sea, by the time I finished my work there I was told that four more telephones had been installed in this formerly luxurious three-hotel area.

Some observers might not consider the Kachavara family to be a very good example of an extremely traumatized refugee family. After all, no family member died during their ordeal, and they were exiled to a location within Georgia itself where they had no fear for their lives. Most of us, I am sure, have read much more horrible stories about refugees around the world. But the Kachavara family, by allowing me to visit with them for five years, gave me an opportunity to learn about their internal processes as they adjusted over a period of years to being forced from their home. By learning what they went through internally, I believe that we can form a good picture of the psychology of dislocated victims due to identity conflicts.

Psychoanalysts have contributed a great deal to our understanding of the internal worlds of the survivors of the Holocaust, most of whom were displaced and forced to settle in places other than their original homes. But the first serious studies of the internal processes and various internal adjustments of Holocaust survivors did not occur until decades after the end of World War II.[32] In general, outside of Holocaust-related studies, there have not been many in-depth, years-long studies of the internal adaptations of refugees. When a catastrophe is in its crisis phase, the ability of international organizations such as the United Nations of High Commissioner for Refugees (UNHCR), the World Health Organization (WHO), the Red Cross, and the Red Crescent to help those affected depends, of course, on the conditions on the ground. For example, the situation may be too dangerous for foreign mental heath workers and others to enter at first. But once a certain level of security has been established and foreign workers arrive on the scene, how they approach traumatized persons is well-documented.

While still visiting the Republic of Georgia for our CSMHI projects, for a short time I was also a temporary consultant to the WHO and visited Albania and Macedonia, where I conducted seminars for local health workers working with Albanian refugees from Kosovo. I became familiar with the official joint manual of the WHO and UNHCR (1996 edition) on the mental health of refugees. This manual only mentioned such things as crisis intervention methods, relaxation techniques, alcohol and drug problems, and professional conduct toward rape victims. After a disaster, the crisis situation takes precedence over other considerations, but when the crisis is over, crucial mourning and adaptation processes continue in full force. There are, of course, other nongovernmental organizations that are also interested in refugees and other victims of wars or war-like situations.[33] In general, their efforts, even though they are often helpful, do not seek to understand the internal work refugees need to do, the length of time that is necessary to do this work, and the difficulty or even the impossibility of bringing such work to a successful conclusion.

There are, of course, various types of dislocations that do not parallel the Kachavara family's experiences. Tales of dislocation experiences throughout human history are presented on a spectrum, ranging from "forced immigration" (a term that does not do justice to tragedies such as when Africans were brought to the Americas as slaves) to "voluntary immigration," such as when an individual leaves one area for another in search of a better life. We can easily imagine many other types of "voluntary immigration," so here I will not study them in-depth, but rather I will continue to focus on situations where people like the Kachavaras were forced to dislocate and made to feel helpless due to large-group identity conflicts. Nevertheless, there are some common elements that underlie the psychology of the "normal" (voluntary) immigrant and the traumatized forced immigrant, such as the asylum seeker, the refugee, and IDP. All of them have to mourn losing part of their selves and loved ones or things, and they also have to deal with guilt feelings for surviving while others may have been left behind or died. All of them, due to their personal psychological make-up or external circumstances, may have complications in mourning and adjusting to their new locations. Accordingly, I will provide a summary of some psychoanalytic theories that pertain to the psychology of dislocated persons.

For a long time the psychology of immigrants and refugees was not studied extensively by psychoanalysts. This is surprising since there were and are many psychoanalysts in the United States and in other countries who are themselves immigrants. Of course, there have been exceptions to this lack of attention.[34] But to my knowledge, the first comprehensive psychoanalytic study of both migration and exile in book form was published in 1984 in Spanish by Léon and Rebecca Grinberg and translated into English in 1989.[35] Having been "transplanted" on several occasions and having worked in three countries, the Grinbergs qualified as "participant-observers" in a real sense.

In their psychoanalytic observations of various types of migration and exile, the Grinbergs note that those left behind, like those departing, utilize various unconscious defense mechanisms to deal with the pain of their loss. As they observe, the Spanish word for "mourning"—*duello*—is derived "from the word for pain and duel, or a two-sided challenge or combat."[36] It refers equally to the pain of the immigrant as well as to the pain of those left behind.

One area the Grinbergs focused on was the task of learning a new language, which is a major problem for any immigrant. (It should be remembered that the Kachavaras were spared this difficulty since they were IDPs.) The Grinbergs studied the theory of the development of language and the impact the mother-child relationship has on it, especially in cases of separation. They described the newcomer's psychological resistance to changing his or her native language and concluded that age was a factor. Children seem able to identify with a new cultural environment relatively quickly and are capable of letting a new language sink in. Adult immigrants face a far more difficult task because of their age; thus they may never succeed in acquiring the "music" (accent and rhythm) of the new language.

In my book *The Need to Have Enemies and Allies*,[37] I describe how it is impossible to truly change a person's ethnic identity after adolescence. When adult newcomers face new ethnic sentiments and investments in a new location, they will have mild to severe difficulties in developing a synthesis of two ethnicities. Some, especially those who migrated voluntarily, if still accepted in the country left behind, may develop a bicultural adaptation upon completion of the work of mourning, as described by Demetrios Julius, a Greek-American psychiatrist. This will enrich them internally. Julius, who has worked with me closely for many decades as a fellow member of CSMHI, states: "I slowly came to an appreciation of the importance of intrapsychic cultural complementarity and, more significantly, to an acceptance of the vast cultural differences of the two countries [Greece and the United States]. I began to accept certain psychological paradoxes and to feel myself bicultural."[38]

A youngster who has not gone through the adolescent passage and who becomes an immigrant may develop a true investment in the ethnicity of the new location. However, this usually becomes complicated due to "interferences" by immigrant or exiled parents or other adult newcomers and nonacceptance by the host country. For example, while most Jews who escaped the Nazis and relocated to America or other nonfascist countries fared relatively well in their adjustments, particularly when their Jewish ethnicity was accepted by people in their new locations, there are, of course, many examples of Jewish immigrants being made to feel unwelcome in this country. Martin Wangh, a well-known psychoanalyst and German-born Jewish immigrant, wrote that shortly after he landed in the United States he received a reply to an application for an internship from a southern hospital that read: "We have found that persons not of our denomination do not feel comfortable working here." He added that "a similar letter was sent to my wife and me from an Adirondack mountain resort. Still later, when we purchased a vacation home in Connecticut, we were quickly informed that the nearby country club (to which we had no intentions to applying) would not admit Jews."[39] I personally observed a similar situation in Charlottesville, Virginia, where I settled in 1963 and where, until very recently, a certain country club there would not admit Jews, blacks, or Muslims as members. For the most part, however, things have changed a great deal in the United States in relation to xenophobia and racism. However, such attitudes still exist here as they exist anywhere else in the world; being technologically and economically "superior" does not change human nature. For example, after September 11, 2001, xenophobia and racism in the United States increased toward Muslims, even those who had long called the country their home.

The Grinbergs drew upon Melanie Klein's psychoanalytic theories[40] and showed how guilt over loss of parts of the self—that is, the immigrant or the refugee's previous identity and his or her investment in the land and people left behind—may complicate the newcomer's mourning process. When guilt is "persecutory" and the individual is driven by guilt to expect punishment from others, the newcomer becomes prone to complicated mourning. If the individual internally acknowledges the loss of the past life and is able to accept the pain—Kleinians call this "depressive guilt"—the individual may exhibit sorrow but will still be able to retain reparative tendencies. Therefore, the immigrant or refugee who has depressive guilt is better equipped to adjust to a new life.

To further explain what Kleinians mean by these two types of guilt, I offer the following summary written by Léon Grinberg:

In patients with persecutory guilt, the notion of time is often governed by the characteristics of the primary process (unconscious). In such cases, we often find a temporality in which past and present are confused. The principal emotions involved in persecutory guilt are resentment, pain, despair, fear, self-reproach, etc. . . . In depressive guilt, on the other hand, time is formed in accordance with laws of the secondary process (conscious). There is discrimination between past and present, and there is also perspective and a future. The most important feelings of depressive guilt are concern for the object and the ego, sadness, nostalgia, and responsibility.[41]

In the case of the refugee, the individual's own psychological organization generates more persecutory guilt than may be found in the person who becomes an immigrant by choice. After all, the refugee's guilt is reinforced by being a survivor while relatives and friends have been killed or remain in danger. If either the immigrant or refugee faces discrimination within his or her host society, however, persecutory anxieties are kept alive.

A recent major psychoanalytic study of the internal worlds of immigrants and refugees has been provided in a book written by a Philadelphia psychoanalyst, Salman Akhtar, who comes from a Muslim family and who voluntarily immigrated to the United States.[42] While the Grinbergs relied upon the Kleinian conceptualizations of psychoanalysis, Akhtar focused on the adaptation of immigrants to a new country according to Margaret Mahler's concept of separation-individuation. Mahler was a prominent psychoanalyst who conducted studies on how children accomplish their own separate individualization from their mothers and how they develop their own distinct sense of self.[43] Akhtar argues that the immigrant's adaptation constitutes a "third individuation," the first having occurred in childhood and the second during adolescence. His study includes creative responses to the difficulty of mourning, as well as the role of nostalgia and the poisoning of nostalgia in the immigrant's or refugee's mind.

In general, it is more difficult and perhaps impossible for refugees and exiles to complete a work of mourning. This is especially true for those who were subjected to helplessness, humiliation, rape, ethnic cleansing, torture, and shame before or during their flight to safety and who were relocated to places where people did not welcome them, did not speak their language, did not eat their food, and did not sing their songs. Extreme trauma associated with a loss interferes with the mourning process. The "normal" mourning process includes the mourner's experiencing narcissistic hurts and the accompanying sense of "normal" anger over being psychologically wounded by the loss. Those who are severely traumatized avoid sensing their own anger, since it becomes unconsciously contaminated with murder and annihilation and accompanying feelings of helplessness, shame, humiliation, and identification with the persecutor's rage. Thus, they avoid experiencing "normal" anger and cannot mourn properly. Such persons first have to become ordinary, "normal" immigrants in order to begin the work of mourning in a genuine way. I think that my being around on and off for many years helped the Kachavara family members to become ordinary immigrants.

In describing the Kachavara family's story as IDPs, I focused on the role of linking objects and linking phenomena as an entry point, if you will, into the internal struggles of dislocated persons. The way they utilize their linking objects and phenomena tells us a great deal about where they are in their mourning for their losses and adaptation to their new environment. For the Kachavara family, the first Charlie and then the second Charlie were linking objects. After the death of the second Charlie, Dali herself acted as the family's linking object. Additionally, "our Vamık's room" and its picture of Hotel Gagribsh partially functioned as the family's private memorial to what they had left behind. (Later in this volume I will describe how memorials to losses have various functions.) A memorial, such as the one the Kachavara family built, is a different kind of linking object: it absorbs the mourner's remaining unfinished work of mourning and locks it within itself. A perennial mourner is preoccupied with a regular linking object and spends energy controlling it and also controlling the struggle between bringing back or "killing" what is left behind. On the other hand, a stable memorial, such as "our Vamık's room," frees the mourner to invest in new things in the new environment rather than to spend energy with the past.

There are also "memorials" that provide an opposite function: the crystallization of perennial mourning. Antonius C. G. Robben, an anthropologist from Utrecht University, provides a good example of this in his examination of Argentina's "Dirty War" that raged from 1976 to 1983. During this time of violence and chaos, many individuals "disappeared," meaning they were abducted from their homes and murdered because they were deemed "enemies" of the totalitarian government. Some parents, as an expression of their perennial mourning, preserved the lost person's room and possessions. This type of memorial became "peculiar" after 1984 when it became clear that the disappeared were dead rather than imprisoned. Robben visited people "between 1989 and 1991 who still changed the sheets on their disappeared daughter's bed or pre-pared every few days their son's favorite pudding so that he could enjoy it as soon as he would appear at the doorstep." In 2002, Slavica Jurcevic and Ivan Urlic carried out a study with families of disappeared sons from the 1991–95 war in Croatia. Their findings are similar to Robben's observations in Argentina. In Croatia many families created "memorial shrines" that resembled some form of altar on which Catholic iconographic symbols, flowers, and candles surrounded the missing person's picture. Such memorial shrines are always located in the room where the family spends most of its time and/or where guests are received.[44]

The struggles to mourn or not to mourn, and to link to what was left behind or to separate from what was left behind, always accompany the refugees' various types of guilt feelings and their internal attempts at adaptation. Under certain circumstances this struggle may result in peculiar individual and collective symptoms. I studied refugees' internal struggles for the first time in 1975 in the northern section of the island of Cyprus. Indeed, it was an odd collective behavior that initiated my study. During the summer of 1974, the Turkish army arrived on the island after the Cypriot Turks faced a disastrous fate at the hands of Cypriot Greeks. This led to the division of the island into northern Turkish and southern Greek sectors. Previously Cypriot Greeks and Cypriot Turks lived all over the island, in all Greek, in all Turkish, or in mixed villages, while Cypriot cities were comprised of both ethnic groups. After the Turkish military stormed the north of the island, the Cypriot Greeks in the north fled to the south, while Cypriot Turks living in the south escaped to the north. Those Turks who came to the north were housed by the newly formed North Cyprus government in the homes, villages, and towns of the

CYPRUS

Mediterranean Sea

Kyrenia

UN buffer zone

Cypriot Turk-administered area

Famagusta   UN buffer zone

NICOSIA

Larnaca

Area controlled by Cyprus Government   Dhekelia
Sovereign Base Area (UK)

Paphos

Limassol   Mediterranean Sea

Akrotiri
Sovereign Base Area (UK)

departed Cypriot Greeks. This created an unusual situation. While the Kachavaras and three thousand other Georgian IDPs from Abkhazia were placed in the Tbilisi Sea, which carried no mental image connected to the enemy, the Cypriot Turks were placed in residences just vacated by their enemies. Obviously the mental images of these locations had a direct connection to the enemy.

I arrived in North Cyprus some six months after the summer 1974 war was over. A high school classmate of mine, Ahmet Savalash, was given a job at the North Cyprus central administrative office. One of his tasks was to assist young college-educated men assigned to one or more formerly Greek communities where Cypriot Turkish refugees were being settled. Each of these men, who were called *kılavuz*, which means guide, was given a house of his own and was put in charge of a building that served as a warehouse. In these buildings were stored usable items that Cypriot Greeks had left behind in their flight, such as beds, sewing machines, food, and televisions. The Cypriot Turkish refugees, meanwhile, were assigned mostly empty Greek houses that were comparable to those they had lived in in the south.[45]

While I was visiting Ahmet at his office, a kılavuz called him to complain about how the new settlers in the village assigned to him were burning the blankets he had provided them from his warehouse. He was puzzled by this strange behavior. Because it was winter, the settlers needed blankets. Why would they burn them? Ahmet said that he recently had received similar reports from other guides, so we decided to investigate the matter and drove to the village, which was located just off the main road linking the capital of Nicosia with Famagusta, the next largest city in northern Cyprus. Male villagers on Cyprus, when not working, spend a great deal of time in coffee shops. So we decided to learn about the blanket burning by visiting the village coffee shop, interviewing the people there and observing the interactions among them.

Indeed, at the coffee shop that day—and in subsequent days—the mystery of these new settlers' peculiar collective behavior was gradually solved. I learned that after the war had ended, the Cypriot Turkish administration did not have enough new bedding to meet the needs of the refugees. An order went out to make quilts from whatever suitable fabric the Cypriot Greeks had left behind. The newcomers knew, then, that the quilts and blankets they had been provided with had been made from Greek dresses, pajamas, and underwear. In effect, if they used the bedding they had been issued, they would be having "physical" contact with the Cypriot Greeks. For the settlers, therefore, the blankets were linking objects to the enemy images. It is not only love that connects us deeply with others; hate does as well. Thus, just as we must mourn the passing of those we love, so too do we need to mourn when intimately hated persons or things are lost, although we usually try to deny this. Although the Cypriot Greeks were traumatized as they escaped to the south, the blanket-burning Cypriot Turks, as is typical in such situations, had no empathy for their tragedy. Still, in the midst of their grief and shock, it was psychologically imperative for the Cypriot Turks to burn these linking objects and create the illusion in their minds of a quick and clear separation from the enemy without going through the requisite mourning process.[46]

These Cypriot Turks, like the Kachavara family, were IDPs since their new location was under Cypriot Turkish rule. They were among people of the same ethnicity and they did not need to learn a new language. But as their original houses and lands in the south of the island were now inhabited by Cypriot Greeks, their mourning process included a preoccupation with Greeks since they now lived in their homes. A year later, accompanied again by Ahmet, I revisited the village to collect more data about their adjustment. Though blanket burning was no longer an issue there, a pile of garbage I had noticed in the center of the village the year before had grown to considerable size, almost as if it were a statue made of trash. The pile was comprised of objects left behind by the Cypriot Greek villagers. There were torn slippers, broken pots and pans, pieces of cloth, and more importantly, faded pictures of some Cypriot Greeks and their children who had fled during the war. Seeing these pictures emotionally moved me, even though at the time I was angry at Cypriot Greeks in general because of the horrible things they had done to my relatives, friends, and other Cypriot Turks.

I realized that this huge pile of junk was connecting the new settlers' selves with the corresponding images of the original Greek owners of the houses and lands they now occupied. For them, the departed Greek villagers symbolically stood for all Cypriot Greeks under whom they had suffered in the past. But the former Greek owners could not be mentally abandoned because of the newcomers' guilt over replacing them in this place. The huge pile of garbage was obviously a shared linking object invested with significant aggressive feelings. It was "out there," in the middle of the village square, facing the coffee shop. Although the junk pile was not as intimate as the blankets, which would have physically touched the skin of the people who used them, it allowed the mourning process to be truly externalized. As I indicated earlier, it is typical for refugees to regress to an oral and anal state of mind and spoil their environment. But this pile of garbage also had another specific meaning as a shared linking object.

While we were sitting in the coffee shop pointing at the garbage pile, Ahmet expressed his and the Cypriot Turkish government's frustration with the new settlers, stating: "We tell them that all they need is a can of gasoline and a match to get rid of this mess, but they do not listen to us. We sent them medically informed persons who told them that having this garbage pile may cause health problems, but they do not listen to us." I noted that if the government was so concerned, they could easily send an outsider to get rid of this mess. Apparently, they had not done so. I wondered if the people in the government unconsciously sensed the psychological importance of this shared linking object and therefore did not touch it.

Seven years after my first visit to this village its appearance drastically changed. First, a huge billboard of a half-naked woman advertising a certain brand of gasoline appeared facing the main road between Nicosia and Famagusta, attempting to lure passing travelers to buy gasoline for their vehicles. The trash pile in the middle of the village was gone. Later small restaurants and even a nightclub opened near the billboard. I visited this village again last year, thirty years after I carried out my studies there. Strangely, no one I spoke with remembered the burning of the blankets or the huge "statue" made of garbage. Perhaps some had repressed the memory of their difficult mourning, and others were caught up in newer developments in the Turkish Cypriot-Greek Cypriot relationship.

Both the Tbilisi Sea and North Cyprus refugees had been dislocated. But in my many decades of observations of communities traumatized by "others," I noted that sometimes people do not need to be physically dislocated in order to become refugees. They continue to live in the same location; what is "exiled" is familiar surroundings. For example, when a community's physical surroundings are drastically changed, houses are ruined, trees are uprooted, and fields are burned by enemy actions, the people who struggle with images of lost persons and things may become perennial mourners; they experience guilt, shame, and humiliation, and in short, develop a refugee psychology. Consider, for example, the Kosovo village of Gjakova, inhabited by 740 Albanian families near the Albanian border. When Serbs under Slobodan Milosevic attacked the village, they killed more than two hundred people, leaving 138 widows and four hundred orphans. Many more villagers were maimed and handicapped. Most of the bodies of the massacred victims were then said to have been burned in Gjakova's incinerators. This meant that the widows, orphans, and other traumatized villagers woke up each morning to see the buildings in which the bodies of their murdered husbands, fathers, and other relatives had been turned into ash. Thus, the villager's previously familiar physical environment had been "exiled," and they behaved as if they were actual refugees.

Similarly, during the fall of 2004, U.S.-led forces acted to uproot Iraqi insurgents from Fallujah, a historic city on the Euphrates. They turned several hundred houses into rubble and made the entire city uninhabitable. Several weeks after "cleaning up" the city of insurgents, the Americans allowed some Iraqis (initially only fourteen hundred of them) to return. These individuals found that their city had been sent into "exile." They expressed anger, resentment, and helpless frustration. As in Gjakova, I believe that they became refugees in their own homes, and I suspect that the population of Fallujah will have difficulty mourning their "lost" city.[47]

As with refugees, people whose familiar physical environments have been taken away from them also utilize linking objects. Such a linking object is dramatically illustrated on a painting by the Austrian architect and painter, Wolf Werdigier.[48] Werdigier is Jewish and lives in Vienna. During World War II, his father, his father's first wife, and their little boy, also named Wolf, had been sent to concentration camps. There, the boy and his mother were murdered by the Nazis, but Werdigier's father survived. In 1945, when the war ended, he met and married a Christian nurse with whom he had a second son, Wolf Werdigier. While Werdigier was raised as a Jew, his sisters were raised as Christians.

Werdigier is well-informed about psychoanalytic concepts and believes that painting psychoanalytic concepts that pertain to national, ethnic, or religious conflicts can provide new perspectives toward understanding the psychology of such conflicts, open new ways of thinking about them, and even open doors to the consideration of peaceful solutions. His paintings have been exhibited in Jerusalem, Tel Aviv, Ramallah, Vienna, and New York. One of his paintings titled *The Power of Soil* shows the agonized face of a man whose eyes are closed and mouth is open. Below his neck, his body disappears into the soil. But around his neck, five large old-fashioned house keys protrude from the ground. Werdigier explained to me how Palestinians whose homes have been razed by Israeli bulldozers often keep their house keys as linking objects. Werdigier's painting speaks louder than words in its illumination of the agony humans experience in the name of large-group identity.

In the next chapter, I will share some observations of the capital city of South Ossetia, known as Tskhinvali to the Georgians and Tskhinval to the South Ossetians.[49] This city, north of Gori, is where Joseph Stalin was born and many people there continue to honor him as a great idealized historic figure. After the 1991–92 war between Georgians and South Ossetians, which I briefly described in Chapter 1, Tskhinvali was, in a sense, "exiled." Indeed, South Ossetians living in this city developed a refugee psychology, which I will explore in the next chapter. The discussion in the next chapter is important for another reason. In describing the trauma felt by South Ossetians, I wish to remind the reader that, in conflicts between neighboring ethnic groups, both sides usually suffer. I also want to remind readers that in regressed large groups we always find persons who are more "immune" to the psychological influences collectively exerted on and by their own large group. By examining such an individual, I will try to clarify the differences between individual and large-group psychology.

When I speak of large-group psychology, I refer to general shared psychological phenomena. Obviously, a large group is not one living organism with one brain or mind, and does not function the exact way an individual does. Nevertheless, there are some parallels. And since a separate vocabulary does not exist, I apply terms used for individual psychology to large-group psychology. For example, we can closely study an individual's mourning process and regression in a clinical setting. But large groups also "mourn" and "regress."[50] While we see some reflections of an individual's mourning process and regression in large-group mourning and regression, the mourning process and regression of a large group can really only be observed in general shared societal, political, and military trends, and also in physical, environmental changes. When we look at a large group that lives under a totalitarian regime, or is composed of refugees, there is an abundance of individual and collective behaviors that help define it as regressed. In such instances of large-group regression, the individuals within the group lose their individuality to one degree or another, follow the leader(s) blindly, and become prone to taking in (internalizing) political propaganda without really questioning its validity. Sigmund Freud's original description of mass psychology outlines this phenomenon, although he did not specifically call it the regression of a large group, nor did he attempt to explain why some members regress and others do not.[51]

Every member of a regressed large group does not exhibit individual regression in the same way, but I do not believe that observations and theories regarding collective psychological behavior are therefore invalid. In certain circumstances, individuals within regressed large groups, such as dissenters, do not themselves regress, or they regress in different ways than the general public. For example, Nodar Sharveladze, a Georgian man I encountered in my work, was able to hold onto his individual mind both while living under the Soviet Union and after the reindependence of Georgia. As I will describe, he played a key role in helping me observe various societal movements in Tskhinvali and introduced me to some fascinating (as well as some scary) South Ossetians, including a beautiful young woman named Irene Bekoeva. Later, I would have the pleasure of becoming honorary "grandfather" to Irene's first born, Sasha (Alexander).

5 "Have You Read *Sophie's Choice?*"

Nodar Sharveladze, a professor of psychology, has a round face, usually bearing a pleasant grin, topped by graying hair and dark eyebrows. His trademark accessories are the scarf he typically wears in place of a tie and the safety chains that hang down from the sides of his glasses, disappearing under his scarf. All in all, he cuts the classic figure of an absent-minded professor. He is not a particularly large man physically, but his work on what he calls the "social rehabilitation" of Georgia has made him, to my mind, a giant figure. Nodar, who has strong powers of self-observation, personifies an "ordinary" man without political ambition who has evolved into a citizen diplomat and healer.

Nodar was born in 1945 in Batumi, near Georgia's border with Turkey, and was the oldest child in a family of four. His father, whom I got to know before his death in 2000, was a truck driver who was not terribly interested in intellectual pursuits. Nodar's mother, whom I never met, was a nurse who collected books and loved to read in her spare time. Nodar takes after his mother, as he is also a great reader and collector of books. As a youth, he greatly admired fellow Georgian Joseph Stalin. He recalls that as an eleven-year-old, when demonstrators were protesting the government in Tbilisi, he went to Stalin's statue, desiring to defend it against potential attackers. Nikita Khrushchev's denunciation of Georgia's native son at the 20th Congress of the Communist Party in February 1956, followed by an anti-Stalin campaign throughout the Soviet Union, alienated many students in Tbilisi, including Nodar. When they organized demonstrations to prevent the removal of a Stalin monument, Soviet authorities sent in tanks that killed dozens and wounded hundreds in the main street of Tbilisi.

Nodar believes that he began to question his attachment to Stalin's image and to free himself from the influence of state propaganda in 1963.

Under his mother's influence, he started to study philosophy independently, reading the works of Plato, Aristotle, Schopenhauer, and Nietzsche. He discovered Sigmund Freud and Carl Jung around the same time, finding books "on the street" containing the works of Freud; most of Freud's early work had been translated into Russian long ago, although it was banned in Georgia, as well as elsewhere in the Soviet Union. These books fascinated Nodar, and he began to ponder not just human nature, but also the societal processes of totalitarianism and nationality. Nodar eventually went to Moscow to become a psychology student. He was so intent on meeting foreign psychologists that he managed to enter, without invitation, a 1966 reception at the Kremlin in order to catch a glimpse of the famed Jean Piaget, who was attending a conference in the city.

He felt that his mind needed to be trained, not unlike the training he had undertaken to become a serious chess player and fearless mountain climber. Just as one has to consider every step one takes when playing chess or climbing mountains, Nodar began taking extraordinary steps in his own life. He studied French, which enabled him to leave the Soviet Union after Leonid Brezhnev's rise to power; he spent a year in France studying social psychology and some psychoanalytic theory. Even though it was illegal, he also opened a private psychotherapy office in Tbilisi in 1980. Determined to know more about human nature and to help others, he became increasingly concerned with notions of freedom and responsibility. When Mikhail Gorbachev introduced his program of glasnost and perestroika, Nodar embraced the reforms that promised new freedoms of expression and information. As a result, though he had not been personally involved in the independence movement, he was deeply shocked when Gorbachev denied any responsibility for the Tbilisi massacre of April 9, 1989, which I described at the beginning of this book.

Only a few months after that traumatic day, Nodar found himself in neighboring Armenia trying to help those affected by a huge earthquake that killed more than twenty-five thousand people. "It was a cathartic experience for me," he recalls. His transformation from youthful Stalin devotee had crystallized: he began to feel committed to doing whatever he could to help traumatized people. Despite his continuing ambivalence about the Soviet leader's response to the Tbilisi massacre, Nodar became a supporter of Gorbachev's "new thinking" and even appeared on television to present the leader's ideas to his fellow citizens. However, as the Soviet Union collapsed, Nodar saw that ethnic and religious differences would be exacerbated throughout the former "empire," possibly leading to serious violent conflicts. He watched with concern as Georgian nationalism surged and foresaw major ethnic conflicts erupting in Georgia.

It was during the early 1990s when, as Nodar put it, "Thanatos won over Eros" in Georgia, and he came to feel it his responsibility as a citizen to counteract the destruction and death. He began a quest to understand the psychology of social diversity and conflict. Upon his return to Georgia from an extended academic trip to Israel, he found that some of his friends had become psychologically injured during the ethnic wars, which moved him a great deal. IDPs were everywhere. He went to visit the Norwegian Refugee Council (NRC) office in Tbilisi and offered his services, preparing a proposal for them in only one day. He gathered about fifteen of his friends, including psychologist Jana Javakhishvili and Manana Gabashvili, who had helped me with my observations at the Tbilisi Sea, and Nato Sharveladze, his daughter. His group also included psychiatrists Nino Makhashvili, Zurab Berberashvili, and Rezo Jorbenadze. His friend, a famous screenwriter, Amiran Dolidze, also joined him. They formed the Foundation for Human Development (FDHR). FDHR's first efforts served Georgian IDPs in various locations around the country, including the Tbilisi Sea, where the Kachavara family had settled, and Gori, where a huge statue of Stalin still stands in the middle of the city and where there also is a Stalin museum.

While working with IDPs in Gori, Nodar met an old man who asked him, "Do you know that South Ossetians also need the type of service that you have been giving us? They are traumatized too." Intrigued, he arranged a meeting with a Russian general in charge of certain negotiations between Georgia and South Ossetia. While seated in a waiting room, Nodar was shocked to overhear the general attempting to profit from the misery of the people: the general was more interested in making arrangements for illegal trade between the two warring groups than in making peace. Once he was called in to speak with the general, Nodar offered to bring people from Tbilisi to collaborate with South Ossetians on some social rehabilitation programs. The general promised to speak with the then-chairman of South Ossetia's parliament, but Nodar did not hear back from either the general or the South Ossetian authorities and decided to take action. One morning he borrowed a NRC car, determined to drive to Tskhinvali on his own. Though this in itself was a dangerous move, he felt it was a necessary one. In Tskhinvali he met, through NRC contacts, some South Ossetian teachers and psychologists. Together they planned—in the first joint Georgian–South Ossetian conflict resolution project—to bring a group of Georgian and South Ossetian teenagers—with their adult caretakers—to a two-week-long summer camp.[52] Shortly after, the NRC in Georgia approved funding for the program.

Nodar had mixed feelings about such a brief venture; the FDHR and his South Ossetian partners had no experience with guiding such a sensitive process. But he was determined to begin somewhere. On the way to the campsite in Kobuleti, a resort on the Black Sea near Batumi, Nodar sat next to a handsome, athletic South Ossetian teenager. Mostly Orthodox Christian in faith, ethnic Ossetians consider themselves to be descended from the Alans, a people who were pushed from the plains into the foothills of the Caucasus in the fourth century C.E. Until the bloody conflict of 1990–92, they had enjoyed relative peace with Georgians. The South Ossetian boys were very excited when the group stopped along the way, as they had never before seen the sea or such lush, well-groomed citrus orchards. Nodar found himself saying to his seatmate, "Now you see what a beautiful country our Georgia is!" He was immediately aware of a sense of competition with this boy, the feeling that he had wanted to put the youngster down. Even when one consciously wants to be helpful to the "enemy," he realized, one may unconsciously have—and act upon—opposite feelings. Nodar was amazed to notice how people in times of ethnic conflict keenly notice the differences between their own large-group identity and the identity of the enemy group. Nodar realized that he wanted to show the boy, who obviously stood for his people and represented his people's shared identity, that Georgians were better than South Ossetians.

At Kobuleti, Nodar realized that there would be no instant miracles and began to appreciate the role identity issues play in fueling large-group conflicts. The lead South Ossetian caretaker, a man named Phillip, repeatedly made hostile remarks about Georgians in front of the children, who were, of course, supposed to be there for conflict resolution, not conflict inflammation. Nodar and his FDHR coworkers Jana and Nato, who accompanied him to Kobuleti, felt that Phillip had come to Kobuleti just to fight, and there was no third-party to intervene. Finally, Nodar's patience reached its limit and he interrupted one of Phillip's tirades with a sharp request for him to be quiet and to let the children speak. Phillip stormed out, only to return later and remain silent. No doubt Phillip was expressing rage by his silence, but Nodar felt guilty that he had "killed" Phillip's spirit. Soon after the Kobuleti outing, Phillip died in a car accident. He had been Nodar's main contact in South Ossetia, so it took some time for the program to get back on its feet. Then, during another trip to Tskhinvali, Nodar finally met Venera Basishvili, whom the Georgians would later call "the South Ossetian Nodar," and a humane link between

Georgia and South Ossetia was established.

When I arrived in Georgia in May 1998, Nodar Sharveladze and Yuri Urbanovich greeted me at the Tbilisi Airport at three o'clock in the morning. Yuri had gone to Georgia two weeks earlier to prepare a meeting between representatives of CSMHI—Andy Thomson, Yuri, and me—and members of the Foundation for Human Development, including Nodar, Jana, Manana, Nato, Nino, Zurab, and others. When we met for the first time, Nodar, with his typical pleasant grin, hugged me and told me that I looked like a Georgian and that I was certainly a *jigari katsi,* a "real man." Later that day we all met at the FDHR office and CSMHI became a partner—by handshake only—as a "third neutral party" in FDHR's ongoing work with South Ossetians to help both sides tame emotions and perform more effective peace work.

Listening with a clinician's ear to Nodar and his colleagues during one of CSMHI's earliest meetings with FDHR, I sensed that they unconsciously linked Phillip's death with their aggression toward him. If this was an accurate assessment, then their ongoing work with South Ossetians was, at least in part, motivated by guilt. In other words, if Nodar imagined he had "killed" Phillip by silencing him, and if this fantasy was "actualized" by Phillip's fatal accident, then they felt they needed to pay penance by helping South Ossetians, especially the children who were the focus of their collaborative project. Doing good out of unconscious guilt, however, may lead to potentially messy psychological consequences: without being aware of it, those who are feeling guilty may act in such a way as to punish themselves, making it impossible for them to relate to the "other" as equals. And without the freedom to approach one another as equals, members of opposing groups cannot generate realistic negotiations or workable collaborations. True altruism does not include this element of masochism and therefore does not self-sabotage: only when a person acknowledges feelings of guilt—and works through their perceived need to do more for the "other" than is necessary (or perhaps even possible)—can he or she engage in genuinely altruistic activities. Fortunately, in this situation, Andy, Yuri, and I were eventually able to help open up the psychological consequences of Phillip's death, which strengthened the FDHR members' sense of altruism once it was purged of its guilt elements.[53]

When I began my visits to Georgia, both official and secret talks between Georgian and South Ossetian authorities were going nowhere. Later, a high-level official at the U.S. Embassy in Tbilisi told me that the American and the Russian governments had agreed not to interfere with the South Ossetian situation since there were no longer any people dying from the conflict. Whether the official's information was accurate or not did not matter. No American official would go to South Ossetia, and the Americans we met in Tbilisi who were in one way or another connected with the U.S. government were surprised that CSMHI faculty members planned to go to Tskhinvali, a dangerous place as far as they were concerned.

Andy, Yuri, and I were told that there were some representatives from international refugee organizations in Tskhinvali and some attempts had been made to build houses and permanent structures for the South Ossetian IDPs there. But these attempts had been plagued by fraud, as some builders used poor materials in their construction, pocketing the savings. As a result, the houses were completely inadequate as protection from the bitter Tskhinvali winters. There had not been—and there still has not been—any public investigations or truth commissions relating to any of the civil conflicts in Georgia. And certainly there had been no serious efforts to build ongoing person-to-person interaction between Georgians and South Ossetians until Nodar's courageous efforts to build a partnership between FDHR and Venera Basishvili, headmistress of Tskhinvali's Palace of Children's Creativity, a recreational and educational center for South Ossetian youth established in the Soviet era.

The first time I went to Tskhinvali, we drove there in two cars, passing through Gori and feeling Stalin's shadow falling on us. The car I was in with Yuri and Jana belonged to Amiran, the screenwriter, who served as our driver. Earlier, Amiran had told me about the "Georgian school" of filmmaking that existed during Soviet times when every script had to be approved by a governmental committee. A writer could not openly express an opinion against communism or the state of affairs in the Soviet Union. Accordingly, the "Georgian school" always sought out symbolic expression. In fact, they often borrowed forms of symbolic expression from the Bible or mythology to fool the committee members. The committee would urge the screenwriters to glorify the Soviet system and the working class. "You Georgians are happy people," they would say to Amiran, adding, "Make people appear happy in the movies." In his scripts, Amiran would oblige, making people appear outwardly happy, while expressing his character's true feelings in other ways. For example, one character might carry a basket full of broken eggs, which would symbolize his broken spirit.

Amiran had written scripts for five Georgian movies between 1980 and 1985 and was well-known and admired by the intellectuals there.

However, after Georgian reindependence there was little money to produce movies. During the Soviet era Georgians made an average of twenty movies per year; in 1998 they made only eight. Amiran did not know English and, of course, I did not know Georgian or Russian, but Yuri, as usual, was willing to help.

Earlier, Yuri, Amiran, and I had gone to the building that housed the Joint Stock Company of Georgian films in Tbilisi. In its garden stood statues of great Georgian film directors. Inside, although there were red carpets and the screening room had comfortable red chairs, everything was falling apart and the atmosphere was somewhat melancholic. We sat in the screening room and watched the 1987 movie *Nylon Christmas Tree*, which Amiran had written. It was directed by the famous Georgian director Rezo Esadse. Yuri interpreted the dialogue for me. I could see Amiran's most clever symbolization of life under the oppressive regime. Like Nodar, Amiran was someone who could maintain his individuality by writing while living in an oppressive political system.

The movie centered on a bus filled with people going home for Christmas. Everyone is "happy," but the crowded bus, as a representation of a regressed large group, is going nowhere. Meanwhile, the bus driver, as a representation of the Soviet leadership, does not care about the passengers. At one point, police stop the bus and the chatter onboard immediately turns to dead silence. All the while, one passenger carries a nylon Christmas tree, which symbolized how the "happy life" of Georgians was only a synthetic imitation.

In the new Georgia, left without an income, Amiran accepted his friend Nodar's offer to join the FDHR. While driving us to South Ossetia, Amiran told us that he was working on a new movie script called The Ceiling. He explained, "If you have a ceiling, it means that you have a home; you are not lost. We Georgians have been looking for a new ceiling for the last ten years." I was reminded of my tent analogy for large-group identity. I am always amazed at how much painters, poets, novelists, and other creative people who have no formal training in psychoanalysis "know" about psychoanalytic concepts concerning human nature.

I will never forget my first sight of the Georgian–South Ossetian border. It was marked with a wooden arm over the road, much like those at railroad crossings in the United States. The border guards were housed in a watchtower structure next to the barricade. Hundreds of trucks were parked in the fields around the barricade while their unsmiling drivers roamed around in the mud. I got the strong impression that this crossing was literally a gateway through which people, money, food, and arms were flowing into Central Asia. There was a sense of lawlessness, and a feeling that these people were trying to find out who they were, and which ethnic or religious cause they wanted to ally themselves with. We had no trouble passing through the border. When I first saw the city's buildings, once more I was reminded of certain places in the Turkish sector of Nicosia, Cyprus, as they were after 1974. The walls of many buildings were marked with bullet holes. The infrastructure of the city was basically ruined. There were few people in the pothole-filled streets.

Finally, we reached the Palace of Children's Creativity, which was also sadly dilapidated. When one hears the word "palace" one generally thinks of a majestic edifice built to house royalty, but the Palace of Children's Creativity was no such place. Its courtyard had been converted into a parking lot. Inside, its once-handsome marble floor was broken in pieces, and the staff rooms were sparsely furnished with old furniture. The entry hall held a bust of South Ossetian poet, painter, and revolutionary Kosta Khetagurov (1859–1906); photos and newspaper clippings of various South Ossetian and, surprisingly, American literary figures were taped to the walls. Headmistress Venera Basishvili and some of her assistants were quite proud of their deep knowledge of American literature and counted Ernest Hemingway, William Faulkner, and Edgar Allan Poe among their favorite writers. When I told Venera (through an interpreter) that I came from the University of Virginia, where Poe had studied and Faulkner had lectured, she seemed very pleased.

Venera was a local ethnic Georgian widow in her sixties whose husband had been South Ossetian, and she had come to identify herself as a South Ossetian. In the midst of emotional and physical devastation she was trying to make the Palace of Children's Creativity a healing place for South Ossetia's children who had been traumatized by the war and the siege of Tskhinvali. As a younger woman, Basishvili had been a well-known and respected educator; she had even taught some South Ossetians who were now in powerful political positions. Thus, as I guessed and soon confirmed, she was a person of some political clout in the breakaway region. So it had been an act of courage when Venera had agreed to work with the "enemy"—that is, when she accepted Nodar Sharveladze's proposal to work together to provide psychological services to a group of South Ossetian children. Since the Georgian psychiatrists and psychologists working with the FDHR had better training and more experience than their Tskhinvali colleagues, it was agreed that Nodar and his FDHR colleagues from Tbilisi, supplemented by NRC funds, would take turns coming to the Palace of Children's Creativity once a month to supervise the work of South Ossetian teachers and psychologists. After learning techniques at their monthly sessions with the Georgians, the South Ossetian caretakers would then begin to hold weekly sessions with the children.

On that first visit to the Palace of Children's Creativity in May 1998, Andy, Yuri, and I only spoke with staff members and did not observe their or the Georgian's work with the children. We explained to them why a CSMHI team would like to observe their efforts: we wanted to help train the South Ossetian caretakers in the hopes that their work with children would provide a sort of "vaccination" against the influence of traumatic events they had experienced and even against violence if another extreme crisis arose in the future. They agreed to be our partners. The juxtaposition between the fearsome Georgian–South Ossetian border and the friendly South Ossetians with their lovingly collected clippings of American literary figures on the walls of the Children's Creativity Palace confused me. I felt I was seeing human nature represented in concrete form—aggression and love, the ugly and the beautiful, standing next to each other. It took some time for me to integrate these opposites in my mind. Visiting a place like Tskhinvali on a cold spring day for the first time, a foreigner needs to do internal psychological work to integrate such polarities in order to carry out a realistic conversation with locals who have adjusted to living with the contradictions of a traumatized society.

When we first parked our cars in front of the Palace of Children's Creativity, we saw four staff members—all women—in front of the entrance to the building. One of them, who was tall and beautiful, was standing on crutches due to an injured leg. She was Madina Gazzaeva, a South Ossian psychologist who would work with us closely for years to come. Madina told us (in Russian) that she was a basketball player and that a few days earlier she had broken her leg while playing. A young woman playing basketball in a rundown city—every building we saw needed repair—forces a foreigner like me to do further internal integrative work: to comprehend how a young woman can have fun playing sports while surrounded by a physical environment that constantly reminds her of the horrors of human aggression.

I decided that listening to Venera, Madina, and other South Ossetians' personal war-related stories would allow them to feel comfortable with the CSMHI members. They spoke for hours about their first-hand observations of various tragic events. Our Georgian friends also listened to them and even showed some empathy. But I knew that some of them wanted to "compete" with the enemy and tell their own horror stories.

During this period of time the average monthly salary of a teacher in Tskhinvali was less than two dollars. Many people had developed a bartering system to survive. Finding heat during the winter was an especially great problem. We were told that one group of old people, knowing that the coming winter would kill them, dug the graves in which they were indeed later buried. Prostitutes, mostly young women and children, we also learned, earned a dollar or two for each favor. The city itself was a concrete example of large-group regression and chaos.

After spending long hours at the Palace of Children's Creativity, we went to see the South Ossetian foreign minister who was, I believe, a former student of Venera. During my long years in unofficial diplomatic work in many troubled spots of the world, I found that paying our respects to an official(s) in the government by a brief visit is always useful. This gives us—the CSMHI faculty—credibility and saves us from being perceived as doing something in secret and hiding something from the local authorities. Visiting the foreign minister's office in South Ossetia, we found a tiny room furnished with a desk and two chairs. The minister himself, wearing a heavy coat indoors, was completely alone in the place with the exception of one female secretary stoking a small fire. Yuri thanked the foreign minister in Russian, the common language used between Georgians and South Ossetians, for receiving us during his "heavy daily schedule!" The foreign minister smiled widely. I think that he had a good sense of humor.

Yuri and I returned to Tskhinvali in November 1998, along with Nodar, Jana, Nino, and Amiran. This time I had an opportunity to observe ongoing Georgian–South Ossetian collaborative work with South Ossetian children. Initially sixty children from ages nine to twelve were involved in the project. Later thirty more were added. They would meet once a week with South Ossetian teachers and psychologists in groups of twenty to twenty-five. Once a month Georgians would come, and the children, in their own groups, would meet with Jana and Nino. The program would allow them to speak about their experiences during the war and express their feelings. The aim was to remove the pathological responses to trauma from these children's psyches and keep them from remaining as living carriers of ethnic hate.

On the icy morning of November 3, 1998, there were twenty-five children at the Palace of Children's Creativity to participate in a two-hour meeting with Jana and Nino. On the right side of the entrance hall, past the decrepit and constantly flooded lavatories—there was no money even for basic plumbing repairs—were the rooms in which the children gathered for their sessions. When I entered one of these rooms I saw the South Ossetian children seated on wooden benches in three concentric circles. Some of them were local, and others came from a boarding house for children from the war-devastated countryside where family structure had broken down and many fathers had left for Russia in search of work. A metal stove stood in one corner, belching smoke into the snow-covered courtyard through a makeshift pipe. Two Georgian consultants prepared to lead the session with the children. I sat with five South Ossetian teachers and psychologists, Nodar and Amiran from the FDHR, and Yuri on higher benches outside the circles, observing. All conversation took place in Russian. My interpreter that day was Irene Bekoeva, a South Ossetian woman, probably in her early twenties, who spoke English with an American accent. I had never met Irene before, and I was so impressed by her command of the English language, I inquired where she had learned to speak it. She told me she had never left South Ossetia except to study English and American literature at the University of Nalchik in the Republic of Kabardino-Balkaria in the Northern Caucasus of the Russian Federation. Irene was beautiful, but I sensed she was like a little wounded bird. I did not know why I had such a thought.

Jana began the meeting by introducing herself and explaining that she and her colleagues had come to the Palace of Children's Creativity to talk to the children. Noting that she already knew most of the children, she urged them not to be shy and asked them to introduce themselves as she tossed a soft yellow ball toward the group. As the children caught the ball, they were supposed to introduce themselves and name their favorite hobbies. They spoke of liking soccer, music, wrestling, and dancing. After almost every child had a chance to speak, Jana introduced a new twist to the game. After catching the ball, each child was supposed to name one "rule" of social behavior recognized by the group. "We smile," one said. "Be friendly," added another. "Listen more and speak less. . . . Accept each other's appearance.... Be polite," they continued.

After about an hour, the children were asked to make up and to tell a story as a group, a technique of working with traumatized children that had been taught to the instructors by some Norwegian-sponsored visiting teachers. From the caretakers' point of view, the storytelling activity would form a kind of shared painter's canvas onto which the children could externalize and project aspects of their internal worlds. Once out in the open, these projections could then be discussed in a way that could be therapeutic. The children began: "There was a man . . . who sailed to an island ... where he searched for food."

I was immediately impressed by the children's abundant references to water. On the surface, they and the instructors would laugh and chatter about how fun it would be to sail on a lake or sea to an island and have a holiday at a beach. But, I recalled, South Ossetia is completely landlocked, with no large lakes, oceans, or inland seas. Since sailing is not a realistic option in South Ossetia, the children's preoccupation with vacationing at a beach seemed to represent a fantasy of being elsewhere. In my psychoanalyst's mind—and based on my experience with war-traumatized children elsewhere—I sensed that the children were, further, trying to send a message to the adults in the room, as if they were screaming, "water, water everywhere." I wondered if the water that they obsessively referred to also reflected the symptom of bedwetting; water is often prominent in the dreams of traumatized children who wet their beds, and bedwetting is often related to feelings of helpless rage.[54] Through their storytelling, I thought perhaps the children sought to reverse a troublesome wetness, that is, to remake it as a pleasurable experience. When I presented this idea to the South Ossetian caretakers after the session, Venera confirmed that bedwetting was indeed quite common among the children, but that it was rarely spoken of openly because it was so humiliating, especially for the older children. Significantly, though, the children's mothers sometimes whispered about it to the esteemed headmistress. Venera had not even discussed it with the younger South Ossetian caretakers or their Georgian colleagues until that very day. For the children and adults in traumatized Tskhinvali, the children's bedwetting was a secret, a symbol of the community's humiliation.

More importantly, however, I sensed that the island in the children's story represented South Ossetia surrounded by "enemies," even though none of the children made any reference to Georgians or to themselves as South Ossetians. At one point in the children's story, the man sees a hostile Iranian boat and wants to fight the people onboard. Studiously avoiding the differences within the room, the children had turned any hostile feelings instead toward "others," Iranians. When aggression surfaced, one of the children would say, rather robotically: "Even though it is difficult to make friends after a war, we want peace!" With a frozen smile on his face, another child drew a stick figure on the island with upraised hands, as if surrendering to an unseen enemy; next to the figure, encased in a square like a cartoonist's balloon, he wrote, in English, as if for the benefit of Yuri and myself, "Help! Help!" I was very moved by his struggle to state directly that he and the other children needed our help, even though he wanted to hide it. But, as if she could not see the "help" message, one of the instructors said to the boy: "Isn't it nice that now you are on vacation on this island, jumping up and down with joy?"

As the two-hour session proceeded, I felt frustrated. Rather than airing the children's anxieties and aggressions, Jana and Nino seemed to be going along with—even encouraging—the children's denial of any negative feelings. I was anxious to discuss all that they had missed in the session—after all, I was there as a consultant and felt I had much to teach these colleagues! Impatient to discuss what I had seen, I turned to Irene, my young interpreter, and asked, "Isn't it amazing that these two instructors missed the children's pleas to discuss their hurt feelings, and instead actively suppressed the children's expressions!" Irene turned and looked at me in amazement. "Jana and Nino, like the South Ossetian teachers and psychologists here, are all aware of what the children wanted to talk about," she said, adding in a whisper, "We are not stupid!" She went on to suggest—quite rightly in my view—that the caretakers, Georgian and South Ossetian alike, were themselves traumatized and therefore not yet able to tolerate the children's pain and fear, as this would open the caretakers' own wounds. She paused a moment, then asked me: "Have you read *Sophie's Choice*?"

On this dreary day in Tskhinvali, watching Jana and Nino as they continued to work with the children, and sometimes trying to keep our hands warm over a smoky stove in this dismal room, Irene told me her story in whispers, with dignity. She had been in her mid-teens when Tskhinvali came under attack by the Georgians. Her father had died just before the war, and she was living with her mother and sister, all in acute states of grief, when the war broke out. An international organization arrived in Tskhinvali during the hostility to transport South Ossetian teenagers out of harm's way for the duration of the conflict, but they could only take forty of them. Representatives of the organization had asked Irene's mother to choose one of her daughters to participate in the program. Once Irene was chosen, she was quickly taken over the mountains into the Russian Federation to the city of Nalchik, where she lived in a dormitory for four months while her mother and sister remained in Tskhinvali. She was the oldest child among the forty who had been taken to safety. This itself separated her from other South Ossetian youth in the dormitory. Once safely settled, Irene, an avid reader, was struck by the similarity between her story and that of William Styron's novel *Sophie's Choice*. She was the chosen one.

While Irene was away, she had no idea what was happening to her mother and sister, she had no friends in her dormitory, and her mind was filled with fantasies of bad things happening to her family while she remained safe. Plagued by nightmares, she ended up hating herself for being the "chosen one." Fortunately, Irene found her family alive and well upon her return, but she had internalized these extremely severe feelings of guilt to such a degree that she now considered herself a bad person. She felt unable to discuss these feelings with family or friends. She told me that she, like the Georgian instructors, would or could not allow the children at the Palace of Children's Creativity to talk about their traumas or memories of horrible occurrences. Since she had been spared such trauma, hearing others talk about it rekindled her intense feelings of guilt. I felt that her internalized guilt was almost palpable. We continued to speak in intense whispers. She told me that her father, who died just before she was sent away, was an ethnic Georgian. After he was gone, Irene's South Ossetian mother told her girls to stop using their father's surname and instead adopt the mother's surname. The girls agreed to do so. To use an Ossetian name in South Ossetia after the war with Georgia was safer and more adaptive. I sensed that to do so created an internal problem for Irene. Her being the "chosen one" and "betraying" her sister Vera was condensed with her "betraying" her father. She was also feeling guilty for "killing" her link to her father.

Irene suddenly looked at me and said, "When I first saw you I thought you were a Georgian man." I realized that she had transferred the image of her dead father onto me; she had "re-created" him and wanted guidance from him/me. I told Irene that since she gave me the privilege of being like her Georgian father, even temporarily, I, as a father figure, could tell her that it would be a crime if she continued to live with guilt. She could drop it. She began crying silently and tried to hide it from the others in the room, but not from me. Then she told me that after returning to Tskhinvali and finding her mother and sister alive once more, she left them for some years, again for Nalchik, to pursue her education. She described how the experience of going to Nalchik for four months as the "chosen one" had contaminated her experience as a student at Nalchik.

After Jana and Nino's session with the children ended, I took Irene aside and we made a plan to share her feelings, step by step, with her mother and sister. I told her to take a walk with her sister, Vera, at least once a month and share with her how she had felt to be the "chosen one." We also spoke about how she could talk with her mother about her guilt feelings concerning the same. She could tell her mother she was grateful to be the one her mother picked to send to safety, but her mother should also know how this was burdensome, as it was burdensome to let go of her father's surname for the sake of realistic safety concerns.

We gathered in Venera's room for a social hour after the sessions at the Palace of Children's Creativity. Despite their hardships, the South Ossetians had prepared food and drink: their desire to display pride and dignity was very moving. Over our meal, as usually happens in gatherings of people from "enemy" groups, minor differences between Georgians and South Ossetians were a topic of social conversation—such as preparation methods for *kapachuri*, a kind of pizza traditional to both groups. It became clear to me that the South Ossetian and Georgian caretakers, as Irene had pointed out, were aware of their own limitations related to the children's attempts to openly express their feelings about trauma and the war era. Nodar, with his unusual capacity for self-observation, was able to make several tactful comments that tried to address the caretakers' own traumas and feelings of guilt.

But it was not until we were back in Tbilisi the next day that our Georgian colleagues from the FDHR were able to talk about how difficult it was for them to travel to South Ossetia. They spoke of their fear of being perceived as traitors within their own Tbilisi communities since they were collaborating with South Ossetians to try to help the children of the "enemy." Jana recollected an incident that had occurred during the social hour after our meetings and discussions at the Palace of Children's Creativity. She had been sitting at a table with the others when a rather tall man entered the room. Her immediate reaction was one of intense fear; she felt that the newcomer was a South Ossetian who had come to take her hostage. "I thought I had never seen him before and did not know who he was," she recalled. "Then someone asked him to sit down with us, and I realized that he was the Georgian driver of the car I had ridden in from Tbilisi, and for about three hours we had talked together in the car on the way to Tskhinvali." Her level of anxiety over being in "enemy" territory had blurred her normal powers of observation. Something similar had happened to Amiran at the Palace of Children's Creativity the day before. At one point during the session with the children he had briefly left the room to smoke a cigarette, but he now explained that his main reason for leaving the room was not to smoke, but to check on a group of South Ossetian men whom he had noticed through the window. They were hanging around his car, and he was afraid that they would damage or attack the vehicle because of its Georgian license plates. Whether his fear was realistic is irrelevant: his anxiety reflected the heightened feelings of danger that sometimes interfered with the primary tasks of the FDHR caretakers. I admired their courage and willingness to try to overcome emotional and realistic obstacles to help others.

I returned to Tskhinvali once more in the spring of 1999, again with Yuri. Andy was with us this trip, too, as well as psychiatrist Gregory Saathoff, another member of CSMHI. During this journey I was preoccupied with the memory of what I thought of as "one full hour of analytic work" with Irene during my previous visit. I knew that in the smoky room of the Palace of Children's Creativity she had sensed my empathy for her; in her mind, I believe, I took the place of a concerned father. Using this role, I was able to help her to speak about her terrible feelings of guilt.

When we arrived at the Palace of Children's Creativity, Irene was waiting for me. She was no longer a wounded little bird. She told me that she had kept our conversation alive in her mind and followed my instructions very closely. Indeed, she had blossomed as a professional and had fallen in love with a young man, who had proposed to her. Irene knew that she could not agree to marry him until she got my "permission." Therefore, she had been anxiously waiting for my return. I gave her my "permission."

I never returned to Tskhinvali after this visit, mainly because Tskhinvali's situation had worsened and the U.S. Embassy in Tbilisi told us directly not to travel to South Ossetia. But I continued to work with Madina and her associates Fatima Turmanova, Inga Kochieva, and Irina Yanovskaia. Whenever I was in Tbilisi they joined CSMHI and the FDHR for further work. The program with South Ossetian children lasted about three years. In late 2002 Madina and others reported to us at a meeting in Istanbul, Turkey, at which Georgians and South Ossetians were present, that criminality and prostitution had become endemic in Tskhinvali, even among young teenagers. But Madina and her colleagues told us that none of the ninety children who had gone through the Palace of Children's Creativity program had become criminals or prostitutes. However, their most striking findings related to the boarding house for rural children. Of the boarding house's two hundred youngsters, only twenty had participated in the Palace of Children's Creativity program. Madina and her colleagues observed that these twenty youngsters had adjusted well as teenagers, while the rest had become criminals or prostitutes.

Such findings on the efficacy of the Palace of Children's Creativity program—however premature—are not atypical. But financial and political pressures are always a significant part of the context in which psychologically informed efforts to heal societal wounds take place, and unfortunately, traditional diplomacy does not usually respond unless "hot" military-political conflict is raging. As I mentioned, the U.S. Embassy in Tbilisi told CSMHI in 2001 that the policy of the United States and Russia toward Georgian–South Ossetian interactions was strictly "hands off ": neither country had any interest in becoming embroiled in the conflict. Even Norway transferred most of its aid from Georgian–South Ossetian initiatives as soon as the Chechen war broke out and thousands of refugees arrived in Georgia. Unfortunately, the international community tends to turn away when deadly political-military conflict "cools" into deadly societal conflict.

This neglect may have grave consequences indeed, and not simply in terms of the societal ills of criminality, prostitution, family disintegration, and the like. While we worked there, Georgians believed that Russia intended to keep Georgia weak and in a state of arrested development, so that it would indirectly remain under the more powerful nation's control. South Ossetians could travel to Russia without a visa, yet Georgians needed one; Russia treated them as two separate countries, though South Ossetia is not an internationally recognized state. September 11, 2001, made Georgia's relationship with Russia even more rocky, as Georgians believed that the international war on terror had extended the rights of war to Russia, which now and then bombed parts of Georgia where it suspected terrorist—meaning Chechen rebel—activity. Obviously, when it came to Georgia, the international agendas of powerful nations such as Russia and the United States did not include the need to alleviate suffering and to reduce ethnic tensions there, as I observed in Tbilisi a few days after the U.S. military arrived in early March 2002. Though the U.S. military had come because of suspected al-Qaeda activity in Georgia, the Georgian IDPs developed a shared fantasy that the Americans were there to help them fight the Abkhazians. I strongly suspected that after awhile, when reality set in and the Americans did not aid them in their continuing conflict, the Georgian IDPs would be left frustrated and retraumatized once more.

When I visited Tbilisi for the last time in March 2002, I was told that Irene Bekoeva would accompany the other South Ossetians to the Georgian capital where they would get together once more with their Georgian counterparts and the CSMHI team. Instead, she sent me a letter by way of the other South Ossetians who came to Tbilisi that moved me very much. The envelope contained two photographs of Alexander (Sasha), Irene's seven-month-old son, whom she was unable to leave to come to Tbilisi. She wrote: "You don't even know how much you mean to me. What a great role you played in my life. Life without fear, without any stress, without feelings of guilt. You taught me to be wise and to receive my fate and everything as it was. You gave me a great lesson on how to be strong." Irene went on to talk about her present happiness and concluded her letter by saying: "Since my son does not have any grandfathers (my father-in-law died a year ago), do you object to having a grandson in South Ossetia? May we call you our grandpa?"

There are occasions when I ask myself why I voluntarily put myself in uncomfortable and often dangerous situations around the world. Besides the intellectual satisfaction of understanding individuals' and large groups' behavior under stress, I am extremely honored to have touched the lives of people like Irene. Though I have not seen her since 1998, her correspondence alone (I heard from her last in June 2005, when she let me know that she, her husband, and Sasha were doing well) has made all the energy I have spent understanding the situation in her part of the world personally worthwhile.

Part II

Societal Trauma
and Transgenerational Transmission

6 From Natural Disasters to Ethnic Cleansing

W hen a massive disaster occurs, such as the one in Tskhinvali that I described in the previous chapter, those who are affected may experience its psychological impact in several ways. First, many individuals will suffer from what is known in psychiatric and psychological literature as posttraumatic stress disorder (PTSD). PTSD is a relatively new diagnostic category in the mental health field, having only been officially recognized by the American Psychiatric Association in 1980. Briefly, it refers to the experience of unexpected mental states in which sufferers' traumatic experiences resurface vividly. They may have recurring dreams, flashbacks, and difficulty concentrating and sleeping. The regulation of emotions, consciousness, self-perception, perception of the trauma's perpetrator, relations with others, and meaning of events are altered. Developments in the neurosciences in recent decades have begun to inform us about how the brain is shaped by experience and how going through traumatic experiences transforms its biology.[55] As I write this book, memos are being circulated among members of the Group for the Advancement of Psychiatry (GAP) and other mental health-related organizations that warn clinicians to prepare for an onslaught of military persons returning from Iraq with PTSD symptoms.

The signs and symptoms of PTSD do not tell us about the traumatized persons' intimate stories, such as the intertwining of the images of external disaster with the internal images of their past experiences, their struggles with mourning over losses and the meanings of what has been lost, and their attempts at adaptation. In essence, PTSD symptoms tell us about the existence of a nightmare but do not tell us the story and meaning behind the nightmare. Obviously, when working in a war zone or a newly created refugee camp, caretakers have no time to deal individually with thousands of traumatized persons. But when time and circumstances permit, more careful work is needed to focus beyond PTSD and understand the affected individual's internal struggles. In the first part of this book I provided a lens through which we can recognize more personalized reactions to massive trauma due to ethnic identity conflicts. When I worked with the members of the Kachavara family and Irene Bekoeva, I went beyond considering PTSD and got to know them, as much as I could, as individuals in their own right, individuals whose internal stories moved me.

Beyond the presence of PTSD among individuals, massive traumas and disasters can also lead to four kinds of reactions among society as a whole. They include: (1) new societal preoccupations; (2) a modification of the existing cultural customs; (3) the building of monuments as shared linking objects; and (4) transgenerational transmissions of trauma. Only through studying these societal responses can we understand how sufferers' medical and psychological problems following a shared trauma can be connected or can evolve into societal, political, and historical movements.

The first response, new societal preoccupations, is directly related to the shared mental representation of the traumatizing event. One example of this is the preoccupation with blankets I described among certain Cypriot Turk refugees—specifically, their preoccupation with the blankets was directly related to their ethnic conflict. In this chapter, I will look closely at similar preoccupations that have initiated new societal processes after recent massive disasters.

The second societal response involves the modification of already existing cultural customs after the experience of a catastrophe. Cultural customs are like designs painted on the canvas of a large group's tent. When the tent shakes or is torn, the large group needs to restore or repaint the designs in order to maintain the protosymbols and symbols of its identity. In this chapter I will give an example of this phenomenon.

Later I will devote two chapters to the third societal response: building monuments as shared linking objects (see chapters 7 and 8).

The fourth societal response deals with the concept of transgenerational transmission. Briefly, members of a traumatized society may not be able to fully perform certain necessary psychological tasks, such as mourning their losses. They then "transfer" such unfinished tasks to the next generation(s) so that their offspring might perform these unfinished tasks for them (see chapter 9). I will later illustrate how sharing transgenerationally transmitted tasks may play a crucial role in shaping societal, political, and historical processes, in inspiring the eruption of massive violence, and in influencing large-group identity (see chapter 10).

Before I turn my attention to these four specific responses to massive disasters, we must acknowledge that there are different types of shared catastrophes. Some massive disasters stem from natural causes, such as tropical storms, floods, volcanic eruptions, forest fires, avalanches, mud slides, earthquakes, and tsunamis. Some are accidental man-made disasters, such as the April 26, 1986, Chernobyl accident that spewed ten tons of radioactive dust into the atmosphere. Other massive disasters are due to the loss of a person who thousands or millions of people share as a symbolically important figure. Such a loss provokes individualized as well as societal responses, as did the assassinations of John F. Kennedy in the United States and Yitzhak Rabin in Israel,[56] and the deaths of the American astronauts and teacher Christa McAuliffe in the January 1986 space shuttle *Challenger* explosion.[57] Other traumas result from political, nationalistic, religious, and ideological propaganda in the form of revolutionary or civil wars that lead to significant loss of life and property, and drastic social changes that turn the lives of many individuals upside down, creating severe shared anxiety. Such traumas usually occur among subgroups that belong to the same ethnicity or nationality.

We know from history that sometimes people humiliate and kill their own kind and create terror from above. Under the dictator Enver Hoxha (1908–85), Albanians humiliated, tortured, exiled, and killed other Albanians. In reality, the Albanian population was divided between "torturers" and "tortured." Such a division was internalized by the citizens, and for many years after the death of the dictator, the impact of this societal division was kept alive within the society and its influence could be felt in Albania's political, economic, and legal concerns.[58] The repressive dictatorships that dominated the Latin American continent from the mid-1960s through the 1990s carried out what became known as "dirty wars" against their own citizens in which hundreds of thousands of individuals, families, and even entire communities were eradicated.[59]

But how are disasters at the hands of "others," which are directly related to large-group identity issues, different from the types of disasters mentioned above? At the end of this chapter I will examine this question and will point to some specific areas of difference. Sometimes, however, it may be difficult to differentiate between all categories of massive disasters. For example, a natural disaster can become intertwined with political and ethnic conflicts. Following the tsunami that struck on December 26, 2004, separatist rebels in the province of Aceh on the northern tip of Sumatra ordered a cease-fire, while the Indonesian government responded by loosening travel restrictions to the area and allowing relief agencies and journalists to visit there.[60] In turn, this created an atmosphere that allowed the government and rebels to sign a peace agreement in August 2005 that may finally put an end to their decades-long war. In Sri Lanka, meanwhile, the tsunami has not contributed to any form of reconciliation between the Sinhalese-dominated government and Tamil Tiger rebels. This is at least in part due to disputes over tsunami aid. If anything, the situation there is more violent than ever.[61] However, given that the tsunami occurred in the recent past it is still impossible to determine what the long-term ramifications of the disaster will be on the region's political and ethnic conflicts.

But the 1999 earthquake in Turkey that killed an estimated twenty thousand people happened long enough ago that we are able to see how this natural disaster stimulated change in theretofore unbendable ethnic sentiments. Just a few years before the earthquake, tensions between Turkey and Greece were very high. They had almost gone to war in a dispute over small islands of rocks in the Aegean Sea just off the Turkish coast known as Kardak to the Turks and Imia to the Greeks.[62] This incident inflamed Turkish and Greek emotions. But after the Turkish earthquake, the Turks welcomed the Greeks' offer of help. By publishing pictures and stories of Greek rescue workers on Turkish soil, Turkish newspapers played a significant role in "humanizing" the Greeks as a large group. When a smaller earthquake hit Greece the following month, Turkey reciprocated by quickly sending rescue workers to Greece. As a result, the earthquakes ushered in a new era of relations between the two nations. Indeed, many diplomats have attributed the positive political developments to what they call "earthquake diplomacy."[63]

I traveled to Turkey two days after the earthquake and provided some consultation to Turkish mental health workers from Istanbul who had visited the affected area. I also interviewed many people about their feelings concerning the Greeks' help, including influential decision makers. Both before and after the Turkish earthquake, I was involved in a series of meetings that aimed to open an unofficial dialogue between influential Turks and Greeks. Well-known retired Turkish and Greek military leaders and ambassadors, as well as scholars from both countries, attended these meetings. Using the participants as representatives of their respective countries, I was able to take a closer look at the softening of tensions between Turkey and Greece after the earthquakes. I concluded that this softening was motivated, above and beyond realpolitik considerations, by deep, mostly unnoticed, psychological dynamics. The shared aggressive fantasies that go along with identity issues, enmity, or opposition had not gone away. Rather, they were covered over by an apparent shared reaction formation. The term "reaction formation" is a psychoanalytic one that refers to the response to an unwanted feeling or thought by exhibiting openly the opposite feeling or thought. A shared unconscious wish that something bad would happen to the "enemy" played a part in the Greeks' generosity. The Turks responded to this with their own shared reaction formation by quickly dropping their irritation with and complaints about Greeks and "forgetting" the pre-earthquake animosity between the two countries.

These negative unconscious motivations that I noticed during my observations did not take away from the reality of the new closeness between the Turks and the Greeks. The crucial issue was whether this closeness could be sublimated. Sometimes positive initiatives in human relations, as well as in international relations, have unconscious negative motivations, but when they become established within the society and institutionalized by diplomatic agreements, what initiated them in the unconscious may no longer be important. After the Turkish earthquake a kind of nostalgia for the old togetherness of Turks and Greeks living side by side in Istanbul returned. Playing and singing Greek songs became popular in Istanbul's *meyhanes* (bars) and nightclubs. Emotional poison in the Turkish-Greek relationship had found an antidote. This did not mean that there would not continue to be ups and downs in the diplomatic, legal, and military activities between Turkey and Greece, but the emotional poison was no longer experienced as deadly.

All types of massive disasters evoke societal responses. While the earthquakes in Turkey and Greece led to a thawing of relations between the two countries, the massive earthquake that hit Armenia in 1988 did not lead to a rapprochement between Armenia and Azerbaijan, its neighboring enemy. Although the earthquake devastated the country, when Azerbaijanis offered help by donating blood, ethnic identity issues prevailed over the urgent need for medical assistance. The Armenians refused to accept blood donated by Azerbaijanis; they resisted "mixing blood" that, in effect, symbolically represented "mixing identities."[64] But the degree to which these responses will be generalized within the large group and how much they will remain "regional" (that is, within the boundary of the affected geographical location, affected tribe, or even affected political party) depends on many factors. For example, the response to the *Challenger* tragedy was so quickly generalized across the entire United States not just because of the blow to America's prestige and its mighty space program but also to the presence of Christa McAuliffe onboard, a civilian teacher who symbolically represented all Americans.

The Chernobyl accident did not remain a regional trauma either. As the winds carried the radioactive matter to far-away places, the accident was quickly generalized and became multinational in scope. For example, the event led to a new societal preoccupation in nearby Belarus, where thousands upon thousands considered themselves, in reality and in fantasy, to have been contaminated with radiation. Fearing birth defects, many chose not to have children. As a result, the existing norms for finding a mate, marrying, and planning a family were significantly disrupted. Those who did have children often remained continually anxious that something "bad" would affect their children's health. Chernobyl even traumatized me. When the accident occurred, one of my favorite young relatives from North Cyprus was attending medical school in Kiev, the capital of Ukraine. After she graduated, she returned to Cyprus as a physician and married, but she soon developed leukemia. I strongly suspected that this was due to her having been exposed to radiation. Months later, she passed away and I still mourn this tragic loss.

The 1972 Buffalo Creek disaster in West Virginia is another example of a shared tragedy. On February 26, 1972, an enormous slag damn gave way, unleashing thousands of tons of water and mud on the Buffalo Creek valley. In fifteen minutes, 125 people were killed, four thousand were left homeless, and fourteen mining hamlets were wiped out.[65] In a similar shared tragedy, on October 21, 1966, an avalanche of coal slurry in Wales engulfed a primary school and several houses in the villages of Aberfan and Merthyr Vale, killing 116 children and twenty-eight adults. Studies of both tragedies include data that goes far beyond descriptions of individual reactions, what today would be called PTSD (this term was not available when Buffalo Creek and the two Welsh villages studies were carried out), and longitudinally examine certain societal processes that followed the catastrophes.

Although both tragedies remained "regional," I am mentioning these events because studying them provides us with two concepts that can be applied to more generalized responses to massive trauma, including that which comes at the hands of enemies. The first concept, "the tearing apart the tissue of social life," comes from Kai Erikson, a well-known Yale University sociologist,[66] while the second concept, "biosocial regeneration," was coined by the British psychiatrist C. Murray Parkes, an expert in the psychology of mourning, who used to be associated with the Tavistock Institute of Human Relations in London.[67] At Buffalo Creek, everything was lost, from family and friends to possessions and mementos. Along with these things, the feeling of community also was lost. For Erikson, the tearing apart of the tissue of a community occurs when bonds that link people together disappear. I find an echo of Erikson's conceptualization of losing the tissue of community in the work of the late Israeli psychoanalyst Rafael Moses, a good friend who described the loss of security in the interpersonal worlds of those who experienced long- or even short-term exposure to Nazi persecution.[68] I also consider what happened in Belarus after Chernobyl to be an example of societal tissue that was broken.

C. Murray Parkes worked with R. M. Williams, a local psychiatrist in Aberfan and Merthyr Vale, researching what happened to the two communities after the disaster. Those who survived were highly motivated not only to repair the damage but also to bring something positive out of the ruins. Williams and Parkes's research revealed that in the five years following the tragedy, the birth rate in Aberfan and Merthyr Vale rose significantly, as if to replace the children who had been lost. Further, the increase in births was not confined to bereaved parents but was spread over the entire population. In fact, only a small proportion of the increased birth rate was attributable to the bereaved parents. These investigators concluded that "the increased birth rate in Aberfan and Merthyr Vale observed during the first five years after the disaster was mainly a consequence of a process of biosocial regeneration by couples who had not lost a child." When the tissue of a community is not completely torn apart, psychosocial transitions after disasters are "not entirely destructive in their effects when viewed from the perspective of the total community in which they occur."[69] Following Parkes and Williams's use of the term biosocial regeneration, I use the term biosocial degeneration in reference to conditions after a massive trauma in which the societal tissue is damaged.[70]

Biosocial regeneration and degeneration are also observable after disasters due to ethnic or other large-group identity hostilities, such as wars. A somewhat indirect biosocial regeneration occurred among the Cypriot Turks during the six-year period (1963–68) in which they were forced by Cypriot Greeks to live in isolated enclaves under subhuman conditions. Though they had been massively traumatized, their "backbone" was not broken because of their hope that the motherland, Turkey, would come to their aid. Instead of bearing increased numbers of children like the inhabitants of Aberfan and Merthyr Vale, they raised hundreds and hundreds of parakeets in cages (parakeets are not native to

Cyprus), representing their "imprisoned" selves. As long as the birds sang and reproduced, the Cypriot Turks' shared anxiety remained under control.[71] The art and literature stemming from the Hiroshima tragedy might also be considered a form of symbolic biosocial regeneration. In the case of Hiroshima, however, the society also exhibited biosocial degeneration and showed "death imprints"[72] for decades after the catastrophe; the society's social tissue was in fact torn, and biosocial regeneration could only be limited and sporadic.

Interestingly enough, if societal tissue is not torn apart, those who are not directly affected by the massive trauma, whether it remains "regional" or is generalized into the total large group, begin telling jokes about the tragedy and its victims. In fact, I consider the appearance of jokes and their being told within the society as an indicator that the tissue of the society is not irreparably damaged. Such was my observation in Mexico City following the September 1985 earthquake that killed ten thousand people, injured thirty thousand, and left one hundred thousand homeless. I traveled there two months after the disaster. My host, who met me at the airport, drove me into the city and pointed out some of the devastated areas as we passed by. Suddenly, this socially conscious woman beamed at me and asked, "What is the similarity between Mexico City and a doughnut?" Since I could not answer, she replied, "The middle parts of each are missing," referring to the hole of a doughnut and the collapsed buildings in the middle of her city. She then proceeded to tell me other earthquake jokes that were circulating in the city and expressed aggression against the disaster's victims.

Similarly, even though the trauma due to the *Challenger* disaster was generalized, it did not break America's backbone, as this tragedy also led to many jokes. They too were colored with aggressive sentiments and acts against those who had died. For example, one joke made reference to mutilated bodies washing onto shore. Since these jokes are tasteless, I do not wish to repeat them here, but it is interesting that most people do not repress the content of such jokes. The appearance of them after disasters is a peculiar phenomenon. Why do we become so callous? Why do we laugh? The psychological reasons for this social phenomenon are multi-determined: they contribute to a reversal of affect (meaning the feeling of sadness is denied); they discharge tension through laughter; they celebrate the survival of those left behind; they express anger at those who inflicted a wound on us by dying; and they allow us to minimize our feelings of guilt for living by portraying the tragedy as if it occurred in a cartoon. In these jokes we also see derivatives of initial individualized grief reactions, such as attempts at reality testing that losses actually occurred, attempts to deny the losses, and attempts to identify with victims and to find a link to them or, conversely, to break such links.

Some initial societal preoccupations, besides the appearance of jokes, may seem bizarre. I already mentioned one: the blanket burning by Cypriot Turks after the 1974 war. Another bizarre societal process that took place in North Cyprus at the same time was the development of a peculiar physical condition. Many Cypriot Turks began visiting physicians' offices complaining of itching. The physicians I spoke with could find no explanation for this mini-epidemic of itching among the citizens. I began to make sense of this new social preoccupation when I heard peoples' theory that the first cases of itching started among those who went swimming in the northern beaches after the Turkish military landed there at the beginning of the war. As there were corpses in the water and on the beaches during the first days of the war, it appeared to me that the itching phenomenon was caused by quicklime that had been strewn over the bodies. If your hand touches quicklime, your skin will burn and you will experience an itching sensation. Traces of white quicklime remained on the ground for months in certain areas. But long after the quicklime was washed away, the itching phenomenon continued, perhaps as a symbolic connection with the dead; itching represented not only feelings of guilt for having survived and for having expelled the enemy from their homes, but also proof that one was indeed alive, as one's skin sensation made clear.

The assassination of a political leader can also affect the tissue of a large group. When societal trauma occurs following the assassination of a leader, it makes a big difference if the killing was carried out by someone who belonged to the traumatized large-group itself or by someone who belonged to the "other." For example, it would have made a great deal of difference to America's societal tissue had John F. Kennedy been murdered by a Soviet agent rather than an American. Even though we learned later about Lee Harvey Oswald's presumed commitment to Marxism, his killing of the president, which became a massive trauma, did not stir up severe large-group identity issues. Similarly, the assassination of Yitzhak Rabin on November 4, 1995, created a severe trauma and a tear in the tissue of Israeli society, movingly described by Israeli analyst Rena Moses-Hrushovski in her book *Grief and Grievance: The Assassination of Yitzhak Rabin,*[73] but in the long run, facing an external enemy, the tear in the tissue of the Israeli large group did not become large enough to permanently damage the state. To illustrate how personal and societal processes often converge, I will provide a brief description of certain events that led to Rabin's assassination and the tear in Israeli society.

From February 1 to May 30, 2000, I had the honor of being an Inaugural Rabin Fellow at the Yitzhak Rabin Center for Israel Studies in Tel Aviv. There I saw a documentary film made by a crew from France 2 Television. Now a part of the permanent archives of the Rabin Center, the film shows the propaganda and incitements to violence proffered by Jewish religious extremists just before Rabin's assassination. For me, watching this film was nothing less than a terrifying experience. Though the propagandists were speaking in Hebrew, a language that I do not understand, their gestures and emotional intensity hit me like bullets. I forced myself to remember that, while most Israelis would react to this documentary (and to the extremists themselves) in the same powerfully negative way that I had, there were others who had heard the propagandists and inciters' words as inspiration. There is clear evidence to suggest that such extreme right-wing, religious-nationalist propaganda, which called Yitzhak Rabin a traitor and demanded he be expelled from Israel for signing the Oslo Accords and shaking hands with Yassir Arafat, decisively influenced Yigal Amir, Rabin's twenty-five-year-old assassin.

Ehud Sprinzak, a professor of political science at the Hebrew University of Jerusalem and a popular radio and television commentator, was well aware of the domestic extremism that grew in intensity after the signing of the Oslo Accords. In the spring of 2000, he explained to me how he had sent several memoranda to Rabin pleading with him to invest more thought and resources into investigating domestic extremism before events escalated. "To my great dismay," he writes in his 1999 book *Brother Against Brother*, "I discovered that the dramatic events were far more powerful than my limited ability to make a difference."[74] According to Sprinzak, the countdown to the assassination began with the February 25, 1994, Hebron massacre. On that day, during the Muslim holy period of Ramadan, Baruch Goldstein, an American-born emergency room physician and devout Orthodox Jew, entered the Isaac Hall of the Cave of the Patriarchs in the Israeli-occupied town of Hebron and shot Palestinian Muslims as they prayed, killing twenty-nine and injuring one hundred. Rabin wanted to evacuate the Israeli settlers of Hebron and nearby Tel Rumeida in order to avert further bloodshed, but advisers informed him that doing so would in fact incite more violence, so he abandoned this plan. This initiated a period of intense confrontation between Rabin and ultranationalist rabbis. A series of suicide bombings by Hamas and Islamic Jihad—revenge attacks for the Hebron massacre—that took eighty-seven Israeli lives and injured more than two hundred further intensified this conflict. Some rabbis began to refer to the legal-religious concepts of *din moser* and *din rodef*: "[A] moser is a Jew suspected of providing Gentiles with information about Jews or with illegally giving them Jewish property. . . . [A] rodef is a person about to commit or facilitate the commi[ssion] of murder. The purpose of his immediate execution is to save Jewish life. This rule does not apply to a killer, caught after the murder, who has to go to trial. Din rodef is the only case in which the Halakha allows Jews to kill another Jew without a trial."[75]

Sprinzak demonstrates that ultranationalists' verbal violence and confrontation tactics created an atmosphere that allowed Yigal Amir to convince himself that by killing Rabin he was saving Jewish lives. When interrogated after the assassination, he admitted that he had discussed the notions of din rodef and din moser with several rabbis. Though none of them had specifically given him "permission" to assassinate Rabin, he added, "If not for a Halakhic ruling of din rodef made against Rabin by a few rabbis I know about, it would have been very difficult for me to murder. Such a murder must be backed up. If I did not get the backing and I had not been representing many more people, I would not have acted."[76] However, Israeli psychologist Avner Falk has found that the psychology of Amir's act of assassination was deeply overdetermined; his personal psychological motives dovetailed fatally with radical religious leaders' acts of incitement.[77]

Amir's parents came to Israel from Yemen in the late 1940s and early 1950s and raised eight children in cramped conditions. Haggai, their first son, was born in 1968; Yigal, the future assassin, was born two years later. Falk's investigation focuses especially on the relationship between Amir and his mother, Geulah, a kindergarten teacher. By Falk's account, she was an unhappy and hot-tempered woman, the dominant figure at home, and was married to a man whom she likely did not love, Shlomoh Amir, an Orthodox Jewish scroll writer and ritual butcher and a passive and dependent man. On the surface, Amir seemed to be Geulah's favorite child. According to Falk, Geulah called him "Gali," an abbreviation of "Yigali," which means both "my Yigal" and "he will redeem me."[78] But little "Gali" seems to have received love from his mother only when he was clever, talented, and amusing—only when he "redeemed" her from her own unhappiness; otherwise, she rejected him.

As he grew older, Amir proved unable to break away from his problematic emotional attachment to his mother. Falk describes how Amir, ambivalent toward both parents, unconsciously searched for better ones in the religious realm to restore the self-esteem that Geulah, his "bad mother," had shattered: "The God of Israel became Yigal's good father, the land of Israel his mother. As it is to many extreme-right nationalists, the land of Israel is not the actual country but an abstraction, a sacred emotional object comprising all the territories of Israel and Palestine. During his trial, before the reading of the verdict, on March 27, 1996, Yigal said: 'Everything I have done, I have done for Israel, for the Torah of Israel, for the people of Israel, and for the land of Israel—it is a knot that will never be untied.'"[79]

Indeed, Amir had persuaded himself that by killing Rabin he was saving not just Jewish lives, but Israel itself. Displacing onto Rabin his rage at his father and his mother (as Falk notes, "the mother, not the father, was the prime minister at home"),[80] Amir unconsciously meant to break out of his "bad mother's" home by vindicating the "good mother," Israel, and God, the "good father," over the "bad," "weak" fathers he perceived at home and in the prime minister's office. Indeed, it worked: as his mother stated after the assassination, apparently without realizing the deeper meaning of what she was saying, "by his act he has left this house."[81] Further, Falk observes, rejection by a girlfriend also contributed to the assassin's fatal decision, perhaps reviving feelings of sibling rivalry and rage against his "bad mother": "He wished to win back his girlfriend with an act of heroism that would make him very special and dear to her. . . . Nava Holtzaman, Amir's only girlfriend, a relationship of five months, left him in January 1995 and married one of his friends, thus humiliating Amir and initiating an overt depression."[82]

Although Amir acted more or less alone, propaganda from nationalist-fundamentalist religious subgroups had created an atmosphere with deadly consequences. The assassination of Rabin, I believe, still remains a sensitive issue that maintains a crack in the tissue of the Israeli large group, but concerns about this issue are put aside due to Israelis' ongoing identity conflicts with their neighbors and its real-world security issues.

Other forms of tragedy may also create a split within a large group. For example, if conflict between ideological or religious subgroups continues for a long time, the tear in the tissue of the overarching large group may not be easily mended or may not be mended at all. If such conflict continues for decades, the opposing masses may slowly evolve as separate ethnic groups, especially when they also reactivate the memories of old frictions and other tragedies between them—that is, if they develop strong attachments to the mental representations of the glorified and traumatic events from their respective histories and become preoccupied with identity issues. Time will tell how the large-group identity issues will evolve in Korea, which is divided principally along ideological lines. Will two Koreas reunite in the future or will they remain as two different countries with two distinct large-group identities? As far as I am concerned, the problems in Northern Ireland have turned into or at least are turning into "ethnic" identity problems.

I briefly mention these two examples, but I know more about the division between the former East Germany and former West Germany and their subsequent reunification. The shared traumas of the Nazi regime and World War II on the Germans themselves and of the political, ideological, and military processes that divided Germany into East and West resulted in large-group identity complications. Ideologically divided Germans began to come together after the fall of the Berlin Wall on November 9, 1989. Nevertheless, the integration between former East and West Germans did not take place instantly after the wall collapsed.

A few months after the reunification of Germany, I visited a friend who lived in Gottingen, a town on the west side of the former East German–West German border. He drove me to a grassy area that had once marked the boundary between the two German states. My friend informed me that the trees in the area had been cut down so East German border guards could more easily protect against defections. The day I was there, of course, there were no soldiers, and the watchtowers were empty. However, I was struck by the eerie silence of the place and also by the way that my friend was whispering. It was as though there was still danger along this former border. We then drove across the old border and into former East Germany, something my friend had not done since before Germany's division. Though the two sides had been formally reunited, the physical disparities between the two were immediately obvious. To the east, the roads were poorly maintained and designed, and even the shape of the electric poles was different than those in the west. It was indisputable that we were now in a different "country."

As we drove through the countryside, leaving heavy traffic behind, my friend took a deep breath and then asked me if I smelled something foul. I could not detect anything out of the ordinary and told him so, but he did not accept my answer. He pointed to a car that was quite far ahead of us and said, "You see that car? It's Communist-made. Those cars smell." I was certain he could not have realistically sensed anything emanating from the car because it was too far away. It seemed that since he "knew" Communist-made cars had an offensive odor, his senses played a trick on him. Seeing the car stimulated his smelling of the car. As a psychoanalyst,

I also came to another conclusion: my friend was externalizing and projecting some unacceptable elements of his own onto East Germans. He was "clean"; East Germans "stunk." I did not verbalize my deduction but sensed that my friend, also a psychoanalyst, had come to a similar conclusion about his experience. He seemed embarrassed and quickly changed the topic of conversation.

Because of the societal trauma associated with having separate ideologies and histories, the two German groups evolved, or at least were evolving, into two different identity groups. Interestingly enough, by having "two" identities, Germans, in a sense, could be helped in handling the Nazi image of the past, an image that included extremely traumatizing actions against others, mainly Jews. As long as there were two German states, one side (mostly unconsciously) could imagine that it was the "other" Germany that was the true heir of the Nazis. Therefore, the reunification of two German states could not take place instantly, psychologically speaking. My trip to the former East German–West German border was a factor in my getting involved in a project with Gabriele Ast, a psychoanalyst who practices in Munich, to study how this reunification was experienced internally (unconsciously) by Germans from both sides during the first year of reunification. This project was not completed due to lack of funds. However, we collected enough data to suggest that each side had projected the Nazi past onto the other side before reunification.

An opportunity to further study the effects of the historical trauma that separated the Germans after World War II and throughout the Cold War era came to my attention in May 2002 at a meeting in Leipzig of the German Psychoanalytic Association. This was the first time the organization had held its annual meeting in the former East Germany. I was a guest of the association at this meeting and closely watched the interactions between those German colleagues who had come from the former West Germany and those colleagues from the former East Germany. Inevitably, I think, this "forced togetherness" made them preoccupied and protective of their large-group identities. When the CSMHI team brought enemy representatives together for dialogues, participants from each side initially did the same thing, so I was familiar with this type of interaction and was not surprised to see it between former East and West Germans. What I observed in Leipzig would become especially palpable during the "academic" discussion of the psychology of reunification. Though I do not speak German, I gathered what was said through a translator and I was able to observe facial expressions (some East German colleagues even cried when they, rightly or wrongly, felt that West

Germans did not consider them to be equal in training and knowledge as far as human nature was concerned). While there, I met Irene Misselwitz, a psychoanalyst from East Germany whose main research interest was the influence of the processes of social and political transformation on the human psyche. She wrote a paper for CSMHI's journal, *Mind and Human Interaction*, and described her own personal experience developing an East German identity:

> During the 40 years of separation, very distinct large-group identities developed in East and West Germany. To use Volkan's metaphor of a tent, we seem to have lived in separate ethnic tents or smaller "sub-tents." During the separation, this was concealed and to a large extent experienced only unconsciously. The differences only began to come clear in 1990 once the border had opened and daily encounters between the two groups began to take place. . . . The German-German encounter has profoundly unsettled both sides. Otherwise it would be hard to explain why both sides consistently try to hide beneath their respective East or West German tent and repeatedly resist inhabiting the newly shared tent of a unified Germany.[83]

Sometimes, if centuries pass, people originally from the same ethnic stock can separate their identities and experience themselves as absolutely distinct ethnic groups. This happened, for example, within the South Slav population. Following different religions and holding onto the mental representations of different historical experiences, especially massive traumas at the hands of the opposite side, South Slavs emerged as, among others, Serbs, Croats, and Bosniaks. If two groups from the same identity stock are in conflict long enough, traumas associated with such conflicts will have similar dynamics as those observed between "foreign" enemies.

With this in mind, let us briefly consider the psychological markers specific to trauma that come at the hands of an enemy with a separate large-group identity, such as occurred in the Republic of Georgia and on the island of Cyprus. In instances of ethnic, nationalistic, religious, or ideological conflict between distinct enemy groups, there exists a deliberate design to humiliate, render helpless, and kill the "other" in the name of large-group identity. Sometimes the enemy is dehumanized before being killed.[84] When dehumanization occurs, a "license" is issued to murder the enemy without guilt. There are two types of dehumanization. In the first type, the enemy first perceives the members of a large group as undesirable and then dehumanizes them, such as occurred in Nazi Germany. The same happened in 1994 in Rwanda when a centuries-old ethnic rivalry became inflamed, and Hutus saw Tutsis as dangerous *cafards* (cockroaches), leading to the deaths of one million people. Many scholars also maintain that suicide bombers dehumanize their victims before detonating their explosives. However, this type of dehumanization is different. It is true that suicide bombers bypass the protection of their own and their victims' individual identities and thus commit both suicide and murder. But they "re-humanize" themselves as the spokespersons for their own large group before turning into live bombs. They also "re-humanize" their victims as representatives for the opposing group. They kill such representatives in order to hurt the opposing group and send it a message.

However, natural or man-made accidental disasters do not shame, humiliate, dehumanize, kill, or destroy physical environments in the name of large-group identity. The December 2004 tsunami, for example, did not have a "mind"; it did not discriminate against any one large group. Even though the tsunami caused massive death, it did not willingly commit ethnic cleansing or genocide as occurred in Rwanda or elsewhere. Individuals who live in natural-disaster zones may consider themselves "unlucky." But when the tragedies occur, they do not feel shamed, humiliated, or dehumanized by nature for deliberately picking on them, rendering them helpless, and killing their loved ones. However, this is not to say that some people will not "humanize" nature. Indeed, many will speak as though a given disaster was by nature's—or a higher power's—design. For example, some might say a region flooded as punishment for its people's acceptance of homosexuality. Some "millennialist" Christians believe natural disasters are a sign of the imminent return of Jesus Christ to earth. In other examples, what is assigned to nature or an accident has more direct connection to large-group identity issues or conflicts. For example, some Muslims may believe that the earth shakes to punish them because of increased Western influence on their large-group identity. Nevertheless, after a natural disaster or accident, assigning a brain or mind to the phenomenon is usually not generalized and does not induce shared shame and humiliation. In the long run such people accept the actions of "God" or "fate" without shame and humiliation.

Another observation that differentiates a massive trauma at the hands of the enemy from other massive traumas that do not include large-group identity issues is that the former can never remain as a "regional" trauma. The feeling of helplessness of the people in the affected sector created by a natural disaster is not prone toward generalization in other sectors of the society, even though the people in other regions may feel sad or grieve for the victims. But shame and humiliation of people at the hands of "others" in an affected region is automatically felt by all those who belong to the same large-group identity. This happens whenever the large-group identity has been threatened. Feelings of shame, humiliation, and helpless rage are crucial factors in spreading large-group sentiments and initiating societal movements to deal with the impact of the traumatizing event and to strengthen or modify the existing cultural norms. Such shared activities aim to patch up the wear and tear on the canvas of the large-group tent.

One quick way of repairing the wear and tear on the tent's canvas and removing the shared sense of humiliation and shame is to exact revenge, especially if the external situation permits such an action. This has its own consequences and typically fuels the conflict even further. In natural disasters, there is no shared wish to take revenge against nature, God, or fate. But a large group that cannot take revenge against its enemy often internalizes its aggression. When such a group tries to increase or reactivate certain cultural customs in order to strengthen its sense of "we-ness" and differentiate its large-group identity from the identities of "others," we often see the internalization of aggression in action. For example, in South Ossetia there is a long-held custom of "kidnapping": specifically, a young man will "kidnap" a woman he loves and then, with the families' blessings, he marries her. Following the collapse of the Soviet Union and South Ossetia's wars with Georgia, such kidnapping rituals became highly malignant. In these instances, young women were kidnapped and raped—not married. I once met a young South Ossetian girl who had been kidnapped, raped, and tortured and then returned to her mother. I tried to be helpful, but in the end I was filled with helplessness and sadness. I knew that my talking with her for a few hours could not undo the damage that had been inflicted on her and her family.

As after natural or accidental disasters, jokes also often appear after a disaster at the hands of an enemy. But these jokes, unlike the ones I described earlier in relation to the Mexico City earthquake and the *Challenger* disaster, do not poke fun at the victims. Jokes after large-group identity traumas generally are in the service of erasing shame and humiliation by degrading the enemy's image. For example, when CSMHI conducted a project in Kuwait a few years after Saddam Hussein's invading forces had been pushed back by the United States and its allies, I heard many jokes from Kuwaitis whom I interviewed. One joke attributed the deaths and disappearance of animals in Kuwait City's zoo to hungry Iraqi soldiers, who were said to have eaten them. Another joke told of uncivilized and ignorant Iraqis who had never seen an ATM machine and who thought that in rich Kuwait anyone could simply press a button on a bank wall to get money. Such jokes are attempts to deal with shame and humiliation by making the enemy look stupid and less than human.

Another marker unique to massive disasters at the hands of an enemy involves the transgenerational transmission of trauma. On an individual level, some adults who are traumatized by natural or man-made disasters, but who for one reason or another cannot carry out the psychological tasks to deal adaptively with such tragedies, will pass on certain mourning tasks to their offspring. However, in cases of massive trauma at the hands of an enemy, the transgenerational transmission of unfinished psychological processes are generalized and are inevitably involved in strengthening the shared large-group identity and even in modifying it. This is a vast and very important topic that I will examine later in this volume.

But first, in the next two chapters, I will discuss the psychology of memorial building, a common societal process following massive trauma at the hands of an enemy. In chapter 7 I will describe the American World War II Orphans' Network (AWON) and its members' involvement in the World War II Memorial in Washington, D.C. Since its opening in 2004, the World War II Memorial has already evolved as a shared linking object for many. Then in chapter 8 I will explore the development of other memorials and examine the broad question: What does an examination of such memorials tell us about the psychology of the affected large group, its mourning process, its attempt to reverse shame and humiliation, its readiness to accept its enemy's "apology," and its willingness to "forgive" its enemy?

7 AWON and Four Thousand Gold Stars

On Memorial Day 2004, a football field-sized World War II Memorial was officially dedicated with great fanfare in Washington, D.C. It honors the 16 million individuals who served in the U.S. Armed Forces and the more than four hundred thousand Americans who died during that war. My family awaited the opening of the memorial with some excitement. Jorma Palonen, the father of my wife Betty, was one of the casualties of the war. He died when he was twenty-nine. Married three years, he had been drafted while his wife was pregnant—three months before Betty was born. On leave from military training, he saw Betty twice before he was sent to Europe. During one of these visits, a picture of him holding his newborn baby was taken.

Jorma died on November 21, 1944, in Italy. Four years later his body was brought back to the United States and buried in the cemetery of the small Massachusetts town of Lunenburg, not far from the New Hampshire border. On Memorial Day 1949, a stone memorial was erected in the center of Lunenburg bearing the names of those from the town who had been killed in World War II, Jorma Palonen among them. Betty, then age five, unveiled this stone memorial in a town ceremony. In 1950, after her husband had been buried on U.S. soil, Betty's mother remarried, had another daughter, and provided a good family environment for her children. She did not speak much about her first husband, but she hung a drawing of Jorma wearing an army private's uniform in Betty's bedroom, and for the rest of her life until her death in 2002, she wore two wedding rings welded together. Because of this, and because relatives on her father's side lived in Lunenburg and maintained friendly relations with Betty's mother and her new husband, Betty grew up with many reminders of her dead father. There were, for example, ritualistic visits to his gravesite. But Betty's relatives, like her mother, did not speak much about

Jorma and his life. As a result, Betty was left to create her father and his life in fantasy.

The U.S. government referred to Betty and the 183,000 American children who had lost a father during World War II as "World War II orphans." But because most of the children still had mothers, they did not feel like "orphans." Walter Linne, a retired Air Force pilot from Indiana who had lost his father when he was two, told me that while growing up he never considered himself an orphan since he still had his mother. When Walter was six his mother remarried, though he understood that her new husband was not his father. Walter states:

> I am pretty sure that I conveyed that to my stepfather so much so that at one point I was asked by my mother to call him dad. From that point forward I felt like I had to protect my mother's feelings by doing whatever was necessary to make her happy. I had put my father on the shelf as it were after his death until I reached a point in my life where my children were raised and I was settling into the genealogy phase of life. In 1985 I started bringing dad back into my life by retracing his final days in Europe. I wanted to experience what he saw and maybe gain some insight into what he felt those last few months. It was never a search about what he had accomplished, but rather what he was about, what kind of man he was.

The U.S. government provided federal funds to the orphans for their education. Indeed, Betty benefited from such funds and was able to attend a private university that otherwise would have been too expensive for her family to pay for. When she and I were married, the drawing of Jorma was transferred to our home. It still hangs on a wall in our living room. Jorma, through this drawing, was introduced to me and later to our children. Betty knew that fate had given her a task: a life-long search to find out who Jorma had been as a real, living person—not just as a drawing on a wall.

Adults who have suffered a significant childhood loss with no—or not enough—actual experience with the lost person while he or she was alive, must make the lost person real in their minds before they can let that person go. It can be more difficult to mourn the loss of a father who is mostly or entirely created in fantasy than to mourn the loss of a father who, before his death, was real for the child. Depending on their ages when they lost their fathers, WWII orphans missed the opportunity to have real interactions with their fathers and to develop mental images based on, or at least modified by, such interactions. This does not mean they could not construct their biological fathers' images in their minds. To the contrary, they had to construct such images, but what they constructed was primarily shaped by needs, wishes, expectations, idealizations, devaluations, and other mental defenses. If orphans' mothers became perennial mourners—even partly—and were silent about their deceased husbands, and if the orphans were not encouraged to speak about their mental images of their fathers so that their fantasies could be corrected by adults who actually knew the deceased, the children were left with only their imaginations.

Millions of children lose their fathers or are born after their fathers' death for various reasons, such as illness, accident, suicide, or murder. All such children respond in their own personal psychological way to not having a father. The form the response takes will depend on the child's age at the time of the loss,[85] his or her psychological structures, and the support the child has in working through age-related developmental tasks. In the case of WWII orphans, however, their losses were directly associated with the image of a historic event and shared public sentiments about individuals who died for their country. Their connection to a major event and their designation by the U.S. government as WWII orphans obviously played a role in differentiating them from other children. Walter, who thought that he was not obsessed with knowing about his father while growing up, states that he felt special as a child "every time someone questioned why my last name was different than my half siblings." He also felt somewhat guilty for "using some of my dad's hero status to feel special."

If the child's image of a dead father created only or mostly in fantasy is idealized—dead soldiers are usually idealized as heroes—the mourning over losing them (their fantasized images) becomes more difficult. There is psychological resistance to giving up a hero constructed in one's mind and making him an average dead man. Also, it is difficult to give up one's sense of being special as a hero's child and becoming an average child with an average dead father. The sense of being special had a deeper source: the young widows, some of whom had been married only a few days or few months when their husbands went to war and never returned, knowingly or unknowingly treated their children from their lost husbands to one degree or another as living linking objects. Children had a secret task connecting their mothers with their dead fathers. These mothers, who were forced to move on with their lives, often had to repress or deny the love or even conflict that had existed in their former marriage.

It must be kept in mind that World War II orphans who might have been treated as secret living linking objects were child mourners themselves, even though in reality they did not know, or barely knew, their fathers. They sensed that something was missing. Child mourners need their own linking objects when they become adults in order to mourn their dead fathers. It is only through the utilization of such linking objects (or phenomena) that the adult with a childhood loss can make the mental representation of the dead person manageable enough to be "buried" in one's mind, and as Veikko Tähkä stated, to make it "futureless."[86]

Betty was rather lucky. Although her mother and her father's relatives did not speak about Jorma and his life, they had kept many items that were reminders of his real existence, such as his letters, photographs, and medals. Using such items Betty could construct her fantasy father on some realistic foundation. If she had not had such items, the construction of a dead man of whom she had no memory would have been more difficult.

With more than 180,000 WWII orphans in the United States, many of them shared the psychological task of searching for their biological fathers and the sense of being special, which itself, psychologically speaking, is a burden. Among this group was Ann Bennett Mix. Growing up, Ann did not know that she was a "war orphan," and only later learned that such a term applied to her. She began wondering about other people like herself who had lost a father during the war and how they had coped:

> I had no idea who they were, where they were, or how many there were (World War II orphans). When I turned to government agencies for help I discovered that they did not know either! It was obvious there was a long struggle ahead, but I was determined we come together and talk about our lives and what happened! As I started finding people and as we did talk I was angered and saddened to learn how few people had ever talked with another war orphan, or had been allowed to talk about their fathers. I learned most of us had spent our lives feeling isolated and knew little about our fathers' service or how they died.[87]

In 1990 Ann began looking for other orphans and took initial steps to form the American WWII Orphans Network. Late the following year, she read an article in *Parade* magazine that announced a tree dedication ceremony for the families of those who had died in World War II. This event, held at Arlington National Cemetery on December 8, 1991, was sponsored by No Greater Love, an organization founded in 1971. This organization provides programs for remembrance and care for families who lost a loved one in the service of the United States or in an act of terrorism. Ann called Carmella La Spada of No Greater Love and asked permission to distribute some brochures about AWON at the ceremony. With Carmella's blessing, Ann flew to Washington and met other orphans and distributed the brochures. It was during this ceremony that Betty and I met Ann for the first time. After the *Washington Post* ran a large article about Ann and her efforts, AWON truly became a reality. Today, the organization has more than eight hundred members.

I became a regular speaker at AWON's annual meetings, starting with its first meeting. Because I am a psychiatrist and psychoanalyst who has extensively studied the work of mourning and its complications, the members of AWON thought that I could be of some help to them. But AWON's greatest benefit came from members finding one another and learning how they shared certain psychological tasks. They told their personal stories and realized that, besides losing their fathers, most of them had also "lost" the mothers of their childhood. The mourning process of their own mothers interfered with certain mothering functions. I learned how difficult it was for a young war widow to adjust to life as a single mother in the 1940s. Some young married women perceived them as threats, as competitors for their own husbands' affection and sexual attraction. Some war widows never married again. Some did the opposite. They remarried and tried to erase any physical link to their first husband and the husband's families, except for the children who served as secret living linking objects. Of course, the efforts to erase physical links robbed their first husbands' children of any concrete connection to their fathers, making these children feel both "deprived" and in a peculiar way special.

I learned how common it was for young widows not to speak about their dead husbands. Getting to know many AWON members as friends, I noted that those who were lucky enough to have physical links to their dead fathers were generally able to have a better psychological adaptation to their adult environment. On few occasions, I was asked if I had an opinion about the reasons why World War II orphans waited until they were in their fifties or sixties to begin feeling strongly about their "father search" and to become actively involved in making their fantasy fathers real. I do not have a definite answer. I suspect, however, that when the orphans' own children reached the ages when their fathers had been killed it stimulated their life-long task of "father search."

AWON members, as adults, expressed their involvement with their fathers' imagined mental images in various types of actions. In these actions, they symbolically searched for their fathers, "magically" found them, "lost" them again, and repeated the cycle many times. For example, some women married men who, in these women's unconscious minds, fit well with their images of their fathers. They expected their spouses to fulfill tasks that their fathers should have fulfilled. But since the husbands were contaminated with the mental images of their fathers, the women also consciously or unconsciously feared that their husbands would suddenly die or leave them. I sensed that a few women unknowingly felt that having sex with their husbands, symbolically speaking, was like incest. This created conflict that led to divorce. Some male orphans as adults had to struggle with living up to their deceased father's idealized images, while others devaluated such images in order to achieve their own autonomy. Many men joined the military as a way of identifying with their fathers. Walter described to me how he and his younger brother took part in risky activities such as flying and auto racing. He added, "From an early age I had decided to join the military because I thought I owed it to my dad and the veterans." Yet, at the same time, he also said as a child he was not preoccupied with his dead father's image. Some, unlike Walter, developed intense antiwar sentiments, perhaps to deny the existence of war losses, including the deaths of their fathers. If there were no wars, no child's father would die in a war zone. In short, for such women and men, there was no escape from the influence of their fathers' mental images filled with fantasized expectations. Of course, I am making generalizations here in order to make this point.

Some WWII orphans had stepfathers or other father substitutes while growing up. If an orphan's relationship with the stepfather was satisfactory and if the stepfather was capable of helping the orphan negotiate certain developmental passages, such as going through the oedipal phase in which a father and his image play a key role, then the orphan's "father search" was tamed. If the relationship with the stepfather, as well as with siblings, was conflicted, the orphan's investment in the biological dead father's constructed image increased, and the child was forced to keep feelings of being special more and more a secret. This had burdensome psychological consequences.

Some AWON members, such as Jack Forgy, who is a retired colonel in the U.S. Army, became researchers and went through government files, hospital records, and other documents to find answers to orphans' questions. Common ones include: "How did my father die?" "Where are my father's remains?" "Is there anyone alive who fought with my father and knew him and who can tell me about him?" The members of AWON wanted to know the truth about the circumstances surrounding their fathers' last days. This reminds me of my psychoanalyst friend Nancy Hollander's work with the relatives of the disappeared in Latin America. She described the case of an Argentinean colleague whose son was abducted during the Pinochet regime, tortured, and killed. Some years later this woman found out the details of what happened to her son and commented: "Knowing the truth, even with its horrific details, gave me a certain amount of peace. . . . Mothers of the desaparecidos called to tell me how lucky I was. My 'luck' was to know that they'd killed my son with a machine gun. The mothers told me that they wished they were in my place. That's how important the truth, the knowing, is."[88]

AWON members, fifty years after World War II ended, began to work in earnest, individually and collectively, to make their fathers' images real. During their annual meetings they divided themselves in small groups and compared stories about their fathers' death or disappearance. One father was shot down while flying over France, while another father's ship was bombed; he was thrown into the sea not far from Japan and was most likely eaten by sharks. The current president of AWON's board of directors, Patricia Gaffney Kindig, traveled thousands of miles to Papua New Guinea, to find her father's missing aircraft in an uninhabitable mountain jungle. The crash site was ultimately discovered and his remains were identified from dental records, which Patricia had kept. She accompanied her father's remains to Wisconsin for a funeral and then to Arlington National Cemetery for burial. Many orphans have visited U.S. military cemeteries in different countries to visit their fathers' graves. U.S. government officials have cooperated fully with AWON members in their searches.

Many moving discoveries surfaced. Sam Tannenbaum knew his father had been killed during the Battle of the Bulge near Ottre, Belgium. But what he did not know was that Tony Vaccaro, a soldier who had befriended his father while both of them were serving in the 331st Infantry Regiment, took a picture of his lifeless body as it lay on the snow in January 1945. This picture became well-known and was displayed in many parts of the world. In fact, Betty and I had once seen it in London at an exhibit celebrating a D-Day anniversary. Growing up, Sam did not even know where his father had been buried. Through AWON, Sam eventually met a man from Luxembourg named Jim Schiltz who provided the clue Sam needed to learn more about his father. Schiltz pointed Sam to a book titled *Luxembourg 1935–1945* that Tony Vaccaro had written.

This ultimately led to a moving meeting between Sam and Tony. Apparently Tony had always wondered about his dead friend's son and had hoped to connect with him. Sam found out that his father was buried in Queens, New York. In one of his and his wife Rachel's visits to his father's gravesite, Tony even accompanied them. And in June 2000, Tony joined Sam and Rachel for the dedication of a monument to Sam's father that was erected on the spot where his father had been killed in action some fifty-five years earlier. The dedication ceremony was attended by more than three hundred people from the United States, Belgium, Luxembourg, Germany, France, and Holland.

AWON members, hearing stories like Sam's, openly grieved during the organization's initial annual meetings. As years passed, as far as I could observe, they became involved in a more silent mourning process similar to the process adults would normally undergo after a significant loss. Meanwhile, many of their stories found their way to the media.[89] For example, when former NBC news anchorperson Tom Brokaw wrote *The Greatest Generation Speaks: Letters and Reflections*,[90] he included Patricia Gaffney Kindig's story as well as that of AWON member Anne Moloney Black. who was born after her father's death and whose mother never remarried, dying in her nineties.

My wife Betty made her own "discovery" in trying to learn more about her father. In August 2002, she traveled with me to Bologna, Italy, where I was giving a lecture. Just outside of Bologna rests the small town of Livergnano. It was on the outskirts of this town where Betty's father, Jorma Palonen, had been shot by the Nazis as Americans tried to liberate it. Thanks to Jack Forgy's research we had an army map and a picture of the hill where Betty's father had been wounded. We also learned that a statue of a U.S. soldier had been erected by the townspeople to express their thanks to the Americans who had saved them. One rainy day, we found time to travel by bus to Livergnano and struck up a conversation with an English-speaking waitress at a coffee shop near the bus stop. We told her we were interested in visiting the statue. As the town had no taxis, she told us we would have to walk about two miles to the other end of the town to see it. She also told us about Umberto Magnani, the town's electrician who was an expert on the history of Livergnano's liberation during World War II. Umberto, we understood, had a small museum where he kept war-related items, news articles, and pictures. If we were interested, she said Umberto would be willing to answer any questions about the war we might have. She tried to reach him by telephone, but he did not answer. Because of the rain, we decided to postpone our walk to the statue for half an hour or so and have a second cup of cappuccino. This turned out to be a crucial decision, for staying at the coffee shop a while longer made it possible for us to meet Umberto.

While we were waiting for the rain to stop, the waitress called Umberto a second time. This time he answered. Some minutes later he appeared at the coffee shop. Umberto, who did not speak English well, kindly gave us a ride to the statue. We were not expecting to do anything besides stand by the statue, take some photos, and look at the tree-covered hills surrounding the area to see if one of them resembled the hill in the picture Jack had provided us with. When we arrived at the statue, the rain stopped. Betty and I got out of Umberto's car and took our time looking around while Umberto sat in the driver's seat. Suddenly, leaning out of the car window, he asked Betty her father's name. Betty told him, and we were surprised that Umberto seemed familiar with it. He got out of his car and asked Betty to write it down. Finding a piece of paper and a pen Betty wrote "Palonen." Upon seeing this, Umberto pointed rapidly at his chest and said: "Palonen canteen! Palonen canteen!" It took us a minute or two to realize that Umberto was telling us that he had Betty's father's canteen in his little museum. Betty started crying and at this moment of surprise, tears came to my eyes, too. Umberto began treating us as if we were his close relatives. He looked at Jack's picture and the map of the hill and promptly drove us to the place where Jorma had been shot.

There were three foxholes in which the U.S. soldiers had tried to hide and protect themselves from Nazi bullets coming from higher ground. What surprised me most was our seeing and touching, fifty-eight years later, petrified crackers that Jorma and his comrades had carried with them during this mission. The place was still littered with shrapnel, electrical wires, and other items from the war. We knew that after Jorma was shot he could not be transported down the hill right away. Betty's earlier research informed us that it took medics twelve hours to usher her severely wounded father away from the front-lines. Eventually he was taken to a military hospital in Florence where he died more than a month later. It was easy to imagine how his canteen would have been left behind when he was taken out of this place.

As Umberto drove us to his museum, the rain started again, this time more heavily. The museum was little more than a storage area that contained an old American flag, books, papers, communication equipment, helmets, uniforms, and one big container in which Umberto kept ten metal canteens. Canteens issued by the U.S. Army did not have names printed on them, so nine of them were in no way remarkable. Jorma, however, by making a series of small indentations in the metal—most likely with a bullet—had managed to write his last name, the year, and the country in which he was fighting on the canteen: "Palonen, 44, Italy." He had also scratched in the word "Mass" for Massachusetts, his home state, and had started to indent the first line of the "M," before he was, as one military record stated, "severely wounded in action." When Betty first held the canteen, she caressed it.

We will never forget Umberto's kindness for giving Jorma's canteen to Betty. It now stands on a table under the painting of Jorma in our house as an object representing the fact that Jorma, as a man, actually existed, fought against Nazis, and was killed. His canteen is Betty's private memorial to her father. After hearing Betty's story, Sam wrote to her and referred to this new linking object in her life as something "from your father's lips to your heart."

AWON members' stories tell us that when a war ends legally or warlike conditions disappear, its psychological damage or at least its influence on individuals, even those in the next generation, continues. AWON members, like families of Latin American *desaparecidos*, mothers of sons and daughters lost in Croatia after the collapse of the former Yugoslavia, and IDPs in Georgia and South Ossetia, were psychologically forced to hold onto—or even create—linking objects and to use them to postpone their mourning processes so that they could be initiated at a later date. I am sure that in the United States the family members of the victims of the September 11 tragedy and the Afghanistan and Iraq wars are busy doing the same. I am also sure that the family members of terror bombing victims in Madrid, Casablanca, Istanbul, Mombasa, Taba, London, and elsewhere will also struggle with difficulty in mourning for generations to come. Traumatized people and their offspring all struggle with the same psychological tasks, even though we have a human tendency not to care emotionally about peoples' tragedies in faraway places.

As I described in the previous chapter, after experiencing a war or war-like trauma, a society must undergo certain processes to adapt to the new reality. One such process involves the construction of public memorials, monuments that function as shared linking objects. In this book, I will follow the definitions of "memorial" and "monument" offered by James Young, who summarized the place of memorials and monuments in contemporary culture. He states: "I treat all memory-sites as memorials, plastic objects within these sites as monuments. A memorial may be a day, a conference, or a space, but it need not need to be a monument. A monument, on the other hand, is always a kind of memorial."[91] Jeffrey

Karl Ochsner, a professor of architecture at the University of Washington in Seattle, argues: "We wish to keep the dead truly alive in memory—alive as life is lived and felt, not just in action, but in human interaction. The difficulty is that memories fade with time. We seek to create objects of remembrance—a permanent public record in the form of monuments and memorials—that will serve as symbols of those who have gone before (or the events in which they participated) so that they may remain alive in the memory of the living."[92] Ochsner goes on to remind us that when we choose to erect grave markers and monuments to commemorate the lives of the dead:

> [W]e do not intend to build linking objects, although objects we do make clearly can serve us in this way. Indeed, the role played by linking objects does not require that they be objects intentionally created to serve this purpose (although they can be) or that they be objects that we personally shared with those remembered (again, they can be). Other objects can serve this role as well, as long as they have sufficient "space" to allow the psychological phenomenon of projection to take place. It is this space and essential incompleteness of the linking object that we feel most power-fully as a space of absence.[93]

He provides a powerful example to illustrate how "other objects" can become linking objects, too. He states that among the most moving expe-riences at the United States Holocaust Museum is the collection of ordi-nary objects "harvested" from people about to be killed, such as shoes, hairbrushes, toothbrushes, and scissors. He writes: "There seem to be little time or distance between these things and their owners and the similar things that we own and ourselves. Thus, these offer the opportu-nity for us to realize the similar humanity of those who were killed in the death camps and ourselves. They can become sites for projection (linking objects), and through them we can experience (project) a close connec-tion to the feeling of the lives of those who died."[94]

Jorma's canteen made us experience Jorma's thirst and humanity. Betty took the canteen with her when both of us joined more than three hun-dred AWON members to participate in the dedication ceremony of the World War II Memorial, which was presided over by President George W. Bush. Before the dedication, Bob Dole, a wounded veteran of World War II who served in the 10th Mountain Division, of which Ann Mix's father was also a member, spoke at the AWON conference.

Ann and other AWON members played a role in the design of the

World War II Memorial. Ann realized early on that the creators of this memorial wanted to build a memorial for their fathers or for veterans, but not for those who died or for their families. She felt that those responsible for choosing the memorial's design were going to build a monument to their "own." As a result, Ann lobbied hard to get the names of the dead incorporated in the memorial. Finding this suggestion was met with resistance, she came up with the idea of using stars to symbolize the dead. It is due to her efforts that there are 4,000 gold stars on the Freedom Wall that surrounds the memorial's Rainbow Pool. Each star represents one hundred U.S. soldiers lost during the war. Therefore, AWON members felt a special ownership of the stars, and seeing the stars on its wall closely connected them to the rest of the memorial. The orphans even decided to carry cardboard gold stars to the opening ceremony and continually waved them as President Bush and others spoke. It was clear that as soon as it opened, the World War II Memorial, especially the stars, became a shared linking object for AWON members. Soon I noticed that it indeed became a shared linking object for thousands more Americans.

The public was told not to leave mementoes at the World War II Memorial site, but by the next day, hundreds of items, from pictures to letters to medals to flowers, had been left there, expressing visitors' emotional links to the memorial. The authorities who decided to pick up the items made a psychologically informed decision and declared that they would put the items left behind in storage, thus symbolically keeping individualized links to a central shared linking object. The same thing is being done with physical items that have been and continue to be left at the nearby Vietnam Veterans Memorial.

When a memorial becomes closely connected with group mourning and serves as a mental representation of not only private losses, but also of shared losses, it becomes "alive," only "dying" after the mental representation of what had been lost fades away decades or centuries later. As long as a memorial remains "alive," the way the group experiences it may tell us a great deal about the group—and teach us about certain large-group phenomena.

8 "Hot Places," Memorials, Apologies, and Forgiveness

The convergence of psychological, social, historical, and political forces can be found all around us, and important clues to their intertwining are not always hidden, obscured, or kept in secret. Yes, sometimes we do have to dig for them to see things more clearly, such as with Dali's second dog Charlie, Betty's father's canteen, and the blankets that the Cypriot Turks chose to burn even though winter was coming. But in other cases the clues are right there in front of us like a giant billboard. I call them "hot places."

A hot place is a term I use to describe a physical location that individually and collectively induces (or reinduces) immediate and intense feelings among members of an ethnic or other large group. It typically is a place where people have been recently killed and/or humiliated by others. Some hot places have long-standing historical significance, some are actual monuments that intentionally recall a specific event, and some occur more spontaneously when a large group perceives a threat to its identity. But all hot places induce shared active or passive feelings of sadness, rage, and victimization, a desire for revenge, and other emotions associated with complicated grief or mourning.

It was not difficult to find hot places during the break-up of the Soviet Union—it was, after all, a very "hot" time. During my numerous visits to Latvia, Lithuania, and Estonia in the early 1990s, I came across quite a few, sometimes on purpose and sometimes by accident.[95] For example, Soviet troops killed a group of Lithuanians who were demonstrating for independence in Vilnius, the capital. Lithuanians marked this location by erecting five- to six-foot-high crosses representing their countrymen who had given their lives. This place was hot and indeed was erected to strengthen and protect shared large-group sentiments. After Latvia separated from the Soviet Union, Latvia's national cemetery—the Cemetery of

Brothers in Arms—also evolved as a hot place when some Latvians wanted to remove approximately two hundred Soviet military officers and leaders buried there. These soldiers had been killed in World War II when the Red Army under Stalin's command seized control of Latvia from the Nazis. They nevertheless were perceived as Russians and foreigners—the enemy—by Latvians. The Latvians wanted to dig up these soldiers to "purify" the cemetery from unwanted "others," even though these "others" posed no threat and had been dead more than fifty years.[96]

While I and my CSMHI colleagues were working in the Baltic Republics in the early and mid-1990s, we became aware that if we took representatives of an affected group to a hot place, they would quickly become spokespersons for their large group. They would vehemently express their group's sentiments about the enemy, refer to realistic or fantasized future expectations about these "others," and speak about their shared magical beliefs concerning their relationship with the "enemy." Valuable insights were invariably gathered. On some occasions the CSMHI team took representatives of both sides of a conflict to a hot place. For example, we were able to take Latvians as well as Russians, whom ethnic Latvians now perceived as "victimizers," to the Latvian National Cemetery in Riga. Likewise, we intentionally took both Estonians and Russians to Paldiski, a massive Soviet naval base that had housed a fleet of nuclear submarines. (Both Paldiski and the Soviet military base at Pärnu had been forbidden places for Estonian citizens and were therefore sources of fear and humiliation for much of the population. As a result, these two former bases became hot places after Estonia regained its independence.)[97]

The comments expressed during such visits would inform us about each side's shared conscious and unconscious belief systems and the group anxieties that typically contaminated and derailed effective communication and peaceful negotiations. When we then brought the opposing representatives together for actual dialogues and unofficial diplomatic talks, we could better deal with the emotional flare-ups and stubborn resistances that thwarted realistic discussions. For example, at Paldiski the Estonians' shared fantasy concerning their history became visible. Since they had lived under "others" for centuries, they were afraid that after they regained their independence they would once more become engulfed and "disappear." This shared fantasy had societal and political ramifications. Accordingly, during their ensuing unofficial negotiations with Russians, we brought this fantasy to the Estonian delegates' attention and helped them work through it. Earlier I wrote that in many ways visiting hot places is "to large-group psychology what recounting dreams is to an individual undergoing psychoanalysis. Both can provide a direct avenue to hidden and symbolic aspects of the psychological environment. By physically taking members of opposing groups to sites that are imbued with traumatic significance, one can often bring to the surface deeply held wishes, sentiments, affects, and convictions that otherwise remain hidden."[98]

Hot places often evolve into actual memorials where a physical monument is built to recall the group's trauma and losses. Conversely, some memorials, at least when they are first constructed, function as hot places. "Ground Zero," where the Twin Towers of the World Trade Center in New York City stood before September 11, 2001, is certainly a hot place. In the memorial service that took place there on October 28, 2001, family members of the victims were given wooden urns containing dust, dirt, and ashes from the site. The meaning of the urns was clear, as the ashes symbolically, if not literally, represented the loved ones who had perished; the family members would have a piece of their loved ones even though their bodies could not be recovered. Through this, they would psychologically link themselves to the people they had lost. I do not personally know what family members did with their urns, but I suspect that most became linking objects. Soon after this ceremony, discussions in public and in the media about constructing a memorial—a shared linking object—at Ground Zero began. Should part of the wrecked area be left as a memorial? Should the images of the Twin Towers be created with beams of light from the ground toward the heavens? During the spring of 2005 the media informed us that the rebuilding of Ground Zero fell on bleak times due to economic and political considerations. But we can easily assume that the chosen design for a memorial at this location will be subjected to long and emotional discussions.

If a memorial is built at a site that is still hot, it becomes a symbolic place that the affected group utilizes in order to keep the shared mourning process and a desire for revenge alive. But eventually a "hot" memorial "cools off" and it becomes a metaphorical box made of stone, marble, or metal that collects within it the unfinished work of group mourning, puts a border around shared group feelings, ands the group complete, for practical purposes, its mourning process. The World War II Memorial that I referred to in the previous chapter became such a box right away, largely because it was built six decades after the end of the war. It effectively symbolizes and honors both the four hundred thousand dead as well as all those in the nation who were affected by the war; the memory of lost ones is recognized and commemorated, making them "futureless."

To further illustrate how large-group sentiments are expressed in and through memorials, I offer a comparison between two very different sites: the Crying Father Memorial in Tskhinvali, South Ossetia, and the Vietnam Veterans Memorial in Washington, D.C. The first one, a combination of a hot place and a memorial, is used to keep large-group feelings inflamed, while the second one has become a place that has tremendously aided America's large-group mourning, thereby taming mixed feelings about the Vietnam War and finally bringing unresolved psychological work to a practical end.

Georgian forces encircled Tskhinvali for many months during the Georgian–South Ossetian conflict in 1991–92. At one point during this siege, three young South Ossetian combatants died within moments of one another. Because the Georgians had captured and occupied the cemetery at the outskirts of the city, the men were buried in the schoolyard of High School #5 on Lenin Avenue in Tskhinvali. One of the victims had attended this school, and the school yard was thought to be a safe place to bury them. Gradually, more and more dead defenders came to be buried there, including thirty who had apparently been killed on the same day. Today the graves there number more than one hundred.

It was during our second visit to Tskhinvali that I heard about this schoolyard. After we finished our work at the Palace of Children's Creativity and were preparing to return to Tbilisi, Nodar Sharveladze suggested that we visit the cemetery at School #5. I believe that he wanted those of us from the United States, the members of CSMHI, to have a sense of South Ossetians' suffering. Even though Nodar is a Georgian, he wanted to be fair and give us an opportunity to better understand the trauma that the Georgian–South Ossetian conflict had created for the other side. I think that Nodar had been to this place before, but other Georgians accompanying us on this day had never seen it. Yuri Urbanovich and I had been to quite a few hot places and knew that foreigners should not visit them without making preparations and without "chaperones" from the affected group. Through Venera Basishvili or other South Ossetians whom we got to know, we could have obtained "official permission" to go to School #5. Although we had not, I did not raise any objections to Nodar's suggestion. His intention was noble and, after all, we had just left the company of some very kind and friendly South Ossetians.

So there we were, Georgians and Americans, walking down deserted Lenin Avenue, jumping over potholes as we followed a rundown wall about five-feet high that separated the schoolyard from the street. We arrived at the gate of School #5 and saw the burial site on the right side of the courtyard. I took my camera out to take some pictures. Suddenly, a van and a car appeared from nowhere. Angry South Ossetian men, in civilian clothes, jumped out and surrounded us. I could see that they had revolvers. It was clear that they wanted to know what we, foreigners, were doing at a location that had become a holy place for them. Were we there to desecrate the honored and idealized memory of the South Ossetian heroes buried there?

I was scared. These men could have easily taken our cameras away, beaten us, or even killed us. Because I could not communicate with these men, I felt paralyzed and silently began cursing myself for forgetting how much emotion hot places induce in members of a traumatized group, and how careful we needed to be in arranging to come to such a place. Nodar introduced himself both in English and Russian, and spoke to them in Russian in a very calm manner. As I learned later, he told them that he was a Georgian professor who had contacts with South Ossetian colleagues, that all of us had come to this place to pay our respects to the dead, and that we had not intended to hurt anyone's feelings. These men who, I suspected, belonged to a South Ossetian paramilitary group, eventually allowed us to return to our cars unmolested. Needless to say, I was very impressed with Nodar's calm behavior. I felt very grateful to him for saving us from a potentially horrible situation.

I never went back to the yard of School #5 on Lenin Avenue in Tskhinvali, but this place remained in my mind as a clear example of a hot place. As my colleagues from CSMHI and I continued to facilitate discussions in the coming years between Georgians and South Ossetians, it remained a topic of discussion. I learned that South Ossetians later built a small chapel and erected a statue called the Crying Father in the schoolyard. Inga Kochieva, a South Ossetian, sent me pictures of the chapel and statue. The design of the small chapel recalled the Arc de Triomphe in Paris, while the Crying Father was a life-size stone statue standing on a square block. Striking a sorrowful pose, the figure wears a traditional South Ossetian sheepskin head cover and a long coat. In South Ossetian, culture men are not supposed to cry, so his paternal tears reflect extreme, ceaseless pain.

Although an iron fence separates the burial place, the small chapel, and the Crying Father statue from the rest of the schoolyard, they are visible from the school. In order to enter the three-story school building, students (who began attending classes again after the fighting in Tskhinvali ended) have to walk by them. From all three floors of the school, students and their teachers can look over the burial and memorial site. The youngsters are constantly reminded of South Ossetians' victimization, helplessness, and losses. During the initial years following the 1991–92 conflict, repeated ceremonies were held in the schoolyard. I was told that South Ossetian authorities used every possible excuse to hold such ceremonies, which ranged from anniversaries to religious holidays. The public supported the authorities by participating in the ceremonies en masse. Youngsters were encouraged to write and read poetry that spoke of victimization and, more importantly, revenge. The image of the enemy was reinforced in order to strengthen the victimized group's identity, and the illusion was maintained that fighting these "others" could enable South Ossetians to recover their losses in the future.

During our continuing dialogue series, South Ossetians' relationship with the Crying Father statue became a kind of indicator of the mood in Tskhinvali and of the nature of South Ossetians' interactions with Georgians. The South Ossetian participants acknowledged that the existence of the Crying Father statue and the repeated ceremonies held at this location were poisoning youngsters attending School #5 and keeping negative feelings about Georgians alive in their own generation. The participants spoke about this to the authorities in Tskhinvali, expressing their concerns. They later reported that, as a result of their efforts, over time fewer ceremonies came to be held in the schoolyard. They also reported that the emotions in the poems read by the students became tamer, due to encouragement from the authorities and teachers. But the youngsters still had to walk by the Crying Father statue, the chapel, and the burial place every school day. The South Ossetians from the dialogue series also began to speak about the need to resolve this problem: they knew they either needed to remove the graves to another location or build a new school. But the first option was unthinkable, because their religious beliefs and cultural traditions forbade them to disturb the dead, and the second option was unrealistic because the town could not afford to build a new school.

After some time, discussions surrounding the memorial and other issues enabled Georgian participants to begin expressing a kind of remorse for going to war against South Ossetians and for the nationalism in Georgia under Zviad Gamsakhurdia that had spurred it on. Georgian participants still felt that fighting against Abkhazians had been a necessity, but some of them now began taking a great deal of responsibility for Georgia's role in inflaming the Georgian–South Ossetian conflict. South Ossetian participants also appeared to be more prepared to "hear" some of the Georgian's sense of remorse for the bloody conflict.[99] When a Georgian said she was moved by the South Ossetians' dilemma and that she wanted to go to School #5 to pay her respects to the dead, the South Ossetians seemed to be pleased, although I do not think the visit ever occurred.

But problems in South Ossetia were not limited to those who fell in combat and their memorialization. After the war, many South Ossetian men left to work in Russia. Leaving their wives and children behind put a tremendous burden on traditional family values. When the women had to go out and find work, they discovered a sense of independence. When their husbands returned, they found that their wives' lives no longer fit into the expected norm of their culture. The number of divorces increased and this, in turn, affected children's lives.[100] Many youngsters became criminals or prostitutes. Meanwhile, South Ossetian authorities became more and more vulnerable to Russian political manipulation, making it more difficult for them to reach a political agreement with Georgians, and the fabric of life in South Ossetia continued to split apart under the lingering stress of the conflict. We knew that expanding our dialogues to include more politically influential persons from both sides could help prevent some negative long-term effects the region would otherwise suffer. But, with the end of open warfare, funds for work in Georgia and South Ossetia quickly dried up.

After CSMHI stopped going to Georgia, we were able to work with the Georgian and South Ossetian participants for another year by bringing them to Turkey—once to Izmir and once to Istanbul. After this, the participants from both sides continued to collaborate in trying to understand certain societal processes, such as increased family violence due to ethnic conflict. But in 2004 a new deadly clash occurred between Georgia and South Ossetia, leading to a complete breakdown of communication between the Georgian and South Ossetian participants in the former CSMHI dialogue series. I am not well-informed about why this occurred, but I continued to be in touch with both sides through e-mail. I learned from one South Ossetian that Nodar Sharveladze had sent Christmas greetings to the South Ossetians in December 2004. Although the South Ossetians were personally happy to receive his message, because of the recent political and military developments, they found engaging in contact with the "enemy" impossible and, therefore, did not write him back. I also learned from the South Ossetians that once more their group was noticing the "tears" of the Crying Father.

As I indicated earlier, I never returned to School #5, but what I learned from the South Ossetian participant's remarks about this location taught me a lesson. It reconfirmed for me that a group's relationship with a hot place or hot memorial can tell us a great deal about the group's mourning, sense of revenge, and ability to forgive. I will return to examine such feelings shared within a large group later in this chapter.

While the monument built in the yard of School #5 was utilized as a shared linking object to keep the South Ossetians' mourning process alive, the Vietnam Veterans Memorial in Washington, D.C., has conversely helped bring one to an end. The building the Vietnam Veterans Memorial and the subsequent reaction by veterans, the families of casualties, and the public, helped Americans accept that their losses were real and that life would go on without recovering those who were lost. Earlier, the American dead from the Vietnam War were mourned by family members and friends and were buried privately. But publicly, their deaths were not collectively acknowledged. Given the mixed feelings about the war, veterans returned home without much fanfare. Many questions about the war remained unresolved in the minds of the American people. Did people die for a good cause or did they perish for a bad policy? Did we lose the war? And, if we did, should we honor those who sacrificed so much? Jeffrey Ochsner tells us that, given American's ambivalent feelings about the war, "the most common response was, in effect, denial"[101] of feelings and thoughts about the dead, about the veterans, and about a societal regression within American society. "However, the construction of the Vietnam Veterans Memorial, with the inscribed names of the dead and the missing, seemed to change all this."[102]

The memorial's designer, Maya Ying Lin, was a twenty-one-year-old undergraduate student at Yale University when competition for the design of the memorial was made public. Lin, in an interview with Carol Vogel that was published in the *New York Times* on May 9, 1994, reported that while at Yale in the late 1970s and early 1980s, her professors had told her that she could be either an artist or an architect, but not both. She added: "I love architecture and I love sculpture, but I could never choose. Sculpture to me is like poetry, and architecture is like prose."[103] While designing the Vietnam Veterans Memorial, both as an architect and an artist, she associated death with a "sharp pain that lessens with time, but can never quite heal over a scar."[104] She wanted to take a knife and cut open the earth, and "with time the grass would heal it."[105] When her design was made public, however, some people found it offensive and labeled it a "wailing wall" or a "black gash of shame."[106]

Although the design of the wall invoked controversy and aggravated the unhealed wounds of the war, the Vietnam Veterans Memorial was dedicated on November 13, 1982.[107] Its main features are long black granite slabs that converge at an angle while rising from the earth. They bear the names of more than fifty thousand military personnel killed or missing in action. The organization of names on the black granite is unusual.[108] Ochsner writes: "Before the Vietnam Veterans Memorial, most monuments that listed the dead and the missing from a war or a battle presented the names within the hierarchy of military organization. . . . On the Vietnam Veterans Memorial, the names are listed chronologically, without indications of military rank. There are no dates other than the two years. Yet a sense of days can be glimpsed from the alphabetical grouping of the names—each subtly indicating the losses each day. . . . As we walk along the memorial, we pass through year after year of losses until we are faced with the enormity of the war's time frame as the dates 1959 and 1975 are found on the opposite faces at the apex."[109]

One of my sons, Kurt Volkan, looked at the Vietnam Veterans Memorial from a psychological angle and like Ochsner perceived it as a shared linking object. Kurt especially emphasizes the psychology of seeing one's own reflection intermingle with the names on the polished black granite. He writes: "Any one artist's figurative or allegorical interpretation of the Vietnam War surely would have less meaning than the human element involved in seeing oneself and one's living environment reflected in stone behind the names of dead soldiers."[110] Since the images of the dead are linked with the corresponding images of the live visitors, this monument truly represents a shared linking object. Kurt states: "By touching the stone and the etching of the names, the living bonded with the dead—after all, a name is a symbolic term that embodies everything about one's existence. . . . The etching of the names in granite, which will stand for thousands of years, makes death official and final in the mind's eye."[111] He goes onto say how seeing so many names side by side on the black granite of the memorial's wall—like seeing so many gold stars side by side on the Freedom Wall at the World War II Memorial—makes a monument a shared linking object, adding: "Thus this Wall can be as personal as a mother crying for her lost son, or as public as a nation weeping for a past history that has yet to be resolved."[112]

With no diplomatic overtures of apology or forgiveness between the United States and Vietnam, the building of the memorial and the American response to it—doing significant psychological work on group mourning—was an important step in neutralizing the relationship between the two countries.

So it would seem that the wounds of the Vietnam War, at least in a collective sense, have healed. The same is not true for South Ossetians, whose responses to trauma have rendered them just as rigid as the stone of the Crying Father in Tskhinvali. It would be impossible for them to respond to any possible gesture of reconciliation from Georgians. During the CSMHI-directed dialogue series between South Ossetians and Georgians, the concepts of apology and forgiveness came up, but when they did, the South Ossetians would quickly return to discussing what the Crying Father meant to them. Certainly, how a group reacts to a memorial tells us about their readiness to hear the other side's apology.

Without mourning, in its psychoanalytic sense,[113] an "apology" and "forgiveness" can neither be given nor received by groups that have been traumatized by others. In international diplomacy this typically matters little since nations and their leaders very seldom make official apologies to those they fought against in past wars. But it has happened. In one well-publicized case, then-German chancellor Willy Brandt apologized to Polish Jews during his December 7, 1970, visit to the site of the former Warsaw ghetto, when Brandt spontaneously fell to his knees in acknowledgment for what the Nazis had done. The dramatic apology became known as the Kniefall and its image lingered in peoples' minds, both within and outside Germany, for many years. Some Germans did not like what Brandt had done; the Polish people in general approved of it. Generally speaking, Brandt's apology was effective because many other political processes in Germany after the Holocaust had prepared the victims to hear an apology; the apology itself did not come across as a magical word. It was also a part of what was known as Brandt's policy of Ostpolitik, his efforts to normalize relations with the Soviet Union and other Eastern bloc countries.[114]

A second well-publicized apology took place in 1990 when then-Soviet leader Mikhail Gorbachev apologized for the WWII Katyn Forest Massacre in Poland. During the spring of 1940 about 4,500 Polish army reservists, including doctors, lawyers, scientists, and businessmen, were taken to Katyn Forest near Smolensk in western Russia. They were gagged, bound, and shot by Soviet soldiers by direct order from Joseph Stalin. After the mass grave was discovered in 1943 by a German soldier, the Germans accused the Soviets of the massacre. The Soviets denied being involved in this tragedy and apparently the Americans and the British went along with this denial and tried to pin the blame on the Nazis as part of the Allies' war propaganda against them. Gorbachev's apology was "heard" because of the many other political and social changes that he had initiated before his apology. In 1995, however, Boris Yeltsin declined to attend a special memorial service at the site of the massacre, once more aggravating Polish-Russian relations.

Nevertheless, after Gorbachev's public recognition of Soviet responsibility for the massacre, the concept of apology, as well as the concept of forgiveness, began to interest practitioners and scholars dealing with international relations. It became a rather trendy topic among some government circles, particularly after South Africa's Truth and Reconciliation Commission (TRC) was formed as a way to deal with atrocities committed during apartheid. The process involved victims publicly telling their stories and forgiving victimizers who had acknowledged and apologized for their deeds.

Acquiring a perceived perpetrator's apology and strongly encouraging such a perpetrator to apologize through a third, neutral party came to be seen as a significant element in the resolution of ethnic, national, religious, and ideological large-group conflicts. Thus, the concepts of apology and forgiveness, which have been closely linked to certain religious doctrines[115] for millennia, came to be promoted as a diplomatic and political practice. Commissions modeled on the TRC sprouted up in various parts of the world. But the problems—and failures—faced by those attempting to recreate the TRC's work suggest that a closer examination and a better understanding is needed of when and how an apology and forgiveness are useful.

Although I knew early on from CSMHI's various dialogue series that parties in conflict cannot decide to make an apology, accept one, and forgive the other without controversy, my participation in one set of reconciliation negotiations highlighted to me the problems that one can encounter when apologies, forgiveness, and memorials are part of discussions between two groups. My involvement in these negotiations began in the late 1990s, when I was contacted by my friend Gündüz Aktan, a former career diplomat who served as Turkish ambassador to the United Nations in Geneva, Greece, and Japan and undersecretary of the Turkish Foreign Ministry. Since retiring from public service, Gündüz has become a prominent newspaper journalist and head of a well-known Turkish research center. As someone who still enjoyed significant influence in Turkey, Gündüz asked me to join him and others as a member of the then newly formed Turkish-Armenian Reconciliation Commission (TARC). The aim of this commission—chaired and facilitated by an American— was to bring six Turks and six Armenians together for a series of meetings over several years to discuss the tragic events of 1915, when hundreds of thousands of Armenians—and significant numbers of Turks—died both at each other's hand and through famine and disease. As both sides have vastly different interpretations of what caused the events, what transpired, and, indeed, how many died, the hope was that such an initiative would eventually lead to some form of reconciliation between them. I learned that both the Turkish delegation and the Armenian delegation included well-known retired politicians and officials, such as a former Turkish and a former Armenian prime minister.

I was hesitant to join the Turkish-Armenian Reconciliation Commission for a couple of reasons. First, discussion of what is generally known as the "Armenian genocide" has been filled with controversy and antagonism for generations. Although I am interested in history because it is intertwined with large-group psychology and identity, I am not a historian and knew little about the history of Turkish and Armenian relations. Debate over this turbulent and horrific time has ensnared prominent historians in countless countries for many decades, so how could I possibly contribute?

Second, I have never been a Turkish citizen. I was born in Cyprus when the island was still a British colony, so when I immigrated to the United States in 1957 it was with a British passport. I became an American citizen in 1964 and have spent most of my adult life in Virginia. My only knowledge of and interaction with Armenians dated to my early years. When I was a boy, my family's next door neighbors were Armenians with whom we communicated in Turkish and got along with very well. Additionally, my violin teacher, Monsignor Bedelian, whom I admired from my preadolescence days throughout my teen years, was an Armenian, and I used to play violin on the stage of an Armenian church. In fact, as a child and as a teenager, I was not aware of any hostility between Armenians and Turks. So I wondered about my suitability to be a member of TARC. But I was assured that other members of the commission had similar backgrounds: one participant was an Armenian-American leader of the Armenian community in the United States, and another was a leader of the Armenian community in the Russian Federation. In fact, I knew the latter from my previous work on U.S.-Soviet and Baltic Republics-Russian Federation relationships. My fellow Turkish commissioners knew that I had limited personal and professional knowledge of Turkish-Armenian relations, but they welcomed me as someone with experiences in unofficial diplomacy and the psychology of international relationships.

I had a hunch that Armenians as a group had been unable to collec-

tively mourn their losses and had internalized their sense of victimization, making it a prominent part of their shared large-group identity.
Much of who they are now as a group appears to be based on what happened to them at the hands of their enemies in the early twentieth century. I also knew that such an observation is not novel, as Armenians
themselves have written about such a shared sentiment.[116] Although I was
no expert on Armenia, I did have some knowledge of other groups with
a victimized sense of identity. In my book *Bloodlines: From Ethnic Pride
to Ethnic Terrorism* I told the story of the Serbians' sense of prolonged
victimization and how it was reactivated by Slobodan Milosevic to
enhance their sense of entitlement for revenge.[117] I therefore expected
that Armenians would find it difficult to hear the "other's" apology and/
or forgive them, since such moves would require a modification of the
existing large-group identity and this would, in turn, initiate a shared
anxiety.

It did not take long for complications in the negotiations to arise.
Indeed, issues related to memorials, apologies, and forgiveness came up
right away at the very first TARC meeting that I attended. This meeting,
which took place in Europe, began with the following statement from
Armenian delegates: "During the last many many decades we were able
to raise a huge amount of money and with it we plan to build a huge
monument in Washington, D.C., for the Armenian genocide at the hands
of the Turks in 1915. If you Turks accept that there was an Armenian
genocide and apologize for it, our monument will show the Turks in a
better light. If you do not accept that there was an Armenian genocide,
the proposed memorial will make the Turks appear as really horrible
people. You have a choice to make!" I knew right away that this meeting
had started on the wrong foot, and any hope for neutrality or objective-
ness among its participants would be difficult at best. In spite of this I
tried to observe some hidden and not-so-hidden group phenomena pertaining both to Armenians and Turks as I struggled to remain impartial.

One thing I noticed was that the sense of Armenian large-group identity was intimately linked to the Turkish large-group identity, and did not
or could not exist independent of it. "Turkishness"—which for the
Armenians was linked to the Ottoman Empire—was internalized by
them as part of their own large-group identity. This was not an unexpected observation for me. An ethnic group who lives under a foreign
central power for decades or centuries will assimilate images of this central power's dominant ethnic group into its own identity while maintaining its own core ethnic, cultural, and religious identity. This is true, I

think, for almost all groups, and not just the various Christian groups who lived under the Ottomans for centuries. When an empire or central power collapses, the newly independent ethnic group cannot suddenly erase the internalized "two identities" that evolved over time. But separation of them becomes more drastic. Usually the part of group identity that is associated with the former ruling group becomes "all bad" and the things that were not "contaminated" by it become "all good." A strong internal clash occurs between the two identities.

The part that is "all bad" is externalized onto the descendants of the ruling group or the heirs of the empire, and watched and struggled against constantly. No one describes what I am speaking about here better than the well-known Greek writer Nikos Kazantzakis. In his book *Report to Greco,* Kazantzakis refers to his childhood in Crete and echoes what had happened to Greeks living for centuries as subjects of the Ottoman Empire. He states:

> To gain freedom first of all from the Turk, that was the initial step, after that, later, this new struggle began: *to gain freedom from the inner Turk* [italics added]—from ignorance, malice and envy, from fear and laziness, from dazzling false ideas, and finally from idols, all of them, even the most revered and beloved. . . . Overflowing the bounds of Crete and Greece, it [the struggle] raged in all eras and locales and invaded the history of mankind. Battling now were not Crete and Turkey but good and evil, light and darkness, God and devil. It was always the same battle, the eternal one, and standing always behind the good, behind the light and God, was Crete; behind evil, behind darkness, and the devil, Turkey.[118]

The Armenians' "two identities" as victim and victimizer had to be present internally, side by side in the shadows, in order to create the visible Armenian identity. Some Armenian participants described child-rearing practices in Armenia, and in Armenian families elsewhere, that demonstrated how these two side-by-side identities are transmitted to Armenian children from the age of two, when they are told stories of victimization. Then, as adults they have to externalize the Turkish part of their core selves in order to be free themselves from the internal struggle between the victim-victimizer. Thus the adult Armenians—of course I am generalizing here—are obliged to devote their lives to being preoccupied with this externalized Ottoman/Turkish part.

The ultimatum I heard during the first TARC meeting I attended, and other observations from later TARC meetings, suggested to me that if the

Turks ever agreed that there was an Armenian genocide and that an apology was warranted, this would greatly disturb the core of Armenian large-group identity. In turn, this would induce anxiety within the community. Accordingly, I concluded that there might be unconscious and conscious efforts on the Armenians' part to keep the status quo of the problematic Turkish-Armenian relationship. All of the Turkish TARC commissioners openly accepted that there was a huge tragedy and victimization of Armenians in 1915, but any time they spontaneously attempted to express empathy for the Armenians' suffering, it seemed that they were quickly rebuffed. Even when Armenian commissioners demanded it openly and strongly, there was no room for them to accept the Turkish commissioners' empathy. I learned that hundreds of e-mail and telephone messages were forwarded from Armenia and the Armenian diaspora to the Armenian commissioners, Armenian organizations, and Armenian media urging the Armenian commissioners not to weaken the international pressure on Turkey by creating a positive image of the Turkish participants, as well as Turks in general (See, for example, www.asbarez.com/Tarc/Tarc.html). No such phenomenon occurred on the Turkish side against the Armenian commissioners or Armenians in general.

But that did not mean that the Turkish side of TARC was without its own large-group identity issues. One problem was the silence within Turkish society about what had happened to the Ottoman Empire's Armenians as it began to collapse and, as I will describe later, a silence about what had happened to the Turks themselves during the same time. The Turkish commissioners of TARC had come from such a "silent" society and it was difficult for them to break away from the existing societal norm.

As I mentioned, I grew up in Cyprus as a Turk, and although I knew quite a few Armenians, I was never aware of any hostility between the two communities. When I later went to Turkey after my teen years to study medicine, no one talked about Armenians. One of my teachers at medical school was an Armenian Turk, but no one seemed to pay any special attention to his ethnicity.[119] There was a silence about the "Armenian problem." In fact, I learned how widespread this "problem" was only after I came to America in 1957. Early in my psychiatric career, while attending a professional meeting, I sat next to another psychiatrist who was my age. When he learned that I was a Turk from Cyprus, he said that he was an Armenian-American and that I was the first Turk he had ever met. He then turned pale and began trembling. I was shocked. I will never forget his fear of me. He was like a small boy seeing the most dreaded monster of his childhood imagination.

Among the Armenian and Turkish TARC participants, the perception of why there was silence was drastically different, making empathic dialogue between them extremely difficult. For the Armenians, the reason for the Turkish silence was simple: Turks felt guilty and therefore they would not speak of what their Ottoman ancestors had done to the Armenians. This was not the Turkish participants' experience, however. The Turks' perception of their silence had a great deal to do with their own inability to mourn their losses during the last century of the Ottoman Empire. From 1821, the beginning of the Greek rebellion against the Ottoman Empire, to 1922, the end of the Turkish War of Independence, an estimated five million Turkish and other Muslim subjects were forcefully displaced from their homes after repeated wars in the Balkans and the Caucasus as the Ottoman Empire shrank. This huge number of people was forced to migrate to the heartland of Turkey, Anatolia, by former non-Muslim subjects of the empire, aided by Christian Europeans and Russians. According to estimates, another five million were killed.[120] European propaganda enhanced the idea that Ottomans were just giving back territories they had held for centuries to their rightful owners, creating a "moral" background and justification for "forgetting" five million who were exiled and another five million who were killed.

What complicated matters further and denied the Turks' mourning over losing their empire, people, homes, and prestige, was the birth of the modern Turkish state with a charismatic leader, Mustafa Kemal Atatürk. In order to create the new Turkey, nationalist Turks fought against other Turks loyal to the Sultan. In other words, the image of the Sultan—and by extension the Ottomans—was perceived to be "bad" by the citizens of the new Turkey. In the initial period of modern Turkey, only selected aspects of the Ottoman past were valued; other parts were denied. There was a general silence about losses, mourning them, and extreme suffering, as if having the new Turkey and its charismatic leader was enough, and they did not have extra time to somehow resolve unpleasant memories and feelings. The specific silence about what happened to the Armenians in 1915 was pooled within this more general silence.

I recall the Turkish commissioners became aware of this when they were alone during a meeting break. They suddenly realized that all, except one whose ancestors had always lived in Anatolia, were children of Turks forced from their homes by the former Christian subjects of the Ottoman Empire. In all their homes mourning had been denied; their ancestors had never complained about their forced exile. This was very different than what they had heard about the Armenians' homes, where wounds were kept open. Their attempt to share this observation with the Armenian members was cut short because the style of the meeting under an American facilitator—a student of the so-called rational "win-win" strategy of conflict resolution—was not conducive to bringing such psychological considerations into the open. Empathetic communication was not possible.

The Turkish members also felt that the Armenians were consciously modeling their tragedy after the Holocaust. The Armenians had spent decades crystallizing this model and making it their shared "psychic reality." They would not allow any discussion that might illustrate drastic differences between what happened in Nazi Germany and what happened in the Ottoman Empire when it was collapsing, and in what ways the genocide of the Jewish population under Nazi control was similar as well as very dissimilar to massacres of Armenians. The issue was not to deny the tragedy, but question how to name it.

After I became a member of TARC, I read a great deal on what had happened in 1915 from Armenian and Western sources. I also read a great deal from Ottoman sources that were printed in the new Turkish alphabet after the birth of the Turkish Republic. I came to the conclusion that, historically speaking, the tragedy indeed was very complicated, and that sorting it out needed to be done carefully by historians from both sides under neutral third-party supervision with all documents made available for examination by each side. I also realized that, due to my observations above, this most likely would not be done under TARC's current embodiment. I also came to the conclusion that a massive tragedy—whatever its causes are and however it is perceived differently by opposing groups— first must be explored gently and slowly in order to create room for empathic communication. Without this atmosphere, I thought TARC discussions would go nowhere.

As I noted, the "rational actor" approach of the American in charge of the TARC meetings—and to this day I do not know where the money came from for these activities—was not conducive to creating such an atmosphere. To make real progress, psychological resistances needed to be taken into consideration so that members could "hear" each other, but instead the American facilitator attempted to turn the meetings into bargaining sessions. After a couple of years, I resigned from TARC even though I had developed a genuine desire to be of some help in making Turkish-Armenian relationships better. I also learned about the existence of more successful meetings between Turks and Armenians on a grass-roots level, and wished that money and efforts would have been spent on a more effective model of unofficial negotiations, such as the ones I will describe in part three of this book

After my resignation from TARC, Gündüz followed me, and then all Turkish commissioners except one resigned from it, although later new members were invited to participate and TARC continued to meet. I understand nothing significant developments occurred in these later meetings. However, in March 2005, the Turkish government, with the full support of the opposition party in the Turkish parliament, proposed an initiative that would bring Turkish and Armenians historians together to jointly investigate national archives under the notary mission of an out-side international organization, such as UNESCO. So far the Armenian government and the broader internal Armenian community has been cool toward the proposal of scholarly investigation.

I was not surprised that there was resistance to even a historical analysis of Armenian and Turkish history, because history and large-group identity had become so intimately intertwined over the genera-tions. When a traumatized group cannot reverse its feelings of helpless-ness and humiliation and cannot effectively go through the work of mourning, it transfers these unfinished psychological tasks to future generations. Psychoanalysts and mental health professionals have shown how these transgenerational transmissions occur, especially in many studies of the children and grandchildren of Holocaust survivors.[121] In brief, such tasks are often transferred through parents' behavior patterns, physical gestures, other nonverbal communications, and the granting or withholding of affection when a child behaves in certain ways. In other words, such transmissions take place mostly unconsciously within the child-parent (or -caretaker) relationship.

Despite the individuality of each child in subsequent generation(s), in a large group whose ancestors have experienced a massive trauma and severe losses at the hands of enemies, the children of ensuing generation(s) are given similar primary tasks: complete the mourning over the losses, reverse shame and humiliation, and turn passivity into assertion. Since all of these tasks are related to the mental representation of the same massive traumatic event, the mental representation of this event connects the members of the group in an invisible way. This mental representation of the event, decades later, evolves into a large-group identity marker. I call these historical hurts chosen traumas[122]—that is, the historical image of the trauma is "chosen" to represent a particular group. Czechs commemorate the 1620 battle of Bila Hora, which led to their subjugation under the Habsburg Empire for nearly three hundred years. In the United States, the Lakota Indians recall the anniversary of their 1890 decimation at Wounded Knee. Once an event becomes a chosen trauma for the next generations, its historical truth is no longer the crucial issue for the group. What is important is that through sharing the chosen trauma, members of the group are linked together. The chosen trauma as a crucial "identity marker" becomes significant in the large-group's life.

Large groups may do various things with the tasks transferred to them, depending upon the historical circumstances. For example, the subsequent generation(s) may become involved in hostilities with those neighbors who are descended from the victimizers and who symbolically represent the original victimizers. If the external political or military conditions permit the descendants of a victimized group to have military or political power, they may get involved in war-like situations or become a political thorn in the side of the "enemy." I do not mean to imply that a large group's chosen trauma causes wars or war-like conditions. Rather, when reactivated, it can inflame a conflict.

When history, myth, and large-group identity are intertwined with trauma and complicated mourning, a memorial can reactivate a large-group's chosen trauma with disastrous results. For example, when Slobodan Milosevic was stirring nationalist sentiments among Serbians after 1987, he—with the help of some Serbian intellectuals and others from the Serbian Church—was instrumental in the building of a huge monument on a hill overlooking the Kosovo battlefield. The Battle of Kosovo had taken place in 1389 between the Serbians and the Ottomans. Throughout the centuries, the mental representation of this battle—and that of Serbian leader Prince Lazar, who was killed during it—had become the prominent Serbian chosen trauma. The building of a monument on the six hundredth anniversary of this event was designed to open Serbians' centuries-old wounds and create enemies; in this case, Bosniaks and Albanians stood in for the Ottomans in the Serbian mind.

The Kosovo monument, standing one hundred feet over the battlefield, is made of red stone, representing blood.[123] Serbians nicknamed the flowers that grow on the battlefield "grieving flowers," since the weight of their bloom causes them to seemingly hang their heads down. The monument is surrounded by cement pillars shaped like artillery shells and on each a sword is chiseled along with the dates 1389-1989. It should be recalled that the Vietnam Veterans Memorial bears the years 1959 and 1975, referring to the timeframe of the actual war. Conversely, the dates on the Kosovo monument suggest that the war remains unresolved and that it was built not to complete the Serbians' six-hundred-year-old mourning process, but to reopen it. It was not intended to allow thoughts of forgiveness, but to stimulate revenge against current enemies who psychologically represented the original ones.

I do not want to suggest that the building of the Kosovo monument somehow caused the tragedies in former Yugoslavia. I do believe, however, that the structure symbolically expressed sentiments that had been passed down over generations. These feelings of victimization were awakened from their "dormancy" by ethnonationalistic leaders through the monument and a variety of means. I will elaborate on this later, but in this chapter by focusing on how a group reacts to some memorials that honor their dead and recall their trauma, I sought to shed some light on the complicated psychology that exists between large groups in conflict. These factors in turn can influence political policies. Therefore, in international relations, the focus should not be on the single (seemingly magical) act of apology, asking forgiveness, or visiting the enemy's hot place. Rather, it should be on developing strategies for helping the victimized group's work of mourning, on modifying such processes for taming feelings of revenge, on increasing a sense of peaceful coexistence, and on creating a political atmosphere in which the victim and the victimizer can find justification for a new type of relatedness.

9 The Bataan Death March and Animal Killings

Various societal responses to a massive trauma at the hands of "others," including building memorials, of which I gave examples in the previous two chapters, are associated with attempts to mourn losses and repair injured large-group identity. Now we can turn our attention to a different type of societal response, the transgenerational transmission of certain psychological tasks, handed down to the affected group's offspring, as if these tasks will complete their parent's original unfinished mourning and unfinished repairing activities. In order to illustrate the concept of transgenerational transmission, in this chapter I will describe in some detail how we can observe it in an individual. Once we see that there is such a thing as transgenerational transmission, I will focus in the next chapter on how shared transgenerational transmissions in large groups may become significant factors in societal, political and/or historical movements.

There are variations of transgenerational transmissions, and as we will see, certain types are more suitable for sharing and for starting a societal, political, and/or historical process. But all types of transgenerational transmissions have something in common: they depend on permeability in the psychological boundary between children and their mothers or other important caretakers. A mother or caretaker's anxiety and other affects, unconscious fantasies, and wishes and defenses against these wishes can pass into the child's developing sense of self. Psychoanalysts have been noticing such phenomena for decades.

An early 1940s study by the well-known psychoanalysts Anna Freud and Dorothy Burlingham illustrated how, during the World War II German Blitz over London, some children sensed their caretakers' anxiety and, in turn, became anxious themselves. If mothers and caretakers remained calm, the children did not experience anxiety.[124] Later, in the mid-1960s, Harry Stack Sullivan was an important psychoanalytic figure, who especially studied people suffering from schizophrenia. His theory on schizophrenia was based primarily on how the mother's anxiety could be conveyed in a poisonous way to the child.[125] In the late 1960s, Margaret Mahler's observations on the so-called symbiotic phase of child development (roughly between four weeks and five months of life) illustrated how in certain areas, a child and mother fuse their mental images and functions and behave as if they are one unit. From five months to thirty-six months of life a child goes through what is known as the separation-individuation phases in order to become, psychologically speaking, an individual in his or her own right.[126] More modern researchers in the 1980s and early 1990s have also referenced how affects and psychological "messages" pass through the permeable boundary between mother and child.[127] Lastly, an ongoing laboratory research project at the Kuopio Medical School in Finland has begun to provide ample evidence of trans-generational transmissions and their psychobiological underpinnings.[128]

Some clinical case reports also clearly show how an individual's symptoms may be best, or least partly, explained by considering what passed through the permeable "border" between a mother and child. For example, psychiatrist As'ad Masri and I described a female transsexual's belief that she was a man and that if her skin were unzipped like a garment, there would be a penis between her legs. We also worked with this transsexual's mother and were able to illustrate that this female transsexual primarily reflected her mother's unconscious fantasy that her daughter was a penis, the mother having transferred this unconscious fantasy to her child. When she delivered her child, the future transsexual, she was living in a foreign country with her husband who was involved in semi-secret military activity and was away from home a great deal. The young mother was frustrated, anxious, and regressed, and wanted some pleasure. Thus, at night she would put her baby girl between her legs and masturbate as if the baby was a penis substitute. After a while her fantasy of her female baby as a penis was so generalized that when she took her baby out in public she covered and hid the baby under blankets as an adult covers and hides a penis while in a public place. Her daughter never knew her mother's story, but her mother's fantasy was, in fact, transferred to her because the daughter grew up believing that she possessed a penis.[129] In another case, psychologist Robert Zuckerman and I reported how a mother with a deformed spine passed the mental image of her physical problem to her son who, in turn, behaved as if his spine was deformed.[130] Such clinical case examples are abundant.[131]

In taking into consideration the permeability of the psychological border between the child and the mother or other caretaker, my focus in this chapter is on what I call depositing an adult's self-image or internalized images of other persons into the developing self of a child.[132] Depositing is a specific kind of transgenerational transmission that is closely related to the well-known concept of identification. But it is in some ways significantly different than identification. In identification children are the primary active partners; they take in (mostly unconsciously) aspects of their adult partners and some of the adult partners' functions, assimilate what they take in, and make them their own. There are healthy and unhealthy identifications. In depositing, the adult is more actively pushing specific self-images and internalized images of others into the developing self of the child. In other words, an adult uses the child, mostly unconsciously, as a reservoir for certain mental images that belong to that adult. Although the child, who becomes a reservoir, is not completely a passive partner, the child does not initiate this transfer of images with their associated functions; it is the adult who initiates this process.[133]

One area in which the concept of depositing can be illustrated clearly is with the so-called "replacement child" phenomenon.[134] Imagine a mother has an internalized formed image of her child who suddenly dies, let's say, at the age of three. She deposits this image into the developing self of her second child, usually born after the first child's death. The second child, the replacement child, has no actual experience with the dead sibling, no image of this lost child. The mother, who does have an image of the dead child, treats the second one as the reservoir in which the dead child can be kept "alive." Accordingly, the mother gives the second child certain ego tasks to protect and maintain what she has deposited in this second child. Obviously, replacement children also develop their own ego functions in dealing with what has been pushed into them. For example, replacement children will be preoccupied with the task of integrating the deposited image with the rest of their self-representation. They may or may not succeed in doing so.[135]

Some adults also may actively, but mostly unconsciously, push their own traumatized self-images, sometimes accompanied by internalized images of others who played a role in the trauma, into the developing selves of children in their care. The actual memories of the trauma belong to adults; children who become reservoirs have no experience with the trauma. Actual memories belonging to one person cannot be transmitted to another person, but an adult can deposit traumatized images into a

child's self. By performing the act of depositing, the depositor external-
izes troublesome images into another person. Accordingly, the depositor
aims to become free of internally carrying the troublesome images and,
to one degree or another, deals with mental conflicts and anxiety associated with such images. On the other hand, a child who is a reservoir is
given a psychological "gene" that influences self-representation, and thus
the child's sense of identity. After depositing troublesome images into the
child the depositor also, again mostly unconsciously, directs the child to
be involved in certain tasks in order to maintain what had been deposited. Sometimes the depositor directs the child to do this or that, or develop this or that character traits in order to modify or heal what the child
is now carrying. The adult in a sense "controls" what originally belonged
to him or her and is now "out there" in the child.

When individuals who have been a reservoir of deposited images during childhood come to analysis, their resistance to the analytic process
and getting well will center at one time or another around facing the possibility of ceasing to function as a reservoir, or at least modifying this
condition, thus changing their sense of their existing identity. To discard
or modify what is deposited into one's self initiates anxiety concerning a
change in one's personal identity, losing the connection with the representation of a mother or other caretaker who was the depositor, and even
psychologically "killing" the depositor. Thus, a resistance to getting well
surfaces. When this happens during the psychoanalytic process, the concept of transgenerational transmission becomes palpable. Transmissions
are shared by all or most children in a massively traumatized large group
at the hands of its enemies, and in the next chapter I will return to the
concept of chosen trauma already described in the previous chapter. But
first I want to illustrate the concept transgenerational transmission with
a case study.

Before the Gulf War that followed the Iraqi invasion of Kuwait, an
experienced psychologist/psychoanalyst, Dr. Paul (not his real name),
came from another city to see me in Charlottesville, Virginia, where I live.
I had met him before, but I did not know him well. He described to me
how he had gone through an unexpected and horrible loss that made him
depressed enough to stop working for about two years. He said that he
had reopened his office recently and one of the people who came to seek
help from him was a man we shall call Peter. Apparently, Peter had picked
the analyst's name from a telephone book. Listening to Peter, Dr. Paul
sensed that the patient's traumatic childhood reminded him of aspects of
his own. He thought that in the past, before his unexpected great loss, he

could have handled the similarity between his and his patients' childhood histories. But after his own recent depression, he was not confident about working with Peter without consultation. He had read some of my books dealing with personality disorders, so Dr. Paul asked me if he could consult with me while treating Peter. Although Dr. Paul's story is not my focus here, I mention the above principally to indicate how I became involved in the process and my relationship with Dr. Paul. Dr. Paul and I ended up meeting once a week throughout Peter's five-year analysis, even though Dr. Paul had to travel some distance to come to see me.

I have referred to Peter's case elsewhere,[136] but here I will give details that were not available before. Briefly, Peter's self-representation was a reservoir of his stepfather's traumatized self-image, as I will soon show. Peter's stepfather, Gregory, was an American sailor during World War II who worked in a submarine where he was in charge of its torpedoes. He was captured by the Japanese while stationed in the Philippines and was forced to participate in the horrible Bataan Death March in the spring of 1942, when roughly 76,000 American and Filipino prisoners were forced by Japanese whips and guns to walk fifty or sixty miles in the boiling sun. About 20,000 prisoners died, 11,600 of them Americans. After that, Gregory was in a Japanese prison camp until the end of the war, where he was exposed to unbelievable cruelty. He observed the beheadings of fellow prisoners by swords; he buried his dead friends in shallow graves and reburied them when floods brought their corpses back to the surface. He experienced helplessness and the loss of dignity and also suffered from many physical ailments.

Soon after he returned to the United States as a thin, tired figure (he had lost sixty-five pounds during his imprisonment), Gregory became friendly with a woman whose husband had left her when their only child, Peter, was three weeks old. Gregory eventually moved in with her, Peter, and the woman's mother shortly before Peter's third birthday. During Peter's early childhood, Gregory stayed at home while the women went to work, thereby assuming the major parental role for Peter. Soon, Gregory married Peter's mother and adopted Peter as his son. He, his wife, and stepson Peter moved to a new house, leaving behind the boy's grandmother, who died when Peter was in his preteen years. According to Peter, when he was a child his stepfather rarely spoke of his horrible experiences during the war. He was good to Peter and continued as the boy's primary caregiver. Little Peter considered Gregory a hero.

Before Gregory appeared on the scene, Peter's mother and grandmother were generally angry with men. When her first husband abandoned her, Peter's mother's terrible rage mostly unconsciously turned on her son and intruded into her child's developing autonomy. In her reaction formation, she overfed him and even force-fed him, making the little boy obese. In the fifth year—during the termination phase—of his analysis with Dr. Paul, Peter began reviewing what he learned during his analysis. In a dream, he symbolized his life with his mother and grandmother as his living under a dome with two women who appeared as aggressive/sexual aliens from another planet. In another review dream, his stepfather enters his life and perceives Peter as a disfigured deer with thick, clumsy legs and no horns (overfed and castrated by the two women) and attempts to save the boy.

Before I illustrate the phenomenon of transgenerational transmission as it appeared in the relationship between Gregory and Peter, it is useful to give a bird's-eye view of Peter's total analysis. This will provide the necessary background for observing clearly the concept of how adults "deposit" images into children's selves, accompanied also by their passing on functions to their children to direct them in how to deal with what has been "deposited" within them.

When Peter sought psychoanalytic treatment he was in his mid-forties and married, with a daughter who was attending a university. Peter was a partner in a firm that was involved in the weapons production industry. He had a long history of heavy drinking. He also had another problem: bulimia. He began overeating and vomiting at age twenty and, at times, gorged and threw up more than once a day. At home he felt a lack of closeness to his family. This seemed wrong to him, but he was not about to take steps to alter the situation. He unenthusiastically let his wife manage their social life and declared, "I don't really like my daughter." His sexual impulses were inhibited, replaced by a passion to kill animals. Often he traveled to far-off places to hunt exotic animals. He was a hunter, but not a sportsman. For example, he would fly over a herd of deer in a helicopter in places such as Alaska and massacre the animals with a machine gun. His hobby was taxidermy.

One day, accompanied by his wife, he was attending a business luncheon in Los Angeles. He drank a lot at the table and then began vomiting in front of guests, soiling the clothes of a very important political leader, symbolically a father figure. His wife became very embarrassed and told him to get treatment. She added that if he did not get treatment, she would divorce him. This is why Peter came to see Dr. Paul.

Peter entered treatment with a certain bravado, eager to demonstrate that he was in control and that he needed no one. He was seeing Dr. Paul just to please his wife. He spurned the couch, and Dr. Paul agreed to work face-to-face until Peter felt ready for the couch, which Peter perceived as evidence of dependency. During the first week of treatment, he stopped drinking. He reported that he had the best abdominal muscles anyone could have and that he could vomit at will. He declared that his bulimic practices were no problem.

Just before coming to see Dr. Paul, Peter's firm was engaged in a half-billion-dollar deal. "I guess I can tell you the name of the missile we are developing," he said patronizingly. "That isn't classified information." He reported how he had "in the necessities of war" killed women and children while serving in Vietnam. After bragging about this or that for three months, he said to Dr. Paul, "You are a nice man, but not an important person. When I was in Vietnam I had fifty doctors under my command; two of them were psychiatrists. I hope you take no offense if I stop coming." At this time Peter was not a likeable person. I think that I helped Dr. Paul to remain in a therapeutic position with Peter. He told Peter that he was not an agent of Peter's wife, that he was simply there to work with him, and that it was up to Peter to decide whether or not to continue treatment.

Peter chose to stay in treatment and began lying on Dr. Paul's couch four times a week, developing what I call a "glass bubble" transference.[137] Peter, we thought, had a narcissistic personality organization contaminated with sadism. We also noted that underneath his bravado he was hiding a hungry sense of self. Analysands such as Peter fantasize an existence of something like a glass bubble that constitutes a kingdom in which the individual is Number One and the Only One, a person who holds sway over a universe of his own. In other words, these people put their grandiose part under a (psychological) protective barrier. They constantly observe what is outside of their metaphorical glass bubble. People whom they consider as existing for the sake of adoring them, they acknowledge; they devalue those whom they consider to be people who do not accept them as God's gift to the earth. (The devalued people symbolically represent the narcissistic individual's "hungry" part). Peter actually spoke of an "island empire" in which he would live alone. Peter expected his analyst to stay out of his imaginary island, since he really did not rate admission. At home he exhibited a similar behavior. He had built a special huge room where his hunting trophies were displayed. He would sit there alone and think about what a great person he was.

On the couch Peter behaved as if he were in a glass bubble. He kept Dr. Paul outside of his personal kingdom and devalued him. Peter was involved in name-dropping and bragging. I supported Dr. Paul in his efforts to tolerate this, since it showed an acceptance of Peter's defensive characterological adaptation before exploring his needy, traumatized self that was hidden behind his surface grandiosity. Now and then Peter would exhibit this needy and hidden aspect of himself. For example, on the surface, he did not care about his wife or his analyst, but if his wife or his analyst went away for a short while, Peter would develop hypochondria.

A drastic change took place toward the end of the first year of Peter's treatment. After hearing that his mother, who then was in her seventies, was ill, Peter felt sleepy on the couch and noted that his mother's hair was still black. He went on to say that although the behavior of bears is quite predictable as a rule, the black bear (symbolically his mother) is "schizophrenic" and attacks without provocation. Shortly after that he flew to the city where his mother and stepfather lived and went to the hospital where his mother was a patient. As soon as he entered the lobby of the hospital he felt faint and was taken to the emergency room. Only later we learned that by fainting Peter was protecting himself from the awareness of his wish that the mother of his early childhood would die.

Peter was puzzled. After returning to treatment, he said to Dr. Paul, "I didn't pass out in Vietnam even when my helicopter was shot down!" After this event, Peter was ready to allow himself to speak of his traumatic childhood and explore the effects of his biological father's departure when little Peter became a target of his mother and grandmother's aggression. His symptoms, which he had controlled since the first week of treatment, returned and he allowed his analyst to inquire about the reasons why he had developed them. He began to bring dreams to his sessions and used them to explore his inner world. He developed a feeling that he was like the character, played by Dustin Hoffman in the movie *Rain Man*, who was taken care of by his brother (the analyst). He was the needy one. But this would alternate with Peter's return to grandiosity. Peter would dream about being omnipotent, like an Egyptian Pharaoh, and his analyst being nobody, like a beggar. Slowly, Peter began integrating his Number One part with his "hungry" part and could enjoy life and tolerate being average in many ways.

When the Gulf War approached, the external war stimulated Peter to get to know the internal war of his early childhood, experientially and with accompanying affects on the couch. He dreamed of fighting with bows and arrows in caves (symbolically his mother's belly). He then unrepressed many early childhood memories. Among them was his being humiliated in front of his biological father. When he was five years old, without any preparation, he was taken to see his biological father who had remarried. His father took him to a fair and, like his mother, overfed him. He became nauseated and vomited on his father. The man never saw his son again. Peter understood that his bulimia had one main cause: he was dependent on his mother and grandmother's attention. After all, they were the only two adults who took care of him until Gregory came into his life. But their aggressive overfeeding was like giving him "emotional poison," so little Peter focused on a solution that became one of his adult symptoms. He would gorge himself with food to receive his mother and grandmother's "love" and satisfy his emotional hunger. Then he would vomit and free himself from such food when it turned out to be "poisonous." He was doomed to repeat this pattern. The other reason for his bulimia had a lot to do with his feeling humiliated and then rejected for good by his biological father. He was so angry at his biological father that, as an adult, he had vomited on a very important political figure (father figure) at a luncheon. As I mentioned earlier, this event brought him to see Dr. Paul.

Before his psychoanalysis was successfully terminated, Peter showed a great deal of remorse for his sadistic war activities. Since the killing of women and children had taken place under war conditions, Dr. Paul was careful not to induce guilt in Peter. Peter also stopped being a serial killer of animals who represented his hungry self, his aggressive mother and grandmother, and his biological father. He was remorseful for killing animals, too. Some months before the termination of his analysis he had a dream: "I was dreaming of hunting, and seeing many deer without killing one of them." Then, looking somber, he said suddenly, "God holds us accountable for animals we kill. I am trying to own up to things." Peter completed his analysis successfully.

My aim here is not to present a clinical case as I would do if I were at a professional meeting with other psychoanalysts, so I am not reporting the details of Peter's internal world or his psychoanalytic treatment here. I am not referring to his transference neurosis and its resolution and Dr. Paul's countertransference responses to him. However, I wanted to give the above background in order to prepare for the study of the role Gregory, his stepfather, played in Peter's life, especially in arming Peter with surface grandiosity and sadism. I will focus on what we learned from Peter about Gregory and Grefory's peculiar relationship with his stepson.

While neither Peter's analyst nor I had any direct contact with Gregory, we learned through working with Peter that externalization (projecting his self-images and/or internalized images of others to the outside world) was Gregory's main psychic mechanism that helped him live a "normal" life in the United States following the unspeakable traumas he experienced in the Philippines. After he and his family moved to their new house in a small city in the Midwest, Gregory built a multistoried purple martin birdhouse in the garden. The pole on which the birdhouse was mounted had a concrete base. Later Gregory would boast that he had used one hundred pounds of cement to erect the birdhouse. For decades this birdhouse remained as a permanent fixture in the garden. Gregory took infinite pains to paint (and repaint when the old paint faded) numbers on each of the many "apartments" the bird families occupied. Every year it was full of purple martins. When their eggs hatched, the birds fed their fledglings and helped them to fly when they were ready. Every year Gregory put a band on one leg of each baby bird after it was hatched. Each band was numbered to correspond with the number on its family's "apartment" in the birdhouse. If a baby bird had an untimely fall from the birdhouse, Gregory would know to which "apartment" it belonged and would then return the baby bird to its proper nest. This was extremely important, because if a baby bird was rescued by a human and returned to the wrong nest, it would be rejected by the adult birds in that "apartment" and would certainly die.

As little Peter grew up, almost like Gregory's shadow, he again and again observed his stepfather's preoccupation with the birdhouse and his activities concerning the birds. During the middle of his analysis, he fully realized that the purple martin birdhouse symbolically represented Gregory's Japanese prison camp where he suffered a great deal and was exposed to the deaths of his comrades almost daily. Gregory saw to it that no baby birds would die while occupying his birdhouse. He changed the "function" of the image of his prison camp; he had created a "camp" where occupants, himself and his comrades, were not allowed to die!

Peter's understanding that Gregory treated him as he did his baby birds evolved slowly during his analysis, especially after Peter fainted while visiting his mother in the hospital. First, we were told how Gregory was preoccupied with making little Peter strong. While home with Peter, his stepfather prescribed certain tasks for the boy and taught him how to exercise, lose weight, and develop an athletic body. Gregory introduced young Peter to guns and taught him how to hunt when the boy was in his early teens. Soon, using his contacts, he made sure that Peter enrolled in a military school. After graduation, as a military man Peter was involved in the Vietnam War where, as we saw, he killed people, including women and children, after receiving orders to do so.

After Vietnam, as a civilian, adult Peter had a high-level position in the military weapons industry, although he liked to define himself as a "hunter." Even after Peter married and moved with his wife and daughter to another city, he kept in regular contact with Gregory who continued his preoccupation with his birdhouse and baby birds. Every year Peter would fly to the Midwest and the two men would take ritual hunting trips. But Peter would also go hunting without his slowly aging stepfather. Peter noted that whenever he felt anxious as an adult, he would make trips to kill animals. He was a "serial killer" of animals. Since he had plenty of money he could participate in such activities in order to "cure" his anxiety.

During his analysis, Dr. Paul and Peter slowly began to understand that Gregory had placed (deposited) his "hunted" self-image, (injured, humiliated, and rendered helpless in the Philippines) into the obese little boy's developing self-representation. Indeed, there was a nice fit between Gregory's deposited injured image and little Peter's own humiliated help-less image as it appeared in his dream mentioned earlier, of a dome dominated by intrusive women from another planet. When Gregory gave tasks to his stepson—indeed, acting like his trainer—he made him (in fact his own deposited image, too) into a hunter who could kill. He could kill not only the hornless and disfigured deer that represented Peter in his dream, but any kind of deer; not only black bears, but any kind of bears. This reversed his helplessness, humiliation, and forced passivity, and made the boy omnipotently powerful and active by getting rid of danger-ous others. Gregory had treated Peter as he treated his baby birds. He saw that Peter stayed "alive" and achieved his "freedom," but to do so he had to be sadistically omnipotent. After his military service and education, Peter became professionally connected with the design and manufacture of most deadly weapons.

Peter's understanding that he had identified with Gregory—and more than that, that he was a reservoir for his stepfather's injured image—became very clear when he and Dr. Paul examined the various meanings of one of Peter's major preoccupations as an adult. Gregory had been preoccupied with his birdhouse and its occupants and adult Peter became preoccupied with his trophy room. What I would focus on here is how Peter unconsciously repeated the memories of the prisoner Gregory sur-rounded by his dead comrades. His hobby also included one of the tasks Gregory had given him: to resurrect the dead and change the function of his prison camp, as Gregory had done when he protected the lives of baby birds. Thus, Peter took pains to make his trophies look alive through skillful taxidermy, spending considerable time and money on taxidermists to achieve this illusion.

Acquiring a father had helped deal with the humiliation little Peter had suffered over rejection by his real father. He recalled that with the advent of his stepfather he had proudly pointed to Gregory, saying, "See! I have a father, too!" His mother and grandmother had devalued his biological father, and repeatedly called the boy's attention to his parental deficit, so it balanced things out to make his stepfather his ideal and make the older man feel comfortable by taking in Gregory's traumatized self. After gaining insight about this, Peter then recalled that when his mother went off with Gregory on a sort of honeymoon, they had appeared for some reason on a radio show to which Peter listened with his grandmother. The following day little Peter broke a toy pistol his mother's new mate had given him, and he realized that he had been angry with the man who had taken his mother away. He had been afraid of being punished when the couple returned, and now vividly recalled Gregory asking his mother what should be done to Peter for breaking the pistol, and his mother saying, "He is your son now. Do what you want!" Peter remembered being impressed by Gregory's choosing not to punish him. But he was also impressed by sensing that Gregory would not stop introducing little Peter to more toy guns and then to real guns. Peter realized that the older man had never in fact been a skillful hunter, but that he had gone hunting with the boy because seeing Peter becoming a more skilled and more aggressive hunter pleased Gregory and made him feel better. Peter now understood that Gregory wanted Peter to grow up to be a hunter instead of remaining as someone who could be "hunted" (by the Japanese). If Peter grew up and became a vicious hunter, Gregory's traumatized self living in Peter would never face a similar trauma again.

Throughout his analysis, Peter had a reoccurring dream. In the dream he was walking on water. The manifest content of this dream reflected his exaggerated grandiosity. In his daily life, he acted as if he were a God. Since he was involved in the design and development of new and ever more deadly weapons, he had contact with high-level politicians and top military men. He believed that America's security rested in his hands—overtly he was superior to anyone.

In the beginning of his fifth year of analysis, Peter's reoccurring dream of walking on water changed. In a new dream a submarine appeared just under the water that Peter was walking on. (It should be recalled that Gregory served on a submarine and was in charge of its torpedoes before he was captured by the Japanese. In the dream, therefore, the submarine stood for Gregory before he was rendered helpless.) He only appeared as if he were walking on water; the walking on water was an illusion. The analysis of this modified dream allowed Peter to see further and acknowledge his peculiar childhood relationship with Gregory, the older man's deposited traumatized image, and Gregory's making him "omnipotent" as a defense against his own (and little obese boy's) helplessness. Soon, in a memorable dream—the last of the series of his dreams of walking on water—the submarine dove and Peter fell into the water. His omnipotence was gone. He swam to the shore as an "average" man, but free from Gregory's deposited image (the submarine). Following this, in real life, he got rid of his dead animal trophies, turned his special room into a greenhouse for his wife, began to enjoy her companionship, and their sex life improved. He could not easily give up his lucrative business but changed his political position. He wished that Americans would build grain silos instead of silos for nuclear weapons. He thought of becoming an environmentalist. His drinking and bulimia symptoms were no longer present.

Just as all indications were that Peter would enter into a successful termination phase of his analysis, he presented a very strong resistance to getting well, and his old symptoms reflecting the hungry self returned: overeating, drinking, and depression. The Gulf War was taking place at this time, and he also exhibited corresponding omnipotent fantasies of blasting Iraq out of this world and capturing Saddam Hussein. Peter's analyst was bewildered. As his consultant, I, too, initially could not understand why such a drastic turn of events was taking place. Slowly Dr. Paul and I understood that Peter's resistance was due to his correct perception that if he got well and stopped being a reservoir for the older man's traumatized self-image, Gregory would be forced to take back what he had deposited in Peter. This process might literally kill Gregory, who was now in his seventies. Peter was facing a major dilemma: to get well and kill Gregory or refrain from completing his analysis and save Gregory's life. His, and our, understanding of his dilemma took place after the following events.

Peter came up with an idea. He would lobby his friends in high places and plan for a special ceremony to honor Gregory (and some other Bataan Death March and Japanese prison survivors) during the fiftieth anniversary of the Bataan Death March. At first Peter was pleased that at last Gregory would be recognized for his sacrifices for the country and receive a kind of psychological compensation and, indeed, a medal. Slowly, Peter began to notice his unconscious motivations: if his stepfather were honored by the presence of dignitaries, it would mean that the older man would acknowledge that he was taking back his own traumatized self-image. Furthermore, outside observers at the ceremony, such as senators, congressmen, and top military brass, would bear witness to the fact that the injured party was Gregory. Thus, through an official ritual, Peter would turn over the deposited traumatized image to its rightful owner and would no longer need to be an omnipotent sadistic hunter in order to eclipse his (and Gregory's) helplessness.

Due to Peter's and others' efforts, a ceremony was held in Washington, D.C., on the fiftieth anniversary of the Bataan Death March. But a week or so after this ceremony, it became clear that losing Peter as a decades-long reservoir for his traumatized self-image also weakened the older man's investment in the birdhouse—besides Peter the most visible reservoir for his externalized injured self and images of his injured or dead comrades. Gregory dismantled the purple martin "apartment building," sold his house, and moved to a beach resort town in South Carolina with his wife, Peter's mother. The week after this move Gregory's physical health quickly and drastically deteriorated and he became depressed. He was obsessed with the now dismantled birdhouse, which was lying on the ground in a corner of a friend's yard for safekeeping. Gregory was only able to stay in the new location for ten days. He and his wife frantically returned to their original location in the Midwest. Gregory wanted to buy back the house he had just sold and resurrect his birdhouse, reversing his loss and re-establishing a stable externalization. He demanded that the new owner sell the house back to him. He even offered the new owner double the money he had received from the latter only a few months earlier. But he was not successful in acquiring his old house. Gregory became a bewildered, depressed, and helpless man. He also developed physiological reactions and felt that his body was deteriorating.

When, in analysis, Peter understood that his "giving back" the deposited image of Gregory's injured self image to the older man was almost killing Gregory, he also fully comprehended his resistance to analysis. I encouraged Dr. Paul to tell him that the dilemma he was facing was a real one and that Peter alone could decide what to do with it as his analyst stood by him.

Peter then came up with a solution: he helped his stepfather buy the house next door to his original house and re-erect the purple martin birdhouse in the yard of this second house, not too far away from its original location. Peter chose not to explain the meaning of the birdhouse to Gregory. "I only want to help him; he does not need 'interpretations' in his seventies," Peter said. Once the birdhouse was re-erected, the older man's physical health improved considerably. However, Peter knew that the newly erected birdhouse was not as strong a reservoir for his stepfather's externalized injured images as the original one had been. Nevertheless, the older man did not die and his helplessness and confusion disappeared to a great degree. Peter then reached a successful termination of his analysis.[138]   The day before Peter's last psychoanalytic session something unusual happened. Peter was alone in his greenhouse, his former trophy room, when he realized that some baby birds were trapped in his chimney. After putting a net across the hearth, he climbed up to the roof of the greenhouse and, putting a long broom into the chimney from above, made the baby birds fly into the net below. After climbing down from the roof, he released the captured birds from the net and let them fly free.

During his last session, after speaking of this unusual event, Peter said that it helped him further symbolize his own personal freedom. He had not only been a reservoir for Gregory's traumatized self-image, but also Gregory's internalized images of his injured or dead comrades. All his life Peter had been interested and involved in the older man's birds as they also represented helpless Gregory and his comrades in the prison camp. Through the incident above, Peter felt he had developed his own autonomy in letting go of traumatized images. He had his own way of freeing the birds all at once, rather than through many years of continual preoccupation with them, a symptom that belonged to his stepfather.

Meanwhile, his daughter had become a biologist. Peter knew that the transgenerational transmission of Gregory's traumatized self and internalized images of others had reached a third generation. Gregory's grandchild, as a biologist, was working on projects to save wild animals, just as her father had killed them. His resistance to recovery now gone, Peter said that he had become a new man, a fully analyzed individual without sadistic narcissism.

An examination of the story of Gregory's traumatized self and internalized images of his dead or victimized comrades, and his externalizing them into birds and little Peter, demonstrates the existence of transgenerational transmissions. I have no direct information about the internal world of any other survivor of the Bataan Death March and Japanese prison camps in the Bataan Peninsula. However, from written accounts,[139] we know that tens of thousands of Americans had traumatized selves and internalized traumatized images of others, all of which were connected to their experiences in the Philippines. Even before the death march began, the Americans and Filipinos had felt helpless since the Bataan Peninsula was besieged by Japanese forces and Washington did not send reinforcements. The chanting of the following verses directly reflects their collective regression and the loss of what Erik Erikson called "basic trust."[140]

> We're the battling bastards of Bataan,
> No mama, no papa, no Uncle Sam,
> No aunts, no uncles, no cousins, no nieces
> No rifles, no planes or artillery pieces,
> And nobody gives a damn[141]

We can surmise that tens of thousands of Americans were connected within an invisible network: all had traumatized images linked to this same historical event. We can assume that while such people held onto their own particular personality organizations, most likely a great number of them passed their traumatized selves and object images onto younger generations, giving these people similar tasks to deal with deposited images. Thus, we can further assume that the next generation (composed of people whose self-representations were "reservoirs") also became linked invisibly by receiving traumatized images that stem from the same historical event and by having similar tasks to deal with them.

While what I have described above is an individual case of intergenerational transmission of trauma, through my involvement in unofficial international diplomacy for nearly three decades, I have collected enough evidence to suggest that such transgenerational transmissions occur regularly on a societal level and sometimes—when external historical events are conducive—on a grand scale.

10 The Political Ideology of Entitlement
and "Chosen," "Acute,"and "Hot" Traumas

The story of Gregory and Peter described in the previous chapter illustrates that the phenomenon of transgenerational transmission is not just a theory, but actually is visible in human nature when studied under a psychoanalytic magnifying glass. As I mentioned in this same chapter, similar phenomena are also evident at the large-group level through what I term a chosen trauma. A chosen trauma is a large group's mental representation of a historic event that resulted in collective feelings of helplessness, victimization, shame, and humiliation at the hands of "others," and typically involves drastic losses of people, land, prestige, and dignity. Like Gregory did to Peter, members of the traumatized group deposit their injured selves, and internalized images of others who were hurt during the traumatic event, into the developing selves of children in the next generation. These children are also given certain tasks, such as reversing helplessness, shame, and humiliation, and turning passivity into activity and assertion. Another task that is passed to the next generation relates to completing the shared mourning process.

When all these images of the historic event and the tasks associated with it are deposited into the next generation, it forms an invisible link among its individuals. If this next generation does not have the political, economic, or military power to conduct its inherited tasks, they may end up transmitting the unassimilated images and unfinished tasks to the children of the generation that follows them. As decades and centuries go by, the large group unconsciously "chooses" to consider the mental representation of the ancestor's traumatic event as a significant element in their contemporary large-group identity. Their chosen trauma symbolizes their sense of we-ness.

Not every trauma suffered by ancestors evolves into a chosen trauma. Sometimes new victimizations replace those of the past, or a leader may consciously or unconsciously select a specific past trauma to rally his or her followers in dramatic ways. In addition, how a society mythologizes a certain event through songs, poems, paintings and other art forms, and what memorials are built, also play a role in making a chosen trauma.

When there is a present danger from "others," the current generation reactivates the group's chosen trauma in order to enhance the group's identity and strengthen it to face the threat. This reactivation, in turn, re-ignites the tasks to be performed. Sometimes this manifests as a stubborn resistance to peacefully resolving ethnic or other large-group conflicts. Here we see an echo of what Dr. Paul and I observed in Peter's case. Peter developed a resistance to getting well because if he ceased to be a reservoir for Gregory's injured images, it would change his inner sense of who he was, his identity. Similarly, a large group may resist giving up the shared societal tasks associated with its chosen trauma because it cannot tolerate the resulting modification of its large-group identity.

Or, as demonstrated in Peter's case, the collective task passed down through the chosen trauma may change function. In other words, basic tasks dealing with the influence of the past trauma do not disappear, but their execution appears to have different aims. First Gregory attempted to deal with his trauma in Bataan by building the purple martin birdhouse and making sure that no harm came to the young birds that fell out—he developed a system so that they would always be returned to their home nest. Peter, primarily because of his relationship with Gregory, had become a vicious killer of animals. But we also learned that Peter's daughter reacted to the process by taking it in an entirely different direction than her father: she became a biologist and conservationist—a protector of animals.

When a large group's traumatization changes function, one result may be its transformation into an exaggerated entitlement ideology that, when the group's identity is threatened, can be manipulated by political leaders to initiate new political programs and/or take new actions supported by this ideology. Exaggerated entitlement provides a belief system that asserts that the group has a right to own what they wish to have, and this can obviously precipitate conflict with others. For example, irredentism is a political entitlement ideology. It became a political term after an Italian nationalist movement sought annexation of lands referred to as *Italia irredenta* (unredeemed Italy), areas inhabited by an ethnic Italian majority but under Austrian jurisdiction after 1866.

There is far more to this example, but to further illustrate a chosen trauma and its change of function into an entitlement ideology, I will use an example from Turkey. Norman Itzkowitz and I have studied extensively how some Christian large groups have reacted throughout the centuries to the fall of Constantinople (present-day Istanbul) to the Turks in 1453, and how in one case the mental representation of this event eventually culminated nearly four centuries later in the the Megali Idea ("Great Idea"), a specific political ideology that demanded the reunification of all ethnic Greeks of the former Byzantine Empire.[142]

Pressure on the Byzantines began about a thousand years ago when Turkic tribes began migrating westward from Central Asia, bringing contact as well as conflict with both Arabs and Europeans. During this time the Turkic tribes adopted Islam as their religion and eventually ruled parts of what today are Iran, Afghanistan, and Syria. In Asia Minor they also encountered the Byzantines, Christian heirs of the Greco-Roman empire who ruled from Constantinople. In 1071 A.D., the Turkish Seljuk leader Sultan Alp Arslan defeated the Byzantine forces under Emperor Romanus IV Diogenes near Manzigert in Eastern Anatolia. Although the Battle of Manzigert itself was not especially decisive or significant, Asia Minor, or Anatolia, as the heartland of Turkey is known today, gradually became Turkified and the gradual decline of the Byzantine Empire was underway. Soon after Manzigert, a group of Seljuk Turks captured Jerusalem, leading to the Crusades. By the time Crusaders entered Jerusalem, the city was no longer under Turkish occupation, but their perception of the Turks as the occupiers of the Christian Holy Land and as the enemy of Christians prevailed.

It was, however, the fall of Constantinople to the Turks, which came three hundred years after the Battle of Manzigert, that became a more obvious chosen trauma for the Christian world. Constantinople was conquered by the successors of the Seljuk Turks, the Ottomans, on May 29, 1453. Historically, this marked the end of one era and the beginning of another as the Christian Byzantine Empire was replaced by the Moslem-dominated Ottoman Empire. Despite the fact that Rome had refused to provide support for Constantinople against the Turks, the city received word of Byzantium's fall with shock and disbelief. The Turkish victory was seen as a knife plunged into the heart of Christianity. Aeneas Sylvius Piccolomini, a future Pope, wrote to Pope Nicholas V on July 12, 1453, that the Turks had killed Homer and Plato for the second time.[143]

The trauma pervaded and persisted in many ways. Since Constantinople was taken on a Tuesday, Christians regarded every Tuesday thereafter as an unpropitious day. The loss even was seen as a reflection of God's judgment upon "the sins of Christians everywhere."[144] It was a punishment that then reopened wounds caused by the fall of Jerusalem, and the European-Christian mourning for this loss could not be resolved or set aside. Christian armies fought to regain Jerusalem, though it was later lost again, but Constantinople's fall only elicited feelings of helplessness, shame, and humiliation. The desire to undo this trauma expressed itself in rumblings about organizing another Crusade. Nothing came of such talk, but the idea persisted. Together, Christians in the Ottoman territories sang the refrain, "Again, with years, with time, again they will be ours," in an attempt to deny the changes that had come and undo the losses they engendered. This would be the seed of an excessive entitlement ideology which would later come to fruition.[145]

Denial manifested in other ways as well. If a continuous link between the Turks and the Byzantines could be found, there would be less need for Byzantines and other Christians to feel the pain of loss. Many Westerners became preoccupied, sometimes in mystical ways, with the ancient origins of the Turks. For example, Giovanni Maria Filelfo, a humanist, declared that the young Turkish Sultan Mehmet II, who had seized Constantinople, was a Trojan. Felix Fabri, a German, studied the idea that Turks descended from Teucer, son of the Greek friend of Hercules, Telemon, and the Trojan princess Hesione. Fabri linked Teucer to a descendant called Turcus, a leader of a band of Trojans who fled into the interior of Asia after the fall of Troy. Having lived in obscurity for millennia, Turcus's descendents reemerged to claim their destiny and revive the "glory of Ilium."[146]

While these pseudohistorical efforts to find continuity between the two sides continued as a way to make loss and humiliation tolerable, a counterattempt tried to unlink them, to dehumanize and demonize all Turks. In Europe, this meant stubborn and systematic negative stereotyping that spread to all reaches of Christiandom. According to Niyazi Berkes, the Fates played a trick on the Turks because of their seizure of Constantinople and Jerusalem.[147] No matter what their achievements, the world would view them with animosity. Berkes claims that European historians of the time had never stereotyped other "strangers" such as Chinese, Arabs, and Japanese to such an extent.

Preoccupation with the Turks as conquerors of Jerusalem and Constantinople even stretched to the New World that Europeans had discovered and were aggressively colonizing. In 1539, for example, Mexican Indians took part in a dramatic pageant that represented the liberation of Jerusalem from the Turks, a victory made possible by the portrayed combining of the Catholic armies of Europe and the Americas.[148] Even now, a variation of this pageant is still performed in Mexico, halfway around the world from Turkey.[149] This globalized stereotyping was even incorporated into old editions of Webster's Dictionary under the definition of "Turk," which read, "one exhibiting any quality attributed to Turks, such as sensuality and brutality." The reference to brutality is understandable given the numerous battles against the Turks as their empire expanded. Itzkowitz and I also tried to understand the reference to sensuality. We concluded that it had a great deal to do with the youthful and virile image of Mehmet II (Mehmet the Conqueror), whose conquest was perceived as a "rape." Constantinople is still experienced by contemporary poets as a symbol of a fallen and/or grieving woman.[150]

But the fall of Byzantium was especially problematic for the Greeks since it represented the last vestige of their own once-great empire. They remained perennial mourners, unable to resolve the loss. As generations passed, the fall of Constantinople evolved as their major chosen trauma and influenced the evolution of the Megali Idea, which crystallized in the nineteenth century. When Greece regained its independence from the Ottoman Empire after the Greek War of Independence (1821–33), they too asked themselves "Who are we now?" The new identity that emerged was a composite of Hellenic (ancient pre-Christian Greek) and Byzantine (Christian Greek) elements.[151] The urge to retain and regain the cultural and religious elements of Byzantium, which had fallen nearly four hundred years before, was articulated by many Greek leaders, including influential individuals such as Spyridon Zamblios and Nikolaos G. Politis.[152]

From this movement evolved a far-reaching program of educational and cultural propaganda aimed at instilling a sense of Hellenic identity not only within the border of modern Greece itself, but also in the very large Greek populations that remained under Ottoman rule. The University of Athens (founded 1837) attracted people from all parts of the Greek world to be trained as students and apostles of Hellenism.

This two-pronged approach, according to Paschalis Kitromilides, would not only unite Greeks within the current borders of Greece but also reunite them with those living in the Ottoman Empire in places "considered as integral parts of the historical patrimony of Hellenism."[153] Thus the Megali Idea was born. Sociologist Kyriacos Markides, originally a Cypriot Greek who, like me, immigrated to the United States decades ago, describes the Megali Idea as "a dream shared by Greeks that someday the Byzantine Empire would be restored and all the Greek lands would once again be united into a Greater Greece."[154] The fantasy that everyone of Greek origin could somehow again be brought together soon became more than a wish in Greece—it became a political ideology supported by the Greek Orthodox Church and politicians, backed by academic theories, promoted by diplomats, and fought for on numerous battlefields as Greeks sought what "rightfully" belonged to them.

To make the Megali Idea a reality, Greece fought in the Balkan Wars (1912-13) and the Greco-Turkish War (1919-22), and entered into long-standing ethnonational disputes with Macedonians, Bulgarians, Turks, Albanians, Italians, and other groups along their borders. Indeed, the Megali Idea persisted well after the end of the Ottoman Empire and the birth of Turkey as a secular, democratic nation. It lingered on in political and military policies as well as in the dogma of Greek terrorist groups. You could hear its echo in speeches, newspaper columns, television programs, church sermons, and barbershop small talk. Can we reduce all of Greek-Turkish relations to the fall of Constantinople and its transformation into a chosen trauma and then the Megali Idea? Of course not. But when a fire evolves into an inferno, its fuel cannot be easily explained within rational-actor theories of international relations. And the fire of the Megali Idea continued to smolder on Cyprus in the late 1950s and early 1960s. Markides writes:

> One could argue that the "Great Idea" had an internal logic, pressing for realization in every part of the Greek world which continued to be under foreign rule. Because the Greeks of Cyprus have considered themselves historically and culturally to be Greeks, the "Great Idea" has had an intense appeal. Thus, when the church fathers called on the Cypriots [meaning the Cypriot Greeks] to fight for union with Greece, it did not require much effort to heat up emotions. . . . Enosis [uniting Cyprus with Greece] did not originate in the church but in the minds of intellectuals in their attempt to revive Greek-Byzantine civilization. However, being the most central and powerful of institutions, the church contributed immensely to its development. The church embraced the movement and for all practical purposes became its guiding nucleus.[155]

After the Turkish military intervened in Cyprus in 1974, the island was in effect partitioned into ethnic Greek and ethnic Turkish sectors. Tensions persisted, but since Greece became a member of the European Union, the impact of the Megali Idea on Greek foreign policy lost its strong appeal. However, the influence of the Greek chosen trauma may still be influencing the country's political behavior. In April 2004, the Greek and Turkish sides on Cyprus separately voted on a United Nations proposal known as the Annan Plan that outlined a kind of loose reunification that would allow all of Cyprus to enter the European Union. The Greek side overwhelmingly voted against such a reunification, the Turkish side overwhelmingly for it. There were many realpolitik causes for the Cypriot Greeks' "no" vote, such as the specific terms of agreements on territorial adjustments, the return of property and displaced persons, and demilitarization, but an echo of the Megali Idea could still be heard in it. Before the referendum certain leaders of the Greek Orthodox Church on the island preached that any Cypriot Greek voting "yes" would go to hell. The Cypriot Greeks' emotional sense of entitlement seemingly prevailed over a legalistic plan that would have established a kind of togetherness with Cypriot Turks.

As I mentioned, I would by no means want to reduce Greek-Turkish relations to the impact of the Megali Idea alone. I do not wish to give the impression that in international relations only one side's issues cause trouble and violence—usually reasons for violence come from both sides. Nor do I deny the suffering of Greeks either before or after independence. The focus of this chapter instead has been more narrow: the relation between a contemporary large group, its ancestors' massive traumas, and the change of function into a pervasive and exaggerated entitlement ideology.

While the Megali Idea has contributed to tensions and bloodshed, the true destructive potential of a reactivated chosen trauma is more clearly illustrated by events in the former Yugoslavia after the collapse of communism. At that time, the Serbian leadership deliberately proliferated political propaganda that reactivated deep and troubling feelings of loss, humiliation, shame, and persecution that prompted the Serbian people to carry out, in horrific fashion, the tasks passed down to them through their chosen trauma.

A simple definition of political propaganda, in its widest sense, would encompass any communication and manipulation from a source of political authority that is directed to its followers and its opposition at home and/or abroad, as well as to those who might be described as neutral. Its aim is to further the propagandist's wishes and ideas and under some circumstances, its political ideology. In the modern world, political propaganda exists in both open and closed societies, especially during periods of national and international tension, war, and war-like conditions such as terrorism. After September 11, political propaganda has increased substantially, both within and outside the United States. It seems to be everywhere.

But the propaganda used in Serbia after Slobodan Milosevic came to power was very unique, specific, effective, and deadly. This propaganda directly targeted the Battle of Kosovo in 1389, a highly mythologized event that came to symbolize the defeat and subsequent suffering of Christian Serbs at the hands of Muslim Ottomans. It is possibly the quintessential chosen trauma—its reactivation caused six hundred years years and dozens of generations to collapse into the present; so strong were the inherited tasks that no time seemed to have passed at all. Serbs would avenge their defeat, take back the lands that were "rightfully" theirs, and reverse their victimization at last.

There are various and contradictory historical accounts of the Battle of Kosovo, and it is impossible to accurately report what happened. We do know that there was in fact a major battle with heavy casualties on both sides; both the Serbian leader Prince Lazar and the Ottoman Sultan Murat I were killed. After the battle, Lazar's body was taken to the central Serbian monastery of Ravanica and canonized, and he was eventually succeeded by his son Stefan Lazarevic. Murat's heart and other parts were buried in Kosovo, but the rest of his body was taken back to Bursa in Anatolia and buried next to his ancestors, and his son Bayezit succeeded him as sultan. We also know that whether or not this one battle was clearly decisive, the Ottomans exerted growing influence in Serbia. Bayezit, for example, married one of Lazar's daughters, and Lazar's son Stefan Lazarevic served with the Ottoman army in their battle against Tamerlane, leader of the Mongol empire. At the same time, Serbia remained essentially independent and enjoyed decades of relative peace and prosperity for some time after the Battle of Kosovo. But in the end, the Ottomans conquered all of Serbia by 1459, six years after the fall of Byzantium.

With time, Kosovo and Lazar became directly associated with the fall of Serbia, and both became heavily mythologized. A shared mental representation of the battle evolved over decades and centuries, transmitted and transformed through strong oral and religious traditions in Serbia. These tales made Lazar a martyr and sacred, Christ-like figure for Serbs, and for them the loss at Kosovo became just as significant as the fall of Jerusalem. As Ottoman control took root, many Serbs moved northward, including the monks who kept vigil over Lazar's body at Ravanica. The legends of the Serbian hero and the Battle of Kosovo traveled with his remains, often through the tales of Serbian troubadours called *guslars*.

According to one legend, Saint Ilya, in the shape of a gray falcon, appeared before Prince Lazar on the eve of the Battle of Kosovo to deliver a message from the Virgin Mary. Lazar was given two choices: he could win the battle and find a kingdom on earth, or he could lose the battle and find a kingdom in heaven. Prince Lazar chose to go to heaven and was associated with the crucified Jesus.[156] Serbian sculptures and paintings portrayed Lazar in a similar fashion, including an adaptation of *The Last Supper* with Lazar as the central figure. Kosovo was emerging as the primary Serbian chosen trauma.

Neither the passage of centuries or Communist control could extinguish the power of Kosovo as a marker of Serb group identity. In fact, after the fall of the Soviet Union, it was quickly revived under the leadership of Slobodan Milosevic. As the six hundredth anniversary of the Battle of Kosovo approached, Milosevic's people literally dug up Lazar and along with him the tasks that had been passed down over six hundred years. With the support of Serbian church authorities and some academicians, arrangements were made to bring Lazar's body out of "exile" and return him to his rightful place of burial. But Lazar's journey back to Kosovo would not be a short one: his remains were placed in a coffin and taken on a year-long tour to every Serbian village and town where huge crowds of mourners dressed in black received them. Lazar's body symbolically was buried and reincarnated on many, many occasions. Religious ceremonies were conducted, and some politicians gave direct or indirect hate speeches. The people began feeling, without being intellectually aware of it, that the defeat at the Battle of Kosovo had occurred only recently, a development made possible by the fact that the chosen trauma had been kept effectively alive—even though sometimes dormant—for centuries. The Serbian chosen trauma would thereby help to solidify a new Serbian identity after the demise of Yugoslavia.

On June 28, 1989, the six hundredth anniversary of the Battle of Kosovo, Milosevic himself came to the ceremonial grounds, a hill overlooking the Kosovo battlefield, where thousands of Serbs were gathered to commemorate the event. Earlier, as I reported in chapter 8, a huge monument made of red stone symbolizing blood had been erected on the site. Now, arriving at this place by helicopter, Milosevic was like the reincarnated Lazar returning to earth from heaven. But the sense of victimization that had once tied Serbs together had now changed: rather than pursuing Lazar's choice of a kingdom in heaven, Serbs would now choose a "kingdom on earth."

They would reverse their losses and avenge their humiliation and reclaim the traditional lands of Serbia now in the hands of "others." In a photograph of this rally, Lazar's six-hundred-year-old call to all Serbs to battle against the Turks can be seen imprinted on the T-shirts of many spectators. The resurrection of Lazar and reactivation of the chosen trauma of Kosovo helped to create an atmosphere for future massive violence against Muslim Bosniaks and later against Albanians in the former Yugoslavia, whom the Serbs perceived as extensions of the Turks. Indeed, Bosniaks and Albanians played a significant role in Ottoman history and the Serbs, under stressful situations, often called them "Turks."

The Serbian reactivation of their chosen trauma also, I believe, is closely connected with the systematic raping of the Bosniak women. During wars or war-like situations, individual as well as large-group regressions occur and sex and aggression become fused in many individual's minds and actions. This may lead to rape. The digital pictures of what the U.S. soldiers did in the Abu Ghraib prison in Iraq are a graphic illustration of the fusion of aggression with sexuality. As I write this, it is difficult to say whether or not further investigations will take place concerning Abu Ghraib, besides those which brought some soldiers who were directly involved to the military courts. These events reflect certain individuals' regression and their mixing sex and aggression through the humiliation and dehumanization of the "other." In Serbia however, the rapes were systematic and sanctioned by an entitlement ideology.

To understand the nature of rapes that took place in the former Yugoslavia, let us first look at an example of Serbian propaganda from the late 1980s and early 1990s:

> By order of the Islamic fundamentalists from Sarajevo, healthy women from 17 to 40 years of age are being separated out and subjected to special treatment. According to their sick plans going back many years these women have to be impregnated by orthodox Islamic seeds in order to raise a generation of Janissaries on the territories they surely consider theirs, the Islamic republic. In other words, a fourfold crime is to be committed against Serbian woman: to remove her from her family, to impregnate her by undesirable seeds, to make her bear a stranger and then to take even him away from her.[157]

This dispatch appeared to warn of a resurrection of the Ottoman devshirme system, and overt plans by Muslims in the former Yugoslavia to start a new janissary army. Briefly, devshirme, a practice that started with the reign of Murat I and continued for the next four centuries, involved the conscription of youth from the empire's Christian orthodox population to serve as state servants. Christian orthodox youth, such as Serbian youngsters, were collected as an extraordinary tax levied by the Sultan, taken from their families, converted to Islam, and educated to serve the Sultan. One of the greatest grand viziers of the Ottoman Empire, Sokollu (Sokolovich) Mehmet Pasha, for example, was originally a Serb who had risen within the devshirme system. Most Serbian (and other former Christian) youngsters, however, would be enrolled in the ranks of the military as members of the empire's feared janissary force.

In the late 1980s and early 1990s, Serbian propaganda aimed to create fear among Serbian mothers that they would lose their sons, who would return as janissaries to subjugate or kill their own people. There was a kernel of truth in this idea, since one piece of writing by the then-Bosnian Muslim leader Alija Izetbegovic had intimated the possibility of an Islamic enterprise in Bosnia. For all practical purposes, however, the possibility of resurrecting the devshirme system was pure Serbian fantasy utilized as propaganda.

Maj. Milovan Milutinovic was one key figure in running the Serbian propaganda machine under the Milosevic regime. In 1991, he was interviewed by American journalist Roy Gutman, who was so shocked by references to janissaries that he asked Milutinovic, "Which century are you talking about?"[158] Milutinovic responded that it was a recent phenomenon, adding, "They are trying to do what they did centuries ago."[159] In Milutinovic's statement, we hear references to the consequences of the reactivation of the Serbian chosen trauma—a time collapse—and an example of a direct though untenable equation linking the current foe with an ancient enemy. I have no way of knowing if Milutinovic really believed what he was saying. The important issue is that his remarks were an aspect of a large-group phenomenon that was dominated by the psychology of time collapse in a regressed society.

Just before and during the systematic raping of Muslim Bosniak women, new Serbian propaganda replaced the old campaign that warned Serbian women of systematic rape by Bosniak Muslim men (as an extension of the Ottomans). This new propaganda added a twist: if a Serbian man raped a Muslim Bosniak woman, a child born as a result of this rape would be a full-blooded Serb and not carry any vestige of the mother (i.e., the mother's non-Serbian large-group identity). American sociologist Beverly Allen, who studied this side of Serbian propaganda, seemed puzzled. In her book, *Rape Warfare: The Hidden Genocide in Bosnia-Herzegovina and Croatia,* she wondered if the Serbs had any grasp of genetics.[160] Of course this strain of Serbian propaganda had nothing to do with science: raping a Muslim woman in order to give birth to a Serbian child engendered a wish to reverse the victimization of their ancestors and was also an expression of identification with their ancestors' Ottoman enemies.

When Milosevic first reactivated the chosen trauma of Kosovo, did he intend to implement the systematic rape of Muslim Bosniak women and the ethnic cleansing of Serbia? Or was he, at least in the beginning, simply a hypernationalist who exploited Serbia's need for "we-ness" as the vehicle for his rise to power? This question may never be fully answered, but history has shown time and again that once the Pandora's Box of victimization is opened, annihilation soon follows. When a large group is regressed and people wonder about their large-group identity, the personality of the political leader becomes an important factor in the scenario, one that has considerable influence on societal and political processes. The leader may inflame or tame ethnic or other large-group sentiments, lead the group toward peaceful coexistence with "others," or fuel a war-like atmosphere, even playing an actual role in starting a war. In my book *Blind Trust: Large Groups and Their Leaders in Times of Crisis and Terror,* I wrote about "reparative" and "destructive" leaders of regressed large groups.[161] The former helps to solidify the threatened or changed group identity without devaluing or ruining of another group. The latter aims to enhance and/or modify the group's new identity by destroying, one way or another, an opposing group. In a five-step process, destructive leaders and their propaganda machines: (1) enhance a shared sense of victimization within the large group following an attack by an enemy group or another disaster, such as an economic one, or even in situations without any visible recent victimization; (2) reactivate a chosen trauma; (3) increase a sense of we-ness (large-group identity), but in a regressed state; (4) devalue the enemy to a degree that dehumanizes it; and (5) create an excessive attitude of entitlement for revenge or reactivate a dormant entitlement ideology.

Through these five steps, an atmosphere is created in which large-group members feel entitled to destroy the current enemy and even become involved in cultural and ethnic cleansing, thereby purifying themselves of any contamination by unwanted and devalued "others." Under certain circumstances the large group, without realistic means to be sadistic toward the current enemy, may idealize their own victimization and become "masochistic." Reactivated chosen traumas and accompanying exaggerated entitlement ideology, especially when endorsed by a political leader, have profound effects on large groups and "other" groups they consider to be their enemies, playing a significant role in the evolution of terror and terrorism.

Presently, we wonder about various aspects of large-group psychology that played a role in making hundreds of thousands or perhaps even millions of Muslims into adorers of Osama bin Laden. Bin Laden consistently referred to three rather recent historical traumas for inciting feelings among his followers and encouraging them to take revenge on the Americans and their allies: the United States's "intrusion" into holy places in Saudi Arabia; the U.S.-led UN sanctions against Iraq and the attendant suffering of Iraqi civilians, especially Iraqi children; and U.S. support for Israel against Palestinian Arabs. Did Osama bin Laden also try to reactivate a chosen trauma? In some of his speeches, he talked about Muslims tasting humiliation and contempt for more than eighty years and stated that after September 11 America was tasting the same. In one speech, he said that "the Islamic world [fell] under the banner of the cross" more than eighty years ago.[162]

Most likely, he was referring to the collapse of the Ottoman Empire and the abolition of the caliphate by the modern Turkish Republic under Kemal Atatürk. Although the abolishment of the caliphate does not seem to be generalized into the everyday concerns of the Muslim fundamentalist followers of bin Laden, perhaps bin Laden made this event his personalized chosen trauma. His irredentist ideology of restoring the caliphate is perhaps part of what gave him "permission" to hurt or murder "others," because only by destroying them will the expansion of his brand of Islam (irredentism) be possible.

In any case, the example of Serbia showed that by reactivating a chosen trauma, the political leadership, using propaganda, turned a "memory" into an acute event. There are also current and acute massive traumatic events that, without being condensed with the image of a chosen trauma and without being contaminated with a time-collapse experience, greatly influence large-group processes and may give birth to new political ideologies. By acute trauma I am referring to a trauma that results in a continuing state of confusion, unbearable grief, chaos, and increased criminality within a group. In such circumstances, the group searches for a leader(s) to act as a repairer or savior, and tries to reestablish a new sense of large-group identity. This itself may lead to violent acts, terror, and terrorism directed toward others, or even internally toward other members of the traumatized group. For example, as I write this book, the people of Iraq, divided along religious (Sunni, Shiite) and ethnic (Arab,

Kurdish, Turkmen) lines, and without a unifying leader of their own to tame emotions, are currently experiencing an acute trauma.

The United States experienced its own acute trauma on September 11, 2001. However, unlike the situation in Iraq, the United States has a defined political leader and institutions, and the country did not descend into chaos. Rather, what exists are political divisions and a shared feeling that cannot be easily defined, that certain things are no longer routine—there is an uncomfortable sense that something is wrong. The events of September 11 ultimately led to an ideological policy known as the Bush Doctrine, which threatens the use of preemptive, unilateral force in the international arena. Whether this controversial doctrine will survive the Bush presidency is a matter of debate.

Indeed, a political ideology that emerges from or accompanies an acute societal trauma does not necessarily become politically institutionalized or a marker of large-group identity. Similarly, each acute massive trauma does not necessarily end up becoming a chosen trauma decades or centuries later. Acute traumas that remain "hot" for a long time, however, are more likely to evolve into a chosen trauma. A trauma is "hot" if traumatized individuals and their offspring remain emotionally involved in mourning and memorializing it. The Holocaust, for example, remains a "hot trauma."

Whatever the source of the trauma, the end result is human suffering. The wish to alleviate at least some of this suffering prompted the creation of the first international NGOs. As these NGOs evolved and began to broaden their scope, many added the resolution of international conflicts to their mandates. But many of the conflicts they tried to resolve were contaminated with the large-group processes described above, and it eventually became clear that in certain conflicts solutions were consciously and unconsciously resisted. The next chapters will therefore discuss strategies that can remove psychological "poisons" within conflicts and allow for their peaceful resolution.

Part III

Identities Side by Side: Is Coexistence Possible?

11 From Formal to Unofficial Diplomacy: An Overview

A variety of factors in the twentieth century led to the rise of NGOs, and then their movement into ever-expanding roles that were once the exclusive realm of federal departments. Diverse experts from engineers to anthropologists were enlisted to understand and help solve international problems, and eventually behavioral scientists and other mental health professionals were also included and interdisciplinary work was encouraged. When I became personally involved, I was in a strange new world. But although I felt like a pioneer, I was of course not the first psychoanalyst to apply my knowledge of individual pscyhological processes to mankind's collective groupings.

In the introduction I made reference to Erik Erikson's concept of pseudospeciation and his thinking about how each human group developed a distinct sense of identity at the outset of human history. In order to visualize Erikson's concept we can close our eyes and imagine one small band of early humans wearing the brown skin of one kind of animal and the red feather of one kind of bird, a neighboring group of humans wearing the yellow skin of another kind of animal and a green feather of another kind of bird, and the two groups dividing themselves into two different species. Erikson wrote:

> First each horde or tribe, class and nation, but then also every religious association has become the human species, considering all the others a freakish and gratuitous invention of some irrelevant deity. To reinforce the illusion of being chosen, every tribe recognizes a creation of its own, a mythology and later a history: thus was loyalty to a particular ecology and morality secured. One never quite knew how all the other tribes came to be, but since they did exist, they were at least useful as a screen of pro-

jection for the negative identities which were the necessary, if not uncomfortable, counterpart of the positive ones.[163]

There must have been some occasions when early humans required the services of a primitive diplomat of sorts when they were not engaged in fighting for the same food source. We can also imagine that the same food source later was expanded to include nutriments for another, emotional, type of hunger: a hunger for belonging to a more elaborate large-group identity.

So psychoanalysts and political scientists do in fact share an interest in understanding how humans behave in groups and how diplomacy can function to regulate them. But finding a middle ground was still not easy. As a psychoanalyst I must accept that in large groups often our minds function in a more "primitive" way than many wish to acknowledge. Political scientists, on the other hand, seem to assume that when in comes to modern diplomacy, we function in a far more "civilized" manner where rationality is dominant. Let me offer two different perspectives to illustrate the potential polarity of these approaches.

J. Anderson Thomson believes that among our inherent primitive and primordial behaviors is one called "male bonded coalitionary violence." He maintains that when we look at evolutionary history and male bonding in early human groups, there exists a natural impetus for indiscriminant violence that was useful for most of our evolutionary history. According to Thomson, four capacities, or innate mechanisms, are involved: (1) the capacity to easily form male coalitions; (2) the capacity to use these coalitions to conduct lethal raids in order to kill; (3) the capacity to direct these lethal raids against humans they have never met and who did not directly provoke them; and (4) the capacity to view members of the out-group with the same cognitive mechanisms we use to view prey. Referring to events of massive violence such as the one that occurred on September 11, he writes, "If we truly want to understand September 11 at its most fundamental level, we have to face the horror of our evolutionary history, the deadly legacy it has left in all men, and the violence that resides at the core of religion."[164] In other words, as Thomson recently told me, "We have latent capacities, useful in certain situations, which group processes may activate and use in ways different from the original design, ways that are deadly."

On the other side of the coin are the tasks of traditional diplomacy, which evolved along with and even helped push along our "civilization." Humanity's aggressive drives, many political scientists would maintain, were tamed by laws, customs, and governments—especially at the international level. Diplomacy provided formal representation within the boundary of another nation, explained, defended, interpreted, and negotiated policies, and created, drafted, and amended many international rules of a normative and regulatory kind that give structure to the international system.[165] Psychoanalysts would call many of these activities ritualizations, the "correct ways" for the representatives of one nation to communicate with those of another. These became part of intergroup protocol that established boundaries to keep emotions from bursting out.

As time passed, more laws and conventions were added to manage relations between nations. Some of our diplomatic practices date back to the Congress of Vienna (1814–15), which established very specific grades of diplomatic status and clearly delineated how and on what topics an attache, consul, ambassador, or minister could interact. The congress also put forward the concept of diplomatic immunity based on three claims of privilege: (1) *droit de chapelle*; (2) *droit de quartier*; and (3) *droit de l'hôtel*. These refer respectively to the right to continue the practice of one's homeland's religion, immunity from arrest by local police, and the exemption of one's dwelling from local jurisdiction and taxation. Other rigidities in formal diplomacy date back even further to the political thoughts of such men as Niccolo Machiavelli (1469–1527), Thomas Hobbes (1588–1676), John Locke (1632–1704), Karl Marx (1818–83) and Friedrich Engels (1820–95), while some theories, such as the need to form international alliances to maintain "the balance of power" hark back to ancient Greek historian Thucydides.

W. Nathaniel Howell, former U.S. ambassador to Kuwait during the Iraqi invasion of 1990 and a long-time resident diplomat at CSMHI, put the need for diplomacy in another way: having played basketball in college, he used the analogy to explain that it was as natural and necessary to establish rules of the game in international politics as it was to design plays in basketball. When they were appropriate to the circumstances and implemented as intended, both a well-run foreign policy and a well-executed basketball play were models of grace, effectiveness, and economy of effort. Nevertheless, Howell maintains, diplomacy—like basketball—can be as much an art as a science since the individual diplomat must rely on his or her own personal style, character, intelligence, and ability to be successful within the "rules of the game."

In addition, formal diplomacy is necessarily connected with concepts of justice and morality. It speaks of *Fiat Justitia, pereat mundus* (Let justice be done, even the world perish). Such notions of morality, justice, and honor represent an efforts to control the ruthless selfishness that seems to be mankind's birthright. But these seemingly precise definitions can become not only ambiguous but also corrupted when the loss of large-group identity, power, self-esteem, and self-determination is threatened.[166] To elaborate on the basketball analogy, imagine a game played on a floor with too much polish. The players will fall down and slide into each other, frustrating themselves and their coaches, as well as the spectators. To return to an orderly game, the extra polish on the basketball floor needs to be removed. Similarly, in certain relations between enemies, there is too much emotion—too many psychological complications. Without trying to deal with them first, a graceful and systematic diplomatic effort will not take place. On various occasions I have had the opportunity to observe some "official" diplomats at work, and often felt uncomfortable when a diplomatic negotiator referred to his counterpart as "my esteemed colleague." This was a rule of the game, but I sensed that he deeply disliked not only what the other diplomat said, but the very nation from which he came. There were poisonous emotions present within both parties and they tried to do their best to deny or disguise them—but they were clearly going nowhere.

So, how could common ground be found between the different orientations of political and behavioral scientists, and could the concepts of Freud or Erikson[167] find any meaningful place in the realm of diplomacy? As Harold Saunders, a former U.S. assistant secretary of state, asks, could we grind new lenses and introduce fresh language when old lenses and traditional language no longer bring the world into focus?[168] I intended to find out, aided by the fact that crucial aspects of diplomacy had been gradually transformed since the Congress of Vienna by many others who came before me.

The establishment of the United Nations on October 24, 1945, certainly changed many facets of relations between sovereign nations, followed quickly by the Cold War which changed many others. On one hand the nuclear arms race was a logical military and political strategy based on deterring enemy aggression through the careful diplomatic expression of "credible" threats of retaliation and "mutually assured destruction." On the other hand, the tangible possibility of horrific worldwide destruction was far beyond logic and caused a great deal of un-acknowledged anxiety that nevertheless found expression in countless books, plays, movies, and paintings. People other than statesmen began demanding to know more about how political leaders behaved. Weapons of mass destruction created a sense of urgency for negotiations at the highest level, as happened during the Cuban Missile Crisis in October, 1962. "The age of summitry," as the late Israeli foreign minister Abba Eban called it, was born, and along with it a desire for regular and structured face-to-face meetings between leaders of opposing or competing nations. This one-on-one form of diplomatic negotiation altered the function of foreign policy organs, such as the Department of State.[169]

The dramatic evolution of rapid communications and instant media coverage also changed how formal diplomacy was practiced. The leaders of large groups, whether they were democratically elected or dictators, could now send messages to their friends and foes and engage in political propaganda by appearing on television, removing the necessity of sending ambassadors or other messengers to deliver their words. Then, in the middle of the Cold War, Sir Harold Nicholson pointed out an additional cause of change: the rise of "democratic" concepts of international relations. He said that because of this, small elite groups could no longer be the only players in diplomacy. Political leaders, statesmen, and other bureaucrats were now obliged to explain themselves to the public constituency within their states or regions.[170]

The appearance of human rights issues as demands arose for foreign authorities to publicly speak about, even interfere with, minority or abuse issues in sovereign countries also brought about a change. So, too, did "globalization." In the international environment, the rise of globalization led to more international meetings, regulations, and treaties, and associated economic and legal agreements conducted by people outside formal diplomatic circles, such as business people. These activities also began to receive more and more media coverage, usually contaminated with political as well as economic propaganda.

The ever-increasing number of NGOs around the globe also began to influence the practice of formal diplomacy to one degree or another. Indeed, a very high-level diplomat at the United Nations headquarters in Europe told me once, off the record, how formal career diplomats like himself, while they were obliged to smile and listen to many of their demands, perceive many NGOs as a pain in the neck.

Lastly, the evolution of so-called "unofficial diplomacy" and the ascendence of conflict resolution and conflict management organizations began to influence formal diplomacy in both positive and negative ways. Here, I will elaborate further on the work and history of such organizations, as in chapters 12 and 13 I will describe a method of "unofficial diplomacy" that I, with the help of my colleagues at CSMH, developed and nicknamed the "Tree Model."

In the early 1980s, Eban noted that the role of private individuals and organizations had encroached into diplomacy's once-sacred territory: "Quakers, church leaders, heads of peace research institutions, professors, members of parliaments and journalists have all attempted to solve or alleviate conflicts which have eluded the efforts of officially accredited emissaries."[171] In tracing the roots of the proliferation of unofficial diplomacy in the United States, he reminds us of comments made by President Dwight D. Eisenhower, who once remarked that private citizens who enjoyed the confidence of their governments might help prepare the way for official negotiations. Eisenhower's attitude was unusual: most political leaders in his era thought that unofficial diplomats were troublesome meddlers, despite their good intentions. Of course, such leaders had a point: because of the enormous number of so-called conflict resolution practitioners, unofficial diplomacy has today become commercialized in the United States.

About a dozen years or so ago when I was visiting Northern Cyprus, I went to see a high school classmate of mine at his home. At that time he had a good position in President Rauf Denktash's presidential office and he appeared on television regularly, providing political commentary. In short, he was a well-known person in the Cypriot Turkish community. I also knew that he had attended some "conflict resolution" meetings along with other influential Cypriot Turks in which they met their Cypriot Greek counterparts. An American facilitating team, after receiving considerable funds from certain U.S. sources, directed these "conflict resolution" meetings. When I went to see my friend, he wanted to show me some pictures of his children. As he opened up a picture album, a large photograph fell on the floor. I picked it up and saw a picture of my friend playing with Legos as if he were a small child building a house. First, I thought that he might be playing with a friend's child since he didn't yet have grandchildren of his own. When my friend noticed that I had seen the photo, he seemed very embarrassed. He told me that the picture was taken during his last "conflict resolution" meeting. The American facilitators apparently had asked Cypriot Greeks and Turks, influential men and women in their communities, to play together with Legos. The idea was that this activity would help resolve the Cypriot conflict. My friend recalled how humiliating it was for him to engage in this activity, and he felt that he had been insulted and treated like a child. He also told me that he decided not to attend future meetings. I am sure that the American facilitators in this case had a logical explanation for their technique. But, to me, this example and other similar ones that came to my attention reflect the simplification and commercialization of the conflict resolution "industry" where people are trained for quick "gimmicks' and "magical thinking," such as creating peace between enemy representatives through game-playing exercises.

There are, of course, also serious unofficial diplomatic efforts, and there are people such as Nodar Sharveladze whom I spoke of in previous chapters, who have contributed to opening dialogues between enemies and helped with societal healing in significant ways. I personally could make a long list of such positive contributors. But what were some of the important developments that paved the way for my own involvement in unofficial diplomacy? I will list a few.

After the breakdown of the 1959 Eisenhower-Khrushchev Summit, Eisenhower supported the Dartmouth Conference—a series of unofficial meetings between influential Americans and Soviets originally organized by Norman Cousins, then the editor of *The Saturday Review*. While early meetings provided an informal forum for communication and the exchange of information, in the early 1980s participants decided to establish small, more sharply focused task forces and also agreed to meet between plenary sessions. In 1986, a political relations task force was established that influenced the processes of *glasnost* and *perestroika*.[172]

During the Cold War, economic entrepreneurs became involved in international relations and unofficial diplomacy.[173] For example, Armand Hammer of the Occidental Petroleum Corporation had ties to the Soviets dating back to the 1920s and functioned as a link between the two superpowers. Private negotiations, such as those involving Wolfgang Vogel, a German involved in the East-West spy swap that included the release of Anatoly Scharansky, also took place. Such private negotiations received a wider audience when they involved the news media. Indeed, some reporters found themselves operating as unofficial diplomats. For example, John Scali, an American wire correspondent, was involved in "backstage" mediation during the Cuban Missile Crisis.[174]

It was not only the U.S.-USSR or East-West relationship that led to unofficial diplomatic efforts. Individuals from outside the small elite group of formal diplomats also participated in the Arab-Israeli conflict. For example, Walter Cronkite is credited with bringing together Israel's Menachem Begin and Egypt's Anwar el-Sadat by satellite. By the late 1970s, unofficial diplomacy became more organized. Representatives of new and emerging peace institutions and "professors"—as Eban called the academics involved—gained actual experience in helping to shape policy.

Herbert Kelman, a social psychologist from Harvard University, discreetly began bringing together high-level Arabs and Israelis for secret dialogues, which he called "interactive problem solving workshops."[175] After Sadat's visit to the Knesset, as described earlier in this book, a team from the American Psychiatric Association conducted a series of unofficial meetings between Arabs (mostly Egyptians and Palestinians) and Israelis between 1979 and 1986. Psychiatrists William Davidson, Demetrios Julius, Rita Rogers, John Mack, Alfred Freedman, and I, participated along with diplomats Harold Saunders and Joseph Montville. Montville termed this process "track-two diplomacy" as opposed to "unofficial diplomacy" and defined it as the informal interaction between influential members of opposing large groups with the goal of developing strategies to influence public opinion and to organize resources of manpower and material in ways favorable to the resolution of conflict.[176] And Saunders later wrote a psychologically informed book and titled it after the phrase Sadat used at the Knesset, "the other walls," referring to the psychological barrier between the Arabs and the Israelis.[177] My experiences in these APA meetings—and elsewhere—led me, with the financial support from the Massey Foundation in Richmond, Virginia, to found CSMHI in 1987. In those days, unofficial diplomacy—or conflict resolution—had not yet become as commercialized in the United States as it is today.

The establishment of the United States Institute of Peace (USIP) in 1984 provided further official support for unofficial diplomacy. An independent, nonpartisan federal institution created by the U. S. Congress to promote the prevention, management, and peaceful resolution of international conflicts,[178] USIP has played a significant role for many scholars and others to think of ways to create a more peaceful world.

Now there are hundreds of people with various professional backgrounds, degrees of education, experience, and knowledge of world affairs calling themselves "experts" or practitioners in "conflict resolution." This situation is very similar to the "democratic equality" of psychotherapeutic approaches in the United States; almost anything fits within a "super-democratic" and "politically correct" frame. I believe that the public is confused about what is a proper psychotherapeutic effort and what is a gimmick. Similarly, it is difficult to separate a serious conflict resolution program based on a theoretical foundation and experience, from a commercialized one.

Now, returning to the time of the APA-sponsored Arab-Israeli dialogues and the collapse of the Soviet Union, those of us who were thrown into world affairs felt like pioneers. I remember my own excitement over studying—through a psychoanalytic lens that also illustrates unconscious societal processes—something about which I knew very little but could learn through hard experience in the field. I asked myself, "What is the exact definition of unofficial diplomacy?" In 1987, I organized a conference at the University of Virginia to ponder this question and invited the few well-known practitioners at the time to offer their insights and descriptions of their respective operating techniques.[179] In the course of our extensive discussions, I concluded that there was no specific definition for unofficial diplomacy, or, using Montville's name for it, track-two diplomacy. Some of the techniques tabled included psychological concepts; many others did not, though all were significant for their nontraditional and human-oriented approaches to international relations.[180]

As time passed, many others emerged with various theoretical and practical understandings of conflict resolution. While some newer practitioners did emphasize the "human dimension" of international conflict, they were usually referring to the observable, surface psychology of bargaining, winning, or loosing and did not account for the psychology of large-group processes, especially identity issues and regression. I realized that diplomats have always had to deal with many highly emotional issues, and advances in the achievement of peaceful solutions to conflicts and peaceful coexistence between opposing large groups may very well depend on examining the emotional components of whatever stalemate is in question. The belief that formal diplomacy should and only does operate in a sterile (only rational and emotionally neutral) environment needs re-examination.[181] And, I began to realize the more I learned, that is where my psychoanalytic background might have something to offer. I remember a passage from Donald Horowitz's work. Horowitz, a lawyer and political scientist, noted that the amount of passion that is expressed in ethnic conflicts "calls out for our explanation that does justice to the realm of feelings,"[182] and that "a bloody phenomenon cannot be explained by a bloodless theory."[183]

12 From Theory to Practice: The Tree Model

After many years of studying international and interethnic issues and facilitating dialogues between enemy groups, I was given a unique opportunity to apply my experience, as well as that of my colleagues at CSMHI, in a comprehensive way. In the mid-1990s, CSMHI received a substantial grant from the PEW Charitable Trust to support an already existing project aimed at helping Estonia separate peacefully from the Russian Federation and develop democratic institutions.[184] After PEW indicated interest in our Estonia-Russia project, I recall one day standing beside a blackboard in the small conference room of CSMHI's building on the grounds of the University of Virginia's Blue Ridge Hospital (now closed). As I was explaining the phases of our Estonia-Russia project to PEW's then program director Steve Del Rosso, I began drawing a tree on the black board. The term "Tree Model" soon stuck to describe CSMHI's method of bringing opposing large-groups together in order to find ways for them to coexist peacefully. Briefly, the roots of a tree stand for a psychopolitical assessment of the conflict, the trunk represent a years-long series of psychopolitical dialogues between high-level representatives of the opposing groups, and the branches refer to taking what has been learned from the psychopolitical dialogues to both the grassroots level and the official level in order to institutionalize peaceful coexistence.

When I was a medical student, I learned that one should make a diagnosis of a patient's problems before commencing treatment.[185] Likewise, it is crucial that the facilitators—in my case, the interdisciplinary CSMHI team—become involved in assessing the problems to be addressed within a large group and between the large group and its enemy. Of course, the situation of the enemy group and its perception of the first group also need to be diagnosed.

For a full assessment of a situation, the facilitators need to travel to the location of the conflict in question. Before traveling to such an area, they must do their homework and study the history and culture of the large groups involved and collect information about the current situation. From the beginning, it is clear that interdisciplinary collaboration is needed and, as I indicated earlier, when I was in charge of CSMHI, our facilitating team included psychoanalysts, psychiatrists, psychologists, former diplomats, political scientists, historians, and, when it was necessary, individuals from other disciplines. Even though a historian on the team may not be an expert in the particular country or identity group concerned, he or she brings a methodology and a way of thinking that contributes to understanding the information gathered. Clinicians bring understanding of the mental images of historical events and how members of a large group may share those images. Diplomats evaluate the real world problems, such as legal and economic issues, as they are reflected in political processes.

The Tree Model's unusual but main tool for assessment is the conducting of in-depth interviews by psychoanalysts, psychiatrists, and psychologists with a wide variety of people from both sides of the conflict, including government officials, "ordinary" adult citizens, and children. The interviewing methodology is not based on simple questions and answers. Data collected in this fashion only gives us a surface picture. We aim to learn about shared hidden feelings, thoughts, and perceptions connected with large-group identity issues and conflicts. Such interviews are conducted by highly experienced clinicians. The reader may get a glimpse of such interviews by recalling my talks with Dali at Tbilisi Sea.

If conducting in-depth interviews and examining common themes in those interviews is the first tool of an assessment phase, then visiting "hot places," as described earlier in this book, is the second tool. I already described the Crying Father Monument in Tskhinvali as a hot place. Ayasofya (St. Sofia) in Istanbul, besides being a tourist attraction, similarly can become a hot place under certain circumstances. This architectural wonder was originally a famous Byzantine church, but when the Turks conquered Constantinople (Istanbul) in 1453, they turned it into a mosque. A visit there in 2000 by Turkish and Greek representatives meeting in Istanbul for unofficial dialogues taught the facilitators a great deal about the Greeks' nostalgia for this place. During times of tension between the two nations, this nostalgia reflex motivates the reactivation of a Greek chosen trauma and Greek attachment to the Megali Idea (see chapter 10).

The assessment phase of the Tree Model is time consuming but essential to understanding the large-group psychologies under consideration. After the collection and review of pertinent data, an overall psychopolitical "diagnosis" is formulated and a list is compiled of the real world issues to be addressed, as well as shared feelings, thoughts, and perceptions that lie beneath the surface. Shared hidden feelings, thoughts, and perceptions often fuel conscious and unconscious resistance to dialogues, interfere with effective discussions of real-world issues, help to mix fantasy with reality, and are easily used for destructive propaganda. Therefore, they must be uncovered and acknowledged at a proper time in order to pave the way for practical resolution of specific issues.

For example, Estonians were naturally euphoric after regaining their independence from the Soviet Union in 1991. But CSMHI was able to uncover other less-obvious aspects of the Estonian outlook through intensive interviews with a wide variety of Estonians and through visits to "hot places," such as the former Soviet submarine base in Paldiski. What we found was that Estonians suffered from an underlying shared anxiety that they would "disappear" as an ethnic group, with their unique culture, language, and identity ceasing to exist. With the exception of a brief period of independence from 1918 to 1940, Estonians have lived under the domination of others during their entire 5,000-year history. When at last they regained their independence, they shared an unconscious fantasy that they would once again be swallowed up by a neighboring large group (Russians, in this case). This shared fantasy contrasted with the surface reality that they were happy to be independent.

There was, in fact, a rational root for their anxiety: nearly 40 percent of Estonia's population was not ethnically Estonian and 30 percent were Russian or Russian speakers. In addition, with a total population of only 1.5 million people, the possibility of disappearing could seem far more possible. Also, during the initial years of their reindependence, when Estonians were still actively trying to find out "who are we now?" they perceived an economic invasion by Western European and American corporations, evidenced by a growing number of European cars and American fastfood restaurants. Although such developments were later welcomed, they initially were perceived as a threat to the survival of Estonian identity. A tragic event in 1994 further illuminated Estonian's fears. A large ferry called the *Estonia* sank in the Baltic Sea, killing nearly 900 passengers and evoking both grief and shame among Estonians. The shame was due to the fact that the tragedy was caused by human error, and the ship's crew was composed of Estonians who had replaced Russians or

Russian speakers living in Estonia (former non-Estonian Soviets). When we interviewed Estonians, we learned that the tragedy was felt even more deeply because it echoed their fear of "disappearing." As Estonia attempted to navigate through the stormy post-Soviet world, would they too make a mistake and sink their struggling nation? Would Estonians drown in a sea of foreign influence?

While there were plenty of real world issues to attend to in the newly reindependent Estonia, the hidden perception that Estonia would vanish caused ethnic Estonians to resist policies that encouraged coexistence with resident non-Estonians. If Estonian and Russian blood were to mix, the uniqueness of the Estonian people might not survive, even though their sense of large-group identity had managed to persist, in fact flourish, despite of or because of their small numbers and adverse conditions over the centuries. CSMHI's assessment then indicated the need to help Estonians differentiate between real issues and fantasized fears as they established themselves as a new democratic state so that they might more

adaptively coexist with the Russians and the Russian speakers living in Estonia.[186]

Let me clarify that here I use the term "coexistence" in a descriptive sense to explore the psychodynamics behind different relationships between large groups. There are similar terms, such as "integration" and "absorption." These are not official diplomatic terms despite the fact that they sometimes appear in diplomatic language as well as in scholarly political science literature. Politically and diplomatically speaking, when they are used "officially," they may mean different things to different parties in negotiations. Other related terms are utilized by diplomats, politicians, and scholars, such as "federation," "unification," "conciliation," and "assimilation." There are also terms that refer to the separation of large groups into political entities, as in the case of the Czech and Slovak Republics. For the purpose of this chapter, I use the term "coexistence" in Estonia to refer to the psychodynamics of interaction between two large groups, Estonians and Russians and Russian speakers living within the same legal state boundary. When we went to Estonia, some Russians and Russian speakers were legal citizens of Estonia, but most of them were not.

For the population of Estonia, the tables were turned overnight. With their reindependence, one million Estonians became the "bosses" of their country, facing half a million former "enemies," the Russians and the Russian speakers living among them. The Russians in Estonia suddenly found themselves to be a "second-class" presence in the country. Many of them still had Soviet passports although the Soviet Union no longer existed, and most of them could not speak Estonian. Some had lived in Estonia for decades, and some for centuries, but even those who had moved there in the recent past were not especially enthusiastic about returning to Russia where crime, corruption, and chaos were rampant. Furthermore, after Estonia regained its reindependence, "hot" problems remained between Estonia and Russia, including disputes about Estonian borders, and the status of Soviet (now Russian) military installations that still existed in Estonia, including a nuclear plant at Paldiski. During the first few years after reindependence, inflamed emotions and the shared "vanishing" fantasy created anxiety, which interfered with decision making on certain political issues, as I will soon describe.

For the next phase of our Estonia-Russia project—the tree trunk phase—we brought representatives of three groups together—Ethnic Estonians, Russians and Russian speakers living in Estonia, and Russians from Moscow—for a years-long series of psychopolitical dialogues.

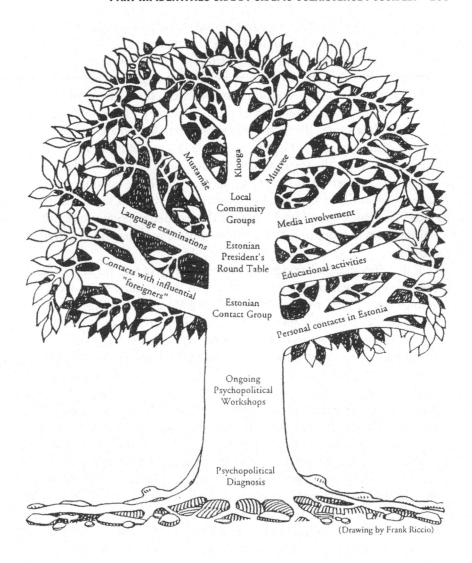

(Drawing by Frank Riccio)

The Tree Model in Estonia

However, before delving into the purpose and methodology of the psychopolitical dialogues we conducted, it may be helpful to describe their general format and structure.

Great care should be taken when choosing the location(s) for the dialogue sessions, for it is important to meet in a site that is perceived as neutral by the participating opposing groups. There may be an advantage to selecting a meeting location that is somewhat isolated, so that participants will not be tempted to skip portions of the dialogue to attend to other business. In addition, there can be a psychological benefit to holding the meetings in a location quite removed from the participants' home territories, even if this means traveling to a country that is not party to the conflict. In all cases the facilitators should remain sensitive to possible slights or disadvantages felt by the participants—sometimes even unconsciously—based on the location and environment of the meeting. I still remember one meeting in Egypt during the Arab-Israeli dialogue series. Suddenly we realized that the hotel for the Israelis and facilitators was named "The Palestinian Hotel." For our three-sided dialogues in Estonia, we always met in Estonia for practical economic reasons, but at different locations.

Ideally, dialogue gatherings should last four days and be held at least three times per year over a period of two to three years. More frequent meetings over a longer time can also be valuable, but funding is often a limiting factor. The same participants should be invited each time, with new participants invited to replace anyone who cannot attend or to add a helpful perspective missing in early dialogues. A group totaling 30-40 persons that includes similar numbers from each opposing group is desirable. Each meeting begins with a plenary session during which a representative of each team summarizes (from their perspective) the events that have taken place since the last meeting and their group's reactions to these events. The rest of the time is spent in small groups (eight-ten persons), each led by two or three members of the neutral facilitating team. In our case, whenever possible we paired a clinician with a diplomat, political scientist, or historian as co-leaders of each small group. The number of small groups depends on the total number of participants, but the same small groups are reformed at each meeting, so that the same participants meet many times with each other over a long period.

During the first and second meetings of these unofficial diplomacy dialogue series, the facilitators convene a plenary session at the beginning and at the end of each day, with small groups in between. As the dialogue series progresses, the plenary sessions become less important and less frequent. At a minimum, the participants meet all together at the beginning of the first day and at the end of the last day of the meeting. At this last plenary session, selected members of each small group share with the others what has happened in their sessions—that is, their findings, suggestions, and suggested action plans. I found that four days is an optimal length for each psychopolitical dialogue meeting. Three days may not allow sufficient time for breakthrough in empathy, communication, and understanding, or for removing psychological resistances and taming inflamed emotions, yet extending meetings longer than four days does not seem, in my experience, to add constructive time. Remember that participants to these unofficial gatherings are very busy persons in their daily lives and it is not practical to have them attend more than three four-day psychopolitical dialogues a year.

During the first two days of a gathering, a tendency for the participants from the opposing camps to focus on protecting their large-group identities underlies much of the discussion. Usually, they are not aware of their intense involvement in this endeavor, and the degree to which they do it varies according to how long the dialogue series has been going on and how familiar the participants are with each other. On the third day, after the facilitators help the participants remove their resistances to hearing one another, more realistic negotiations take place. The fourth day is usually devoted to coming up with practical suggestions to ease the tensions between these large groups. This is when the diplomats and political scientists in the facilitating team come to the fore.

In addition to the plenary and small-group sessions themselves, participants and facilitators eat meals together and have other occasions for informal social interaction. Thus all participants become aware of what goes on in each small group, even if they only participate in their own. It is often during impromptu conversations that important humanizing communications take place. Outside the formal sessions, the facilitators remain on the lookout for derivatives of conscious and unconscious processes that influence the dialogues. It should be noted that the relationships among the facilitating team members are quite important to the success of the dialogues. When I headed CSMHI, the key members had worked together since the 1979–1986 Arab-Israeli dialogues and had removed the natural competition between the disciplines. They could speak one another's "language" and effectively call on those whose skills were most needed at any particular time.

During the series of dialogue meetings, there are actually two parallel processes taking place. One is the evolution that occurs within each four-day meeting, and the other is the larger process that takes shape over the entire two- to three- or four-year series.[187] It is important to understand that certain patterns of interactions and behavior may repeat themselves at different stages in a single meeting and over the longer cycle of the series. The process is not linear—that is, progress made on a particular day, or during a particular four-day meeting of the series, may appear to be repressed when participants revert to less constructive behavior at a subsequent meeting. The facilitators always wonder about the causes of such repressions. Most of the time, they take place when representatives of one opposing group perceive a threat to their large-group identity.

What types of participants should the facilitating team choose to be involved in a Tree Model process? When we get to know a person such as Nodar Sharveladze in Georgia during the assessment period of our model, we obviously felt lucky. Often, however, when going to a foreign land, the facilitating team does not have the luxury of knowing in-depth who in the conflicted locality will be most suitable for this particular type of unofficial diplomacy. But as a general rule, the facilitators should seek out individuals who are influential within their respective circles (government, academia, media), and who are willing to participate in an unofficial capacity and on a voluntary basis.[188]

Facilitators should strive for balance and symmetry between members of the opposing groups and representatives from a variety of sectors. Although the capacity of participants to influence others outside the dialogue group will ultimately determine the impact of the process on the community at large, CSMHI has found that it can be counterproductive to include top political leaders in the process.[189] Often, it is members of the next level down in government who make the most suitable participants, since they can be freer from political pressures and more able to change their attitudes, while still being influential.

Obviously, each participant in the dialogue series has his or her own personality organization, professional and social standing, and political orientation. To varying degrees, each is also influenced by large-group conflict, existing political propaganda, and personal sentiments. During the discussions, individuals may feel as if they are under attack and may feel compelled to defend their personal identity along with their large-group identity, directly or indirectly. There will inevitably be occasions when the clinicians on the facilitating team note expressions of thorny personal issues. When this happens, facilitators should try to direct attention back to the large-group conflict as quickly as possible. The facilitators' aim is not to create small therapy groups for individual participants but to encourage participants to be spokespersons for their respective large groups. Because the principal focus is on large-group conflict as reenacted during the dialogues, small-group dynamics pertaining to the participants as individuals should only be taken into consideration when they get in the way.[190]

Crucial to the series is the establishment of an environment that is psychologically safe for dialogue. This is accomplished first and foremost through the facilitators' neutrality. Neutrality involves showing the participants that the third party is truly interested in the process rather than in suggesting or imposing particular solutions. The facilitators' neutrality entails avoiding the humiliation of either party and exploring in tactful ways the anxiety that is related to participants' large-group identities. Usually, there is asymmetry between large-groups in conflict. For example, Russia is much bigger and more powerful than Estonia. CSMHI facilitators obviously were aware of this. But during the dialogue series, they dealt with the representatives of the opposing groups as equals.

Unlike the dialogue participants from opposing groups, the facilitating team is not facing an enemy, and thus is less prone to responding impulsively to ethnonationalistic, religious, or ideological sentiments. The maturity and success of the facilitating team's approach will depend on clearly defining its task, developing a working alliance among its members, and having a nonregressed relationship with its leader. The leader of the facilitating team will be perceived as the leader of the whole gathering, so it is important that he or she be capable of establishing and maintaining a leadership role and helping the leaders of the antagonist parties define their respective tasks. Frequent debriefing among facilitating team members is essential during the psychopolitical dialogues. For example, at the end of each day, CSMHI team members would meet to share their observations and work through potential difficulties they might be experiencing. Some facilitators may knowingly or unknowingly favor one antagonist group over the other. Like the participants, they may develop positive or negative attitudes toward particular participants or toward political leaders who are not in the room. When such issues become problematic, they need to be worked through during the times when the facilitators meet among themselves. Participants, on the other hand, may develop unrealistic expectations of the facilitators.

In the Estonian-Russians dialogues, for example, it was clear that one of the regular participants from Russia, Yuri Voyevoda, was suspicious of the CSMHI facilitating team's motivations for conducting the dialogues. Then a member of Russia's State Duma, Voyevoda fantasized that CSMHI was connected with the U.S. Central Intelligence Agency (CIA). Not surprisingly, this made the CSMHI team and its leaders rather uncomfortable. One night, during one of the dialogue meetings, Voyevoda invited Yuri Urbanovich and me to join him at the sauna and asked questions of me for over an hour. At the end of this "interrogation," Voyevoda summed up his thoughts by quoting Confucius: "It does not matter what color the cat is—what matters is whether the cat catches mice!" implying that he was still puzzled by our motivations, but willing to go along because the results were helpful. Such impromptu exchanges with participants are sometimes necessary and often pivotal, and facilitating team members must be willing and able to engage participants in a variety of ways in order to further the process.

Although psychopolitical dialogues are not the same as working with an analysand in a clinical setting, some concepts can be carried over. In the psychoanalytic setting where an individual undergoes psychoanalysis, in a sense the analysand plays the "music" he or she composes while on the couch, but the analyst is the orchestra leader. Similarly, in the Tree Model the representatives of the opposing large groups play the music each composes while the facilitating team behaves as the conductor, so that the opposing teams can hear their own compositions and modify them when it is needed. But more importantly, they have a chance to hear the "enemy's" musical notes and respond to such notes. Again, I would like to remind the reader that the facilitating team includes clinicians who are highly psychoanalytically informed and experienced in conducting small group meetings. Accordingly, the Tree Model cannot be imitated unless some key members of the facilitating group have studied human nature and large-group psychology in-depth, both in theory and practice.

Another principle that I took from clinical analysis and applied to the Tree Model is the idea that there is no preassigned agenda for any of the meetings. In a sense, the participants are invited to give "free associations" as an analysand is told to do during analysis. Obviously, the task of these gatherings is clear: representatives of opposing groups come together to unofficially discuss the conflicts between them, negotiate for solutions, and come up with strategies and actions. Facilitators do not give advice to the representatives of the opposing groups about what they or the authorities of their respective large groups should do. Rather, facilitators are present to help remove psychological resistances to more realistic negotiations by bringing to the surface fantasized fears, by separating what is real from what is fantasized, by reversing the time collapse—bringing together feelings, thoughts, and perceptions about a chosen trauma and current events—and creating a time expansion. Examples of such an approach will be given later.

Lastly, I look at these dialogue series as a process similar to the one an individual lying on a psychoanalyst's couch goes through. Thus, the facilitators of the Tree Model are not particularly interested in ending each meeting in the series with good feelings between the representatives of the opposing large groups. They are, however, interested in keeping in mind the process toward more realistic negotiations, uncontaminated with fantasized expectations about the future.

There are also certain concepts that can provide meanings for some events that occur during the dialogue series, mostly in small group settings, but also during plenary sessions.[191] These events are, on the surface, unconnected, but the underlying meanings associated with large-group identity issues do connect them. I will begin with the concept of miniconflict.

Sometimes, at the outset of a dialogue meeting, especially during a meeting at the beginning of the series of dialogues, a disruptive situation evolves abruptly and absorbs the attention and energy of all participants. Such a situation is usually marked with a sense of urgency, yet the content of the "crisis" is essentially insignificant in comparison to the salient aspects of the ethnic, national, religious, or ideological conflict for which the dialogue meeting has been organized. It is reminiscent of the extended debates on who sits where at a conference table that sometimes occur prior to important official negotiations between nations. These miniconflicts may seem inexplicable and incongruous, but are much like the masques that precede an Elizabethan tragedy that provide condensed and symbolically suggestive treatments of what will be explored dramatically later in the play itself. Through the miniconflict, many of the urgent concerns connected with large-group identity issues and tensions are reduced to a more local and accessible realm.

I first noticed the occurrence of miniconflicts during the Arab-Israeli dialogues that took place years before we clearly systematized the Tree Model methodology. Once during the Arab-Israeli unofficial diplomacy series, we were meeting in Switzerland a few days after the assassination in Portugal of Issam Sartawi, then the Palestine Liberation Organization's roving envoy. An argument erupted over whether to hold a moment of silence in Sartawi's memory. The Palestinians naturally wished to do so, but the Israelis did not want to pay this honor to an associate of Chairman Arafat. Both sides threatened to leave the gathering, and this crisis had to be resolved before the unofficial negotiations could begin.

Another example of a miniconflict took place in another Arab-Israeli meeting and concerned the issue of spouses, for the spouses who had accompanied participants were restricted from joining in the dialogue itself. One participant demanded that his wife be allowed to attend the meeting in an official capacity, and this unexpected development quickly took on seemingly critical importance. The large-group identity issues were obscured and forgotten for the time being.

Although individual personalities may be predisposed to causing such disruptions, I believe that miniconflicts have much to do with bringing "enemies" together face-to-face. The individual and large group's sense of self (-identities) are heightened in circumstances of physical closeness, thus threatening the paradoxical equilibrium that exists between enemies—they "need" each other for dialogues, yet must avoid perceiving that they are too "close" or similar to one another, and therefore must maintain a degree of distance. By creating miniconflicts, derivatives of aggression are displaced onto an event that is essentially insignificant in comparison to the magnitude of the national, ethnic, religious, or ideological conflict at hand. A miniconflict reflects a mental defense mechanism (displacement) to cover up the anxiety that is at the heart of the real conflict.

While miniconflicts, which typically appear at the beginning of a gathering, aim to derail the dialogue, paradoxically they can actually perform a useful function in the process: they can help the leader of the facilitators establish or reestablish his or her leadership role. There are inherently multiple leaders in such gatherings, those who are present and represent different large-groups as well as different professionals, and even political leaders of enemy groups who are not present—although their mental images are. If the head of the facilitating team is able to "resolve" the miniconflict, that person establishes authority and can redirect participants to work together, thus turning attention to the large-group conflicts at hand. When the leader of the facilitating team establishes his or her role as the "conductor" of the "orchestra," the participants then perform their tasks.

The miniconflict concerning the death of Sartawi came to an end when I declared that participants could honor the memory of anyone they wanted during the minute of silence. The Israelis decided to go along with this gesture but openly declared that they would not honor Sartawi. They chose instead to honor a recently fallen Israeli, Emil Grunzweig, who had been active in Israel's Peace Now movement. The miniconflict regarding a participant's demand that his wife attend the meeting was resolved by my declaring, as leader of the facilitating team, that all spouses were welcome. (None actually attended after this invitation.) Miniconflicts should not be allowed to drag on as if they were the main focus of the meeting, for if this happens, the entire meeting can be derailed.

Other external events can similarly intrude into a dialogue. When representatives of opposing sides open a discussion, the "echo" of recent events involving their large groups can often be heard in their exchanges, further igniting emotions that exacerbate resistances to adaptive discussions. I call this an echo phenomenon. During psychopolitical dialogues, I have seen the shadow of some recent military or political development fall over the work group. It then becomes necessary to acknowledge and assimilate this shadow and its meaning for the opposing group before realistic negotiation can continue.

In the opening plenary session at the Arab-Israeli workshop following the one-minute of silence in memory of Sartawi and Grunzweig, many aggressive remarks were heard, but the affect was flat. I pondered how the shadow of the assassinations seemed to inhibit the expression of emotions, especially aggressive emotions related to vengeance and a desire to "get even." I wondered if the enemy groups' participants' anxiety over their own aggression in the Arab-Israeli conflict might have induced in them an unconscious identification with the assassins or else a hidden anxiety that they might be assassinated themselves. In the case of the meeting described above, the echo of the assassinations of Sartawi and Grunzweig seemed to have induced a variety of feelings among the participants: vengeance, identification with the aggressor, fear of being a target of aggression, and also heightened shame.

When we went to a restaurant for dinner in Vevey, Switzerland, where this meeting was held, we were aware of the precautionary security measures that had been taken. Swiss police patrolled the street outside, and a Palestinian participant, the late Elias Frej, who was then mayor of Bethlehem, was careful not to sit in front of an open window, I suspected in order to protect himself from being shot by an assassin. I was seated between an Israeli psychoanalyst and a Palestinian lawyer. When the latter expressed a desire to learn something about schizophrenia, the Israeli psychoanalyst, the late Rafael Moses, and I replied from our professional perspectives. Then the conversation returned to violence and aggression: the lawyer wanted to know if John Hinckley, the would-be assassin of then president Ronald Reagan, was schizophrenic, and he bemoaned the impossibility of protecting society from "crazy killers." I noted that the lawyer might be trying to rid himself of aggressive impulses and feelings, in a displaced fashion, by speaking of Hinckley. Tragically, not long after this conversation took place, this Palestinian was himself brutally murdered in Gaza by an extremist Palestinian group.[192] This shook me up and reminded me of when my apartment mate from my medical school days was killed by Cypriot Greek terrorists. I personally became aware of the fact that people not only kill in the name of identity but also for believing that someone of their kind, the victim, is not protecting it. Throughout the years, I have observed that participants who voluntarily become involved in unofficial dialogues with the enemy are seen to some degree as "traitors" by those in their own community who are against all communication with the enemy. These participants may also experience shame for talking with the enemy, which is intensified if and when the enemy carries out some violent act while the talks are going on. After the death of the Palestinian lawyer, it was then clear to most of the facilitators that participants' sense of being "traitors" was not just a fantasy, and we became more aware of the realities facing participants as they "reentered" their communities after attending our dialogues.

After that dinner at Vevey, Frej spoke with humor of the security measures in a London hotel where he had recently stayed with his wife. Apparently conversation at his table, as at mine, had dealt with security, protection, and the fear of assassination, albeit indirectly. I felt that the shadow of the killings of Sartawi and Grunzweig and the associated large-group identity issues had fallen heavily on the group, so I brought it up at the plenary meeting the next day. My observations helped lift the mood of the meeting so that a less-distracted dialogue could ensue.

The influence of external events on participants in a psychopolitical dialogue is not always indirect. Whenever a recent military or political move has disturbed one side, feelings about it must be aired before negotiations can begin or resume. In one meeting in Estonia, the echo of Russian nationalist Vladimir Zhirinovsky's increasing popularity at that time caused increased anxiety among Estonian participants. Zhirinovsky had recently been in Finland, where he had made remarks skeptical of Estonian reindependence, and had promoted nationalistic policies for Russia's "near abroad" that Estonians considered threatening. Estonians' fears of a surge in Russian aggressiveness and heated discussions on the subject pervaded the meeting until the facilitating team helped the Russian participants reassure the Estonian participants that the Russians who were present did not hold the same views as Zhirinovsky.

Official diplomats take great pains to strategically plan the timing of official meetings, yet unforeseen events sometimes occur after a meeting date has been agreed upon and an agenda has been set. The echo phenomenon suggests that close attention must be paid to such incidents, even when they do not seem directly related to the agenda of an official gathering. There are also responses to events of a more personal nature that are clearly related to the echo phenomenon. Although diplomats may well consider the potential influence of any recent military or diplomatic event, events of a personal nature are often overlooked. One example of this was provided by David Rothstein, a psychiatrist who served on the Warren Commission that examined the assassination of John F. Kennedy. Rothstein wrote about a meeting that took place in New Jersey between then president Lyndon B. Johnson and then Russian Premier Aleksei Kosygin. Shortly before this meeting, Kosygin's wife had died, and Rothstein considered the effects of that death on the meeting's outcome: "Could Premier Kosygin have feelings or thoughts whatsoever about his wife's death while he was meeting with President Johnson, or could he have kept those feelings entirely isolated from his participation in the talks?"[193]

Another concept, which I call the accordion phenomenon, also occurs in dialogues. As the dialogues take place, the participants from opposing large groups may suddenly experience a rapprochement. This closeness is then followed by a sudden withdrawal from one another and then again by closeness. Small groups or social gatherings repeat this pattern, which can be seen numerous times in the plenary sessions. I liken this to the playing of an accordion—squeezing together and then pulling apart. Derivatives of aggression within the participants toward the "enemy" groups—even when they are hidden—and attempts to protect large-group identities are the underlying basis for this behavior. Each party brings to such meetings its shared images of historical injuries and conflicts and each experiences conscious and unconscious feelings of aggression toward "the enemy." Initial distancing is thus a defensive maneuver to keep aggressive attitudes and feelings in check, since, if the opponents were to come closer, they might harm one another—at least in fantasy— or in turn become targets of retaliation. The initial distancing also reflects the participants' wish not to contaminate their large-group identity with the enemy's large-group sentiments. When opposing teams are confined together in one room, sharing conscious efforts for "peace," or at least for a civilized negotiation, they must deny their aggressive feelings as they press together in a kind of illusory union. When this becomes oppressive, it feels dangerous, and a new distancing occurs again.

I first became familiar with this phenomenon again back when we were working with the Arabs and Israelis. During this dialogue series, we frequently witnessed sudden harmony among the opposing participants during which times they would enthusiastically note their mutual similarities. Statements such as "we are all brothers and sisters, descendants of a common grandfather, Abraham!" would be heard during these periods of unity. But before long participants from each group would reassert their differences and then distance from one another, and the cycle of contradictory attitudes would continue. Similarly, at a meeting in the dialogue series in Estonia, representatives from both Estonia and Russia blamed the extremists in each camp for the problems between the two countries. Thus, the participants from each side squeezed together and appeared extremely friendly in their common assertion that extremists were the problem. Such feelings of togetherness were generally short lived, however, for when two opposing groups become friendly, the perception that they are far more similar than they previously thought causes anxiety because this threatens their large-group identities. Enemies feel obliged to maintain what I call a "principle of non-sameness." I will discuss this further later in this chapter.

It is my belief that more effective discussion of real-world issues can not take place unless one allows the "accordion playing" to continue for a while so that the pendulum-like swing in sentiments can be replaced by more realistic and stable conceptualizations and more secure feelings about participants' large-group identities. If an agreement is reached during a period of premature closeness, it is likely to be broken or renounced when the groups redistance themselves.

Another concept that is useful in helping us understand what happens during the dialogue phase of the Tree Model is known in psychoanalysis as projective identification.[194] From childhood on, human beings utilize certain mental mechanisms to get rid of unpleasant aspects of themselves and assign them to others. Members of one group in conflict may attempt to define their identity through externalizing and projecting unwanted aspects onto the enemy. For example, it is not we who are troublemakers, but them. Often such processes lead to the creation of a clear "us and them" dichotomy of rigid positions: we are "good," they are "bad."[195] But during a dialogue series, externalizations and projections can also evolve into an even more complex relationship between representatives of the two opposing groups in a pattern similar to the mechanism of projective identification that psychoanalysts see in individual patients. At the group level, one team may project onto the other its own wishes as to how the opposing side should think, feel, or behave. The first team then identifies with the other that houses its externalizations and projections—this other is perceived as actually acting in accordance with the expectations of the former. In effect, one team becomes the "spokesperson" for the other team, and since this process takes place unconsciously, the first team actually believes their remarks about their enemy. However, the resulting relationship is not real since it is based on only one party's process. An illustration may be helpful here, for projective identification can cause stubborn resistances to dialogue that must be addressed before progress can be made.

Russian participants at one of our meetings in Estonia began to make long statements about how Estonians feel, think, and react, and what Estonians believe in, what they want and why, and so on. Estonians responded in turn with their summaries of what the Russians thought, felt, and wanted. While appearing to address each other, the two sides were really talking to themselves, conducting a dialogue between their own position and what they believed (or expected or fantasized) was the position of the other. Facilitators then interceded and clarified for the group that what the Russians were saying about Estonians might be what they wished or feared the Estonians would think or do, and likewise for the Estonians in regard to the Russians. Both sides' initial projective behavior had some roots in reality and was probably based on genuine concerns, yet in other respects it may also have been inaccurate and exaggerated, or even wholly false. If both sides are allowed to speak for themselves, then they can begin to modify any faulty perceptions and "tame" externalizations and projections. We therefore asked the Russians to allow the Estonians to report on their own feelings, thoughts, and actions so that Russians could perceive a "reality" that was not colored by fantasized and projected expectations. The same was asked of the Estonians.

All of the above concepts deal with the threats to large-groups' identities when the enemies meet. They are all intertwined when members of opposing teams enter into a dialogue, which frequently evolve into a competition to list historical grievances (chosen traumas) and past triumphs (chosen glories). In addition to the past traumas and glories themselves, other derivatives of more recent events are also usually chronicled. Since chosen traumas are more effective than chosen glories in promoting group cohesion and identity, listings of past group traumas during a dialogue tend to be more prominent than references to past successes. Furthermore, chosen traumas bring to mind past helplessness, and thus magnify the perception of present danger, especially if one's group remains passive. This, too, plays a role in a group's preoccupation with past shared injuries. At unofficial dialogue meetings, especially at the outset, the competition to list grievances seems involuntary and occurs according to the principle of the egoism of victimization:[196] there is no empathy for the other side's losses and injuries.

During the Estonian-Russian dialogue series, Estonians repeatedly brought up grievances against Russians concerning several aspects of their history. They recounted the 1944 Soviet bombing of Tallinn (Estonia's capital); they described the numbers of Estonians deported, imprisoned, killed, or removed from their homes during the Soviet period; and they bemoaned the humiliation of being forced to learn Russian and relinquish their ethnic traditions under Sovietization. Their chosen trauma did not seem to refer to any specific past event. It reflected instead the reality of their having lived through many centuries under "others." Russians, on the other hand, especially when feeling humiliated, would speak of a specific chosen trauma. They would hearken back to their centuries of being attacked and occupied by the Mongols, or to the Nazi period when they suffered disproportionate losses and sacrifices "to protect the civilized world." Russians also recounted the many advances and advantages that Estonians had gained under Soviet tutelage, such as industrialization and modernization. Russian participants directly and indirectly referred to their legacy as the sons and daughters of a powerful empire with many important achievements, thus boosting their shared self-esteem and holding onto the memories of their chosen glories.

In such exchanges, there is little realistic integration of what "they" did to us, what "we" did to them, or what "we" did for them. If left unchecked, both sides will continue to list their chosen traumas and glories and more recent grievances back and forth in a seemingly endless and victorless competition. However frustrating such exchanges may be for the facilitators, I believe that they are necessary to the process itself, because reactivated chosen traumas and chosen glories as large-group identity markers serve to strengthen participants' hold on their large-group identities. If participants do not feel secure in their large-group identities, they will have great difficulty negotiating more realistically with the "other" when the time comes. During listings of past and current grievances, the task of the facilitating team is to absorb the outpouring of the parties' emotions through active listening, to avoid taking sides, and thus to become a model of empathic listening. When eventually the opposing teams begin to "hear" each other, more realistic discussions can ensue. Mutual recognition of one another's suffering creates a favorable atmosphere for progress in negotiation because underneath there is a mutual verification of each other's large-group identity.

When chosen traumas and their derivatives are reactivated, the emotions and perceptions pertaining to them are felt as if the trauma occurred recently—they become fused with emotions and perceptions pertaining to the present and are even projected into the future. What is remembered from the past, felt now, and expected for the future, come together in a time collapse. Understandably, this time collapse complicates attempts to resolve the conflicts at hand. To counteract this phenomenon and to encourage a time expansion, facilitators must allow discussions to take place concerning the chosen trauma itself and participants' personal traumas pertaining to the large-group conflict. I have noticed that such discussions usually are "taboo" in an official diplomacy setting. "Don't go back to the past; stay at the present time" is what is usually demanded of the participants during official dialogues. Here I am pointing out how sometimes it seems necessary to speak about past traumas and air out feelings. If feelings and issues about the past can be distanced and separated from present problems, then current problems can be more realistically discussed. This same phenomenon occurs not only as a time collapse in relation to an individual's ancestors' trauma, but also as a kind of time collapse that individual participants experience about a past event in their own lives. The facilitators should pay attention to an individualized time collapse if it becomes connected with the task of dealing with large-group identity issues.

During one meeting in Estonia, Arnold Rüütel, the then deputy speaker of the Riigikogu (Estonian Parliament) and a former president of Estonia who had led Estonia from the end of the Soviet period into independence, shared an account of a meeting he had with Mikhail Gorbachev in Moscow. Rüütel had traveled there to discuss with Gorbachev Estonia's desire for independence from the Soviet Union and was kept waiting alone in an anteroom for two hours past the scheduled time of the meeting. This incident, which had happened more than five years prior to this particular meeting, and which had been a humiliation to Rüütel, seemed to color his view of Russians at the dialogue, for he appeared to rigidly hold onto strong nationalistic views and to distance himself from the Russian participants, whether they were from Russia or Estonia itself. After facilitators empathically acknowledged the humiliating nature of this experience with the Soviet system, the Estonian politician appeared to tame his anti-Russian rhetoric and interact less stiffly and more congenially with Russian participants. It was as if the burden of combining his past and present feelings about Russians had been eased, enabling him to deal more comfortably with the present relationship between the two countries now that time had "expanded." In turn, Rüütel's shift in attitude affected the other Estonian participants, and they, too, seemed to participate in this time expansion.

Still another concept deals with minor differences that are utilized to protect and maintain one's individual and large-group identities.[197] As a psychopolitical dialogue meeting room develops into a laboratory for large-group conflict, aspects of large-group rituals become prominent in the small group discussions. When parties become more empathic toward each other, they may become anxious if they begin to perceive themselves and their group as similar to the enemy. As each side's externalization and projection of unwanted aspects becomes unstable due to the perception that the other is similar to one's own group, participants may exaggerate the importance of minor differences between them to maintain their separate large-group identities. The "principle of non-sameness" becomes activated. Minor differences thus function as a stubbornly held border separating the opposing parties so that their respective identities remain intact. A seemingly trivial disparity may then take on monumental importance and turn positive discussions sour.

I have found that minor differences between opposing groups are often psychologically harder to deal with than major differences, such as language or religion. At a meeting when Estonian and Russian participants seemed to be expressing increasingly similar views, one Estonian abruptly got up and announced that it was the birthday of a Russian-speaking participant. Everybody was asked to sing "Happy Birthday." While on the surface this seemed a gesture of camaraderie, it was in essence a defensive act. Coming close to an agreement had made this participant anxious, but he was really responding to the anxiety of participants from both sides. By bringing up the birthday, the participants could be distracted from reaching an agreement and thereby remain different from each other. In such situations, it is helpful for the facilitating team to interpret the meaning of the minor difference and its significance in the dialogue and to reassure all participants that coming to an agreement does not mean losing one's large-group identity.

In the Tree Model technique, instead of telling the opposing groups' participants what to do, the facilitators simply explain the meanings of their anxieties and help them to work through and tame them. As expected, sometimes there are interferences due to the personal issues of a participant. While clinicians on the facilitating team sense the development of such interferences, they should refrain from probing their full meaning in relation to what a given participant may be reactivating from his childhood or other past experiences. Getting involved in this way would turn the dialogues into "pseudo-therapy" sessions, an unproductive and even dangerous development. Thus, facilitators only call attention to interferences from personal issues when a participant may be making connections between individuals or large groups.

When Rüütel told his story of being made to wait at the Kremlin, for example, facilitators felt it was appropriate to point out how he was transferring responsibility for the humiliation he experienced from Mikhail Gorbachev to Russians as a whole. Of course, I do not know whether Gorbachev actually intended to humiliate Rüütel. There may have been other explanations for why Rüütel was made to wait so long before being received, but in any case, the result was that Rüütel felt humiliated. We did not investigate whether in Rüütel's mind Gorbachev represented someone "bad" from his childhood, but only focused on how this event might be a factor in some of his stubborn perceptions of Russians in general. When the psychoanalysts on the CSMHI facilitating team sensed some manifestations stemming from a participant's own development, they used such insights to enhance the process of communication. To be productive, the discussions should become "laboratories" in which individuals become spokespersons of their large-group psychology and where facilitators help them address conflicts and anxieties pertaining to these issues.

As the dialogue series continues and the "enemy" participants get to know one another in an emphatic fashion, the nature of the tree trunk starts to change. We have now moved up to the area where tree branches will begin. While at this point we will still see events and concepts described above—especially new unexpected threats to large-group identity that occur—from here on out, especially in the latter part of the series, there will be less preoccupation with chosen traumas and less concern with minor differences. The participants voluntarily bring up personal stories concerning large-group conflicts that belong to them and this clearly shows that there are multiple perceptions and experiences within each team. Seeing the different ways they relate to large-group identity issues among themselves, in fact, helps to keep "enemy" participants from acting in unison and also helps them accept the differences between themselves and those in the opposing group.[198]

Initially, personal stories often reflect an "us" and "them" (or "me" and "them") psychology in a black and white manner—the other is seen as all "bad" while one's own group is experienced as all "good." As empathy evolves, however, stories begin to include mixed feelings, attitudes, and ambivalence about the "other" and begin to acknowledge the other's personal identity as a total being who is both similar and dissimilar, liked and disliked; the other begins to become more human. Such exchanges allow the participants to see how their personal identities are intertwined with their large-group identities and what events have led them to hold onto their specific sentiments or ideologies. Personal stories also allow the facilitating team to indirectly encourage members of the opposing team to come up with similar stories and to underline empathic understanding. This leads to the development of empathy from members of the opposing team both for the person and for that person's large-group. Personal stories also influence perspectives within a group. Participants who belong to one large group typically share certain perceptions, but through personal stories, it may become clear that the groups are not nearly as homogeneous as they had previously believed. When participants are able to note differences within their own group, it enlarges their flexibility in dealing with many other complex aspects of the overall conflict.

After Estonia regained its independence, the issue of who could become an Estonian citizen became critical. Among other requirements, non-Estonians had to pass a language examination as a criterion for citizenship. Most Russians who found themselves in Estonia when it broke away from the Soviet Union did not speak or write Estonian, and it became evident that the language examination requirement contained hidden agendas. The examination was not standardized and required a one-on-one interview between an Estonian examiner and the Russian or other Russian-speaking applicant.[199] During the dialogue series there were many rational discussions pertaining to the language examinations. Russian speakers wanted Estonians to provide language classes to help them prepare for this part of the citizenship requirement. Estonians countered that they lacked the resources to implement such a policy. Many on both sides agreed that the examination should be standardized. Some suggested a review panel, while others suggested a multiethnic board to design and administer the program. Solutions to overcome many of these obstacles were available, at least in theory, yet progress was elusive.

Gradually, after listening to the personal stories of Estonians and Russians living in Estonia, we realized there were other reasons for the obsession with the language exam. Estonians did not want to standardize or systematize the exams because, consciously or unconsciously, they really wanted the Russians and Russian speakers living in Estonia to leave the country altogether. If the language examination were to be officially institutionalized, this would mean, for the Estonians, that the presence of a substantial percentage of Russians and Russian speakers in Estonia would also be institutionalized. On another level, in its unstandardized format, the language examination was a tool of revenge for the Estonians against the Russians and of protection against the shared sense that their large-group identity would "disappear." On the other hand, many Russians living in Estonia did not really want to learn Estonian, not simply because of the practical obstacles to it, but because doing so would be a painful and shameful acknowledgment of their minority status in a country where they had recently been dominant. At the time of our dialogue series, Russians and Russian speakers were not ready to acknowledge this loss in status. During our discussions, the facilitators verbalized these previously hidden meanings, thereby allowing a deeper understanding of the issues. For example, early in the series, Vladimir Homyakov, an ethnic Russian and a physician who lived in the predominantly Russian-speaking city of Narva in northeastern Estonia, related personal horror stories about being forced to learn Estonian. But later in the series, he one day proudly announced with a happy grin on his face that his daughter had just successfully passed an Estonian-language test. Soon, Vladimir told us that he himself was taking Estonian-language instruction.

As a meeting series progresses, a symbol or metaphor may emerge from within the dialogue that represents important aspects of the conflict. The participants begin to "play" with this metaphor, to kick it around like a ball. The metaphor captures the attention of the participants and transforms diffuse emotions and blurred realities into a more concrete understanding of the problem. The playful metaphor connects the participants, allowing them to share in the game, while at the same time addressing a critical issue. As this play continues, poisonous emotions begin to disappear and laughter often accompanies the banter. Realistic discussion of issues can then ensue. It is important to note that the facilitating team should not introduce or fabricate a metaphor or "toy" for the participants to play with—it must be created or provided by the participants themselves. When anxiety-provoking feelings are represented by symbolic objects and named, they become less threatening. One can better tolerate an enemy who is defined and in the open than an unknown enemy lurking in the shadows.[200]

At one meeting in Estonia, a Russian introduced a metaphor equating Russia with a friendly elephant—big and strong, but not aggressive. An Estonian participant added that if Russia was an elephant, then Estonia was a rabbit. It was difficult, the second participant noted, for the rabbit and elephant to have a relationship even if both were friendly, for the rabbit cannot help fearing that he will be stepped on by the elephant. A different participant then observed that if such were the case, then Russian speakers in Estonia were like elephant eggs in the rabbit's nest—at any moment they might hatch and squash the rabbit and his home, or the elephant might protect them if it thought they were in danger. For days, the participants played with these metaphors; indeed, three months later, at the next meeting, they returned to the same "game."[201]

When an anxiety-producing relationship is symbolized and played with, participants come to a better understanding of some aspects of the relationship between them. Also, they begin to modify their perception of each other. For example, through the elephant-rabbit metaphor, the Russians upgraded their image of Estonians from being "ungrateful" for past "help" from the Soviet Union, to being simply cautious. They sensed that out of necessity the Estonians had to be careful and not too friendly with the Russians, for even a friendly elephant might step on a rabbit by mistake.

When an acceptance of changed attitudes about the enemy and an acceptance of the enemy group's identity as described by the enemy itself becomes crystallized, references to mourning are heard during the dialogue series. This is the clear indication that for all practical purposes, the second phase of the Tree Model is coming to an end. Opposing parties come to unofficial diplomacy meetings with aspirations, hopes, and opinions that tend to be rigid and often unrealistic. A successful psychopolitical dialogue series seeks to tame and loosen such positions, but this is difficult if the losses that result from an altered position or status are not mourned. As I described in detail earlier in this book, human beings must mourn when they give up something or when they lose a stubbornly held position. Mourning in this sense does not refer to observable behavior such as crying, but to psychodynamic processes that occur after loss that leads to acceptance of a new reality: the loss becomes real.[202]

In Estonia, we observed that the mental representations of past hurts during the Soviet period—such as the deportation of Estonians to Siberia—have not been effectively mourned. As the mental representations of such destructive events were passed down from one generation to the next, they changed function and became absorbed into the Estonian shared fantasy of being a "vanishing" ethnic group. Even after regaining independence, this sense of endangerment remained and influenced policy decisions. During the dialogues, the facilitating team brought this observation to the surface so that Estonians could begin mourning past losses, and hence make way for accepting the present reality by taming their shared fantasy that they would disappear as a people after their reindependence.

Another mourning-related event occurred in the Estonian-Russian dialogues. When Estonia regained its reindependence, a border dispute existed between Estonia and Russia over an area extending about 40 miles east of Narva. Estonians wanted this land to be returned to them, since they perceived that it rightfully belonged to them according to the Tartu Peace Treaty of 1920. Russia did not recognize this treaty (in part because doing so meant recognizing that Estonia was independent at that time), and kept the disputed land when Estonian reindependence occurred. At the beginning of CSMHI's dialogue series, this border issue was a hot one. "Losing" this piece of land meant different things for different Estonian participants, but all seemed to share a feeling that they had lost some prestige and power to a giant foe. Ironically, however, if the territory had returned to Estonia, it would have meant a substantial increase in their Russian population since all the area's inhabitants are Russian. Thus, there was also some relief in "giving back" this piece of land to Russia. The simultaneous desire to keep and to give up this territory created ambivalence for Estonians that made the mourning process difficult. The Estonians' concerns over the border issue were sucking up their energy. My CSMHI colleagues and I realized that if, due to these complications in the mourning process, the Estonian participants continued to be pre-occupied with this issue as the dialogues wore on, they would have difficulty engaging in realistic discussions with Russians on other issues. We helped the Estonian delegates to bring their ambivalence about returning the land into the open, which eased the complications in their mourning process, and eventually liberated them so they could turn their attention to other matters. Meanwhile, Russians in Estonia, such as Vladimir Homyakov, felt abandoned by Mother Russia following the collapse of he Soviet Union and they had to mourn their own loss.

During long-term interethnic or interreligious dialogues, rigid and hostile positions can be loosened, allowing the mode of discourse to shift from accusations and recriminations to explanations of each side's position, and from there to a genuine negotiation. Because large-group identity issues are at the root of the original rigid positions, participants will not acknowledge the need or have the will to change unless they recognize that previous strategies have not worked. The situation must be addressed through encouraging time expansion, taming projections, identifying hidden sentiments and fantasies, modifying black-and-white thinking, and initiating mourning. Some of the aspects of psychopolitical dialogues described earlier, such as exaggerated attention to a miniconflict or the expression of chosen traumas, are more common in the first day or two of a meeting and/or during the early meetings of a long-term dialogue. Other aspects, such as genuine mourning and time expansion, typically appear after the work group has progressed through several meetings. Although emotions will continue to flare up and resistances will be encountered throughout a series of dialogues, the parties ultimately become better equipped to talk and listen to each other, respond, and seek clarification of differing views. Gradually, they begin to understand each other's anxieties, fears, hopes, and historically based perceptions, and to build a way of collaborating while maintaining their differences. Certainly, the regression that appeared due to the perceived threats against their large-group identities slowly disappears. They can now negotiate as nonregressed individuals or better, as individuals who resist the influence of large-group regression.But the goal is not to make former enemies into close friends or to encourage assimilation of the different groups into one larger group, but rather to help them find ways of coexisting that do not involve discrimination, violence, or aggression against members of the other group.[203] Participants of the dialogue groups then become the allies of the facilitation, and the third phase of the Tree Model begins.

As Abba Eban noted a long time ago, unofficial diplomacy is of no real use unless it affects official diplomacy when the latter focuses on solutions for conflicts.[204] One aim of psychopolitical dialogues is to arrive at critical meeting points where findings can be reported and made useful in official diplomatic and policymaking arenas. Thus, as the dialogue series progresses, facilitators also seek out and maintain contacts with decision makers who are not participants in the dialogue series, but who are in a position to affect policy. When I first became involved in unofficial diplomacy within the APA-sponsored Arab-Israeli dialogues, I was rather shy in my thinking about getting involved in "critical meeting points." I think this was a realistic position for me. I was a novice and did not have much to offer. We left it to Arab and Israeli participants to come up with their own unofficial "briefings" for the authorities in their own groups. By the time my colleagues and I began working in Estonia in the early 1990s, however, I had more experience in understanding international relationships and had concluded in my own mind how important it was to develop branches of the "tree" and to institutionalize positive findings stemming from a psychopolitical dialogue series. I also learned that personal contacts with influential individuals and policymakers outside of a dialogue series were very important. When I did such things, I would share my activities with members of the CSMHI team and when necessary with the participants of the dialogue series.

In Estonia, one point of contact with officialdom had to do with the Estonian-language examinations of prospective citizens, mostly Russians. One of our facilitators, Joyce Neu, who is now the executive director of the Joan Kroc Peace and Justice Institute at San Diego University, was then with the Conflict Resolution Program at the Carter Center in Atlanta. She was permitted by the Estonian authorities to observe several language examination sessions. She watched more than 30 people take the test, consulted with members of the Estonian-language board and with directors of language schools where exams were administered, and shared her findings with Estonian authorities as well as with the Organization for Security and Co-operation in Europe's High Commissioner on National Minorities. I believe that Neu's actual presence in such sessions tamed the examiners' (conscious and unconscious) feelings of anger and vengeance as well as the examined persons' shame and resistance to learning the language of people they had recently dominated. Estonian authorities sought her advice as to how to modify the examination appropriately. Neu provided "samples" from other locations in the world where there were similar language issues. Eventually, Estonians came up with a fair examination system that became the official one.

Cultivating relationships with Estonian officials in other areas was made easier by the fact that a former president (Rüütel); a former cabinet member (Klara Hallik); four then current members of the Riigikogu (Estonians Toomas Alatalu and Arvo Haug, and Russian-Estonians Sergei Issakov and Sergei Ivanov); and a famous Estonian poet, Jaan Kaplinski, who in 1995 was a nominee for the Nobel Prize in Literature, were among the Estonian dialogue participants. From Moscow, we had parliamentarians and officers from the foreign ministry, as well as the Russian ambassador to Estonia himself, Alexandre Trofimov. As a younger man Trofimov had been assigned to the Soviet embassy in Ankara, Turkey, and had to learn Turkish. He felt particularly close to me and Norman Itzkowitz, a CSMHI member and well-known Princeton University historian who could also speak Turkish. CSMHI facilitators frequently briefed the U.S. ambassador to Tallinn and other U.S. embassy officials, as well as ambassadors and officials from Scandinavia and the other Baltic countries. We also arranged appointments at a variety of government ministries in Estonia to brief official authorities. The

Estonian foreign ministry assigned Paul Lettens, then the counselor to Prime Minister Siim Kallas, to join the dialogue groups in an unofficial capacity. He later made it possible for the CSMHI team to brief the prime minister on the dialogues.

Another key contact was Ants Paju, with whom I developed a very special relationship. Paju's family had been exiled to Siberia and had suffered a great deal at the hands of the Soviets. An Olympic-level discus thrower, Paju had been denied permission for political reasons to travel outside the Soviet Union, and had thus been prevented from participating in the Olympics—another "injustice" that he blamed on the Soviets. Not surprisingly, Paju, not unlike Arnold Rüütel, had very strong Estonian nationalist sentiments when I first met him when he was a senior adviser to Lennart Meri, the then president of Estonia. In his office, he had a long, thick wooden club like the ones seen carried in caveman cartoons. When Yuri Urbanovich and I entered his office in the presidential compound, he greeted me while holding the club in his hand. A huge man, Paju began looking into my eyes intensely for a few minutes. I did not feel frightened, but felt somewhat amused. At that time Paju did not speak English, although later he would learn enough English to speak with me directly. He told Yuri, in Russian, that he was testing me. If I blinked, I would not be worthy of his trust. Since I did not blink, he thought of me as someone worthy of his attention. On CSMHI's periodic visits to Estonia for the dialogue meetings, I had long discussions with Paju, in restaurants, in saunas, at his office, wherever the opportunity arose. Sometimes he would drive for hours to come to see me and began calling me his "teacher." Keeping my psychoanalytic identity in mind, I never told Paju what he should do when he asked my advise on a matter. Instead, I would explain the possible underlying psychological processes of certain political issues he would bring to my attention. He perceived me as his "teacher," because he said that I was teaching him about human beings and humanity. Over time, I could see major changes in Paju's attitudes—in particular, a broadening of his attitude concerning coexistence politics—and knew that with his influence in the Estonian government, his newly found insights were sure to have a wider impact. I learned that he later played a significant role in bringing together local government officials from both sides of the Estonian-Russian border to deal with issues of transportation, trade, and border security to prevent criminal activities.

The most formal "critical meeting point" in the Estonian-Russian dialogues had to do with an official round table created by Estonian president Lennart Meri in 1993 to study the minorities in Estonia. When Estonia regained its reindependence, it was obvious that the Estonian government would face practical and political issues pertaining to non-Estonians (such as citizenship criteria). The Round Table on Minorities was conceived as an unofficial consultative group to address such issues. They met monthly, sometimes more often, and made decisions and recommendations only by consensus. Between 1993 and 1995, Estonia's prime minister and interior minister consulted with the group several times. The round table members included representatives from three groups: (1) the Russian-Speaking Representative Assembly (representing the interests of noncitizens, as well as businesses and unions); (2) the Union of Minority Ethno-Cultural Organizations (established in 1988 to continue the traditions of small ethnic groups living in Estonia, such as Hungarians, Swedes, Jews, Latvians, and others, with an educational and cultural focus); and (3) the Riigikogu. When CSMHI began its work in Estonia, Paju was the head of the round table and three of its members participated in our dialogues. Thus, there was a direct intersection between the unofficial dialogue series and the official task force. When Paju was elected to the Riigikogu and left the round table, another Estonian from our psychopolitical dialogue series became its leader.

Another kind of meeting point, in addition to developing personal relationships with people in power, is creating organizations, facilities, and institutions to support peaceful coexistence and decrease ethnic tensions. In turn, these grassroots efforts by community members must have meaningful contacts with the government so they can have a broader impact and become known by other communities and other parts of the country.[205] After many psychopolitical dialogues in Estonia, it was evident that branches were growing from the "trunk" of our tree. But would these branches bear fruit, and could the seeds from this fruit sprout in other parts of the country? We were about to find out.

13 A Fourth of July Party with Heavy Artillery Fire

The process of psychopolitical dialogues promotes development of a healthy "trunk" of interethnic communication and neighbor-state relationships. It can serve as a critical buffering or stabilizing role in a region where ethnic, national, religious, or ideological conflicts and tensions simmer and flare up with regularity. As with a tree in need of pruning, healthy growth within and between large groups can be thwarted by inflamed large-group identity animosities that cause the undue spending of energy to be spent on counterproductive issues. This phenomenon is reminiscent of the way in which a tree's growth is stunted by "suckers," the detrimental shoots that form at the base of its trunk. To counter these hazards, it is crucial to engage conflicting groups in psychopolitical dialogues that can ward off dangerous escalations and consequences of inflamed animosities. With a healthy trunk, new "branches" can then begin to grow. I have already mentioned some branches that reflect our taking to official levels what was learned during the psychopolitical dialogues. Other branches stand for our taking the same knowledge to the grassroots level in order to build societal institutions supporting coexistence. The psychopolitical groundwork achieved during the dialogues provides a necessary foundation to support actions and new institutions, for without first creating alliances and removing psychological resistances to change, such institutions risk being short lived and ineffective.

Before one can implement programs or actions proposed by the dialogue participants, a local contact group must be formed. The role of this contact group, whose members are chosen by the facilitating team in consultation with participants of the dialogue series from opposing parties, is to coordinate the process of turning proposed action scenarios into real projects. Facilitators encourage the contact group members to interact as a unit and to evolve into a "work group" so that they will not fall back into externalizing and projecting their fear and expectations onto members from the other side. When fully formed, the contact group should evolve into an extension of the facilitating team. The contact group should have local people trained in psychology, people whose training could be enhanced by consultations with the clinicians among the facilitators.

Eventually, the contact group should evolve into an NGO committed to promoting intergroup understanding and reducing ethnic tension by building community support. Having assimilated techniques from the facilitators and having gained a deeper understanding of the conscious and unconscious roots of the conflict, the contact group steps into a new leadership role as the facilitating team begins to withdraw and becomes a model for nonregressed ways of dealing with societal problems.[206]

Once it is cohesive, the contact group, with close consultation with the facilitating team, selects potential "branches," practical projects to be organized and implemented, in a sense to replicate a part of the "trunk" in a different location. This is the real test for the contact group, for it must be able to deal with the same problematic dynamics of the original psychopolitical dialogues, as well as new challenges specific to the project environment. It is therefore helpful if the facilitators are available for some years, first on location and then from afar, to provide continued technical guidance and encouragement along the way. Guidance may also be provided by the original psychopolitical dialogues if they are continuing, and by the growing networks of individuals and organizations that have been connected through the dialogues.[207]

After the 1994–96 psychopolitical dialogues in Estonia, CSMHI developed local projects over the next three years supported by a major grant from the Pew Charitable Trust. Three sites were selected for the development of NGOs and projects promoting democratic, interethnic community building: Mustamäe, a suburb of Tallinn; Mustvee, a town near Lake Peipsi, which lies on the border of Estonia and Russia; and Klooga, a small village twenty-five miles from Tallinn. Each location had a population with roughly equal proportions of Estonians and Russians, but they were also quite different from one another and personified the diversity of issues surrounding relations between Estonians, Russians, and Russian speakers living in Estonia.

With the help of the contact group, we selected ten Estonians and ten Russians (or Russian speakers) in each location. Our technique to begin the process was simple: we met with the twenty participants in each location and told them that we wanted them to meet for a year or so, at least once a month, and come up with a project (or projects) that would be mutually acceptable to all residents in their community. The head of the contact group, in this case, Estonian psychologist Endel Talvik, a veteran of the original psychopolitical dialogue series and then president of the fledgling Estonian Psychoanalytically Oriented Society, would (along with his Estonian and Russian assistants) help them with their deliberations. Faculty members of the CSMHI would also visit with them every four months or so and offer consultations. When they decided on the project, CSMHI would give the local group (that would evolve as into an NGO) $50,000 provided by the Pew Charitable Trust to implement their project.

I will now briefly describe what we did in Mustamäe and Mustvee and then will give a more detailed account of our work in Klooga.[208] Mustamäe, a suburb of Tallinn, has a high proportion of young children and many schools. Estonian and Russian schools in Estonia were separate, each instructing in their own language. The Mustamäe group consisted of Estonian and Russian teachers and parents who sought to develop programs to promote coexistence between Estonian and Russian kindergartners (ages three to six). For a year and a half, the contact group conducted sessions with the teachers once a month based on the principles of the psychopolitical dialogues described earlier. The CSMHI team joined these meetings three times per year to observe and supervise.

After much deliberation, the Mustamäe participants settled on a program. They wrote and published psychologically informed textbooks for teaching Estonian language and culture to Russian children, and they hired seven teachers to teach Estonian to classes of Russian kindergartners.[209] Their program also included opportunities for the Russian children in the language classes to meet and play with Estonian children once they had acquired some language skills. There were field trips to museums and an Estonian puppet theater, visits to each other's schools, and a summer camp for Russian and Estonian children.

While the progress of the Mustamäe group seemed impressive, psychological interferences were nonetheless evident. Many Estonians, even the most intellectual ones, believed that if Russian and Estonian kindergartens were integrated, Estonian children would end up learning Russian instead of the Russian children learning Estonian—a symbolic expression of the "vanishing" fantasy that I already described. Adults were convinced that even if only four Russian children were placed in a class with sixteen Estonian children, the Russians would dominate. The CSMHI team interpreted that this belief, which first surfaced during the original psychopolitical dialogues, was based on Estonians' internalization of victimhood and the projection of their own aggression onto Russians. Despite such fears and misgivings, when the Estonian language program actually took place, the Russian children in Mustamäe exhibited no aggressive tendencies and were curious, playful, and eager to learn Estonian. "Seeing is believing" was actualized in Mustamäe. This one program showed everyone that four Russian children would not dominate sixteen Estonian children. After the first year of implementation, the language program became so popular among parents, teachers, and schools that the demand soon outnumbered the student spaces available. After CSMHI left Estonia, the Estonian government supported the work in Mustamäe and approved it as a teaching model.

Mustvee is a rural town five hours by car southeast of Tallinn near Lake Peipsi that is home to people of both Estonian and Russian heritage, including a sect known as the Old Believers who fled religious persecution in Russia in the seventeenth and eighteenth centuries. Few of the residents therefore were "newcomers," and most had lived for centuries without conflict, although there were nevertheless ethnic and religious differences among them. Here CSMHI's aim was to help the villagers remain on peaceful terms as they sought to develop new industry to rejuvenate their economy, which had collapsed with the Soviet Union. The Mustvee group chose to promote ecotourism in their town and region.

Psychological internalization of the Soviet system[210] was evident in each of the three project sites, but it was most evident in Mustvee. When the ten Estonians and ten Russians (including Old Believers) began to meet to discuss developing a community project, participants tended to give speeches instead of engaging in genuine dialogue with each other. While one person stood to speak, the other participants would talk among themselves and show no interest in the speaker's statements. They seemed to be only going through the motions of a democratic gathering, expecting someone in authority to make decisions for them. They needed to learn how to make independent decisions, both as individuals and as a community.

This unfamiliarity with independent decision making was evident in Mustvee even before the community program began meeting. When CSMHI facilitators were investigating the area as a possible candidate for the community dialogues, Mustvee's new Estonian mayor spoke to us about his impending decision concerning the purchase of new sewer pipes. In the past, a Soviet engineer would have surveyed the town, consulted his procedure manual, and supplied the pipe according to rigid guidelines. Today, responsibility for getting the job done rested with the mayor, and it was obviously causing him considerable anxiety.

Learning how to make decisions as a team and how to prioritize the many needs of the town in order to write a proposal for funding from CSMHI proved challenging for the Mustvee group. Eventually, however, they established a local NGO and submitted project proposals. The community group organized and furnished a center to provide information for tourists in several languages. They printed promotional materials, put up signs to assist tourists who at this time were Finns coming to Lake Peipsi for fishing, and attended professional meetings and trade shows on tourism. They bought equipment for their sports center including an electric scoreboard that would allow them to host tournaments in volleyball and other sports. Eventually, they learned how to develop ecotourism.

I believe it is not only the dialogue Endel Talvik and his people and my colleagues and I conducted in Mustvee that caused these country folks to move away from their Soviet ways of doing things, become active, and adjust to a new way of life. I have come to believe that people in places such as Mustvee (or in refuge camps, such as the ones in the Republic of Georgia) need a libidinalization of their psyche. They were traumatized and I believe depressed. Libidinalization means that through interaction with a caring other, a person learns how to love him or herself and become actively and pleasurably involved in new things. I see this kind of process, for example, when analyzing previously depressed persons. The caretaker, while not impeding the "autonomy" of those who attempt to get out of their depression, becomes a "life-loving" model. Thus, our institution-building not only refers to intellectual planning but also to "humanizing" interactions, so that those who will build institutions do so with increased self-esteem. A psychoanalytic clinician's understanding of society was our guide. Accordingly, we decided to hold a Fourth of July party in Mustvee and brought people from our psychopolitical dialogue series there. Some influential people from Tallinn who attended had never been to such a "faraway" place. The townspeople felt that now Tallinn was noticing them.

At one point, CSMHI team members became "guinea pigs," the first customers of an evolving ecotourism site. Since there was no hotel in Mustvee, candidates of ecotourism among the townspeople opened their homes—for a small fee—to provide lodging for us. Now I recall with some amusement and nostalgia how Steve Del Rosso, then the program director of the PEW Charitable Trust, and I were paired to stay in a house. We were brought there around midnight by members of our contact group. An Estonian lady who did not know a word of English welcomed us. Del Rosso and I had beds in her living room where she had hung a bedsheet like a curtain from the ceiling to separate her bed from ours. She immediately began snoring. To reach the bathroom, a hole in the floor, we would need to remove the curtain and jump over our hostess' bed, something neither of us wanted to do. Thinking about that night, I always wondered if her local lodging for new tourists ever improved.

My fondest memory of Mustvee, however, is my first visit there in the winter. We drove there, on ice, going seventy miles an hour in a bus driven by a former tank driver in the Soviet army. Once in Mustvee, the townspeople put us up in a building that had "good heating." The hallways were lit with red bulbs. The rooms were clean. The next day we learned that we had stayed at the town's brothel. The ladies who worked there took the night off so the townspeople could provide us with warm lodging. The townspeople loved us and we loved them. This is what I call libidinalization of a depressed and regressed society.

In May 1998, CSMHI brought representatives from the three localities, Mustamäe, Mustvee, and Klooga, to Tallinn where they presented their programs and progress at a meeting that included participants from the psychopolitical dialogues, government officials, and news media. The presentations showed what could be achieved in Estonia through the hard work of Estonian and Russian community members supported by both local and CSMHI facilitators. The presentations described models for coexistence and community building that could be applied in other parts of Estonia as well as in other parts of the world. In May 1999, CSMHI convened a final conference in Charlottesville, Virginia, as a capstone to the full five-year initiative in Estonia. In attendance were sixty participants, including conflict resolution specialists, sociologists, psychoanalysts, journalists, diplomats, and historians. Five of our Estonian partners and supporters were also present, including Estonian-Russian parliamentarian Sergei Ivanov; senior policy adviser to the outgoing Estonian prime minister, Paul Lettens; vice president of Euro University and professor at the Institute of International and Social Studies, Peeter Vares; Mustamäe local coordinator Ly Krikk; and contact group leader, Endel Talvik.

There are inherent difficulties in scientifically evaluating the effectiveness of the Tree Model, just as there are in evaluating the progress of an individual psychoanalysis. The psychopolitical dialogues in Estonia, for example, were influenced by and exerted influence on many variables at many levels. First, there were the participants' own attitudes and feelings, their personalities, their positions and level of influence in the government or society, and their personal investment in interethnic dialogue. External political events that took place during the dialogue period within or between the two parties involved also affected the meetings. The duration of the dialogue series and the amount of funding available to support it determined in some ways the scope of what was accomplished. Some of the most critical elements, but also the most difficult to measure, were the unconscious shared perceptions and resistances held by the participants and how these may have changed in the course of the dialogues. Did the Estonian, Russian, and Russian-speaking participants alter any of the unspoken perceptions that they share with other members of their ethnic group?

Many of the changes caused by the dialogue process cannot be reduced to statistical terms; in fact, empirical research focusing on a single facet of government or society can even be misleading, as it can never tell the whole story, and may not produce any data on what really matters. CSMHI's experience is that the best way (and indeed perhaps the only way) to evaluate this kind of work is through detailed recording and reporting and, when possible, videotaping of the process itself. While such "anecdotal" evidence is sometimes dismissed out of hand as being trivial or unscientific, it is the only way to show what happens in the human psyche (in individuals as well as in large groups), and the only way to integrate all the complex levels and variables involved without distorting them. When the process is documented systematically and carefully, it can give clues to what has happened "inside" the participants and can indicate their potential to act upon what they have learned in their continuing interaction with members of the opposing group. This, after all, is the goal: to promote peaceful coexistence in a democratic environment and prevent the kinds of interactions that lead to violence and conflict.[211]

The most visible evidence that the Tree Model was successful in Estonia is the degree to which the community projects and institutions founded during the process continued on their own after CSMHI's involvement had ended. Some received direct support from the Estonian government and others sought funding from other sources. Endnote 212 presents some examples of the concrete outcomes of the application of the Tree Model in Estonia and indications of its sustainability and suitability for replication.[212] This list does not include reference to our work in Klooga, which I will summarize here.

How can I describe Klooga as it existed in early 1996, the first time my CSMHI colleagues and I were taken there? Think of a three-mile long and one-mile wide garbage dump, virtually in ruins. Klooga is only seven miles from Paldiski, the site of a former Soviet nuclear plant. During the Soviet times the Soviet nuclear navy was in Paldiski, and Klooga housed a Soviet military installation. Most of Klooga—like Paldiski—had been off-limits to Estonians, but after the withdrawal of the Soviet military from Estonia, barracks, houses, apartments, an officers' club, a hospital, libraries, and children's' playgrounds became available to Estonians who wanted to find inexpensive housing and settle in this area. Most Estonians who had just arrived had relocated from the nearby capital city, Tallinn, and were struggling economically. In old Soviet-style apartment complexes where hundreds of families could live, only a few apartments were reasonably safe to house the newcomers. The infrastructure was gone and reliable heating systems were nonexistent. There was no garbage collection and there was no law enforcement. I heard that there might be two policemen stationed in nearby Paldiski.

I recall being driven to Klooga for the first time in Endel's car one cold day. We parked beside a little waterfall that might have been a pretty place during Soviet times. There was a small coffee house nearby, which was closed. In my mind's eye, I could imagine Soviet officers and their families relaxing outside the coffee house, listening to the noise of the water. Now, as we looked around quickly, we were careful not to leave the car unattended for a long time since Endel told me that it might be vandalized. Then we drove to the center of Klooga and met some people who were waiting for us. Klooga's population—about 2,000 individuals at that time—was half newly arrived Estonians and half Russians (including a few Russian speakers, such as Armenians). The Russians in Klooga were mostly noncitizens, primarily women with children who were left behind when the base was shut down. The whereabouts of many of the husbands was unknown. Thus, when CSMHI arrived, Klooga was in some sense a "dump" full of people searching for a better life: Estonians with limited resources and the discarded wives and children of Soviet military personnel. The downtrodden nature of the population was compounded by the physical dilapidation of Klooga.

I first thought that the former Soviet military had ruined the place as they withdrew from Klooga in an expression of their humiliation and rage over being kicked out of a location that they considered theirs. My perception was incorrect. I learned later that the former Soviet military left their barracks, apartments, and an officer's house in an orderly fashion. Someone told me that the military even left behind flowers in the vases in the dining area of the hospital. It was mostly the newcomers who had vandalized this place; Klooga's ramshackle state was an expression of the Estonians' rage. Of course, poor Estonians were searching for anything that they could use. They had no use, however, for Russian books, although they all knew Russian. Thus, the inside of the former Soviet library in Klooga was filled with hundreds and hundreds of books that were piled up on the floor, their shelves having been taken away.

Soon I learned new facts. Since there were no reliable heating systems, the Russians who remained in Klooga and the "newcomer" Estonians had a hard time in the winter months. Mothers were afraid that their children might freeze to death, so people went after anything they could burn to heat their apartments and houses. Thus, doors, windows of empty apartments and houses, bookshelves from the library, and so on were taken. Vandalism and crime spread and generalized, becoming facts of life even during warm weather. No true sense of community existed. Klooga housed a regressed society. Since Russians and Estonians did not know each other and since the political situation in Estonia had turned upside down only a few years earlier, the ethnic division was severe.

CSMHI's aim in Klooga, therefore, was to develop some level of community cohesion without causing further interethnic conflict. Russians (and some Russian speakers) who were left in Estonia, whether they were citizens or noncitizens of the new state, had nowhere to go. New Russia, having its own economic and political problems, would not take Russians living in Estonia into Russia. Thus, it was obligatory that a form of coexistence would have to take place within Estonia's boundaries between Estonians and Russians (and Russian speakers). We thought that if we could help to evolve a peaceful coexistence between ethnic groups in Klooga, we could provide a model for peaceful coexistence in the whole country.

My own feelings about our choice of Klooga as a place to work was that we were experimenting with solving an impossible task. To tell the truth, I had no idea how to go about this experiment, except to begin it; we turned to our contact group and Endel, its leader, to find ten Estonians and ten Russians, form a dialogue group, and meet with them once a month. They were told that if they, after about a year or so of discussions among themselves, came up with a project that would benefit the community, we (CSMHI) would give them $50,000. At that time in Estonia in a place like Klooga, this was a considerable amount of money. I now think that one cannot even buy a good missile for this amount of money. For the sake of large-group identity, we spend more money maiming or killing people than giving them a place where they can work, play, and laugh.

Endel, in conducting the discussion with the twenty individuals, would "copy" what we had done with the original psychopolitical dialogue groups, as I described in the previous chapter. Endel and his lovely family lived not far from Klooga, in an apartment complex between Klooga and Tallinn. Once I was driven by their home and met Endel's children playing in a field in front of the apartment complex. During our five years of intensive work there, I can remember only one occasion when CSMHI members were invited into a house of an Estonian or Russian living in Estonia. In time, I sensed that this was due to cramped living spaces and their lack of financial means to be good hosts. Endel's living near Klooga was a wonderful bonus as he could go to Klooga whenever he thought he was needed. Like most Estonians, Endel is rather silent and does not pour out his emotions. But he turned out to be the best "psychoanalyst" we could find for the problems in Klooga and he began to conduct the dialogues there.

Later, as our project in Klooga was coming to an end, I interviewed Endel about his own experiences. He told me how difficult it had been for him to initiate meaningful dialogue among the twenty persons. Initially, they demanded that the $50,000 be used for a new heating system. They would talk about nothing else. Surely, they needed a heating system, but giving them the money right away would be against the aim of the project. Endel and CSMHI wanted these people, the Klooga Group, to "learn" how to speak with one another and develop a democratic nucleus for the village. The village had no mayor and no official leader, and the authorities in the county where Klooga is located paid no attention to this miserable place. Endel told me about the people's hopelessness and how their feelings would be transferred to him. "I needed a stiff drink after each meeting there," he recalled. It was Endel and his assistants' commitment to this project that changed the twenty people, and they, working with other Estonians and Russians in the community, eventually evolved into an NGO and chose their own leader, with Endel as their consultant.

When there were conflicts between certain individuals in the Klooga Group, he visited them separately, listened to them, and "interpreted" resistances, while trying to avoid negative intrusions into the process that the group had begun. When the CSMHI faculty from the United States visited the place every three or four months, we were basically put in the position of observers. We only "supervised" Endel, although in fact, he did not need much supervision. I learned a great deal from this man who is much younger than I am. Eventually, through the efforts of the Klooga Group and then the NGO, a cohesive community was built in Klooga, and Estonians and Russians learned to coexist peacefully.

When we began working in Klooga our hopes for success were not very high—the challenges of daily life there seemed well beyond the reach of what we could offer. But what happened in Klooga surprised us all and happily proved us wrong. Since Klooga's inhabitants had little hope for the future and nowhere else to go, eventually the Klooga Group viewed our team, as well as Endel's presence, as a genuine resource for support. We became for them a source for libidinalization. They could slowly internalize and utilize our compromise functions for the development of their community. In clinical settings, we see a similar process when a child or a regressed adult patient slowly borrows and utilizes their analyst's ego functions. The people in Klooga joined the group in cleaning up their village. This was not an easy task, but hard work as a group became another source for libidinalization.

Over the next three years, Russians and Estonians in Klooga got together, organized a politically informed, democratic NGO, and elected Olga Kamyshan, a Russian woman from the original Klooga Group, as its first director. With $50,000 from CSMHI, they rented and renovated the town's old Soviet library and transformed it into a community center. Men and women, Estonians and Russians, old and young, put their energy into building a "home." Certainly this village needed a community center where village people could gather for social or educational events, but nostalgia for the Klooga of Soviet times also played a role in building this center. The Russians in the NGO were openly nostalgic about the comfort and beauty of Klooga as it had existed when an orderly Soviet military was there. They recalled how nice the officers' club was. Mait Prass, the first Estonian to move to Klooga (from Tallinn), was also nostalgic about the beauty of the Soviet military clubhouse. During the last days of the Soviets in Estonia, Estonians were allowed to come to Klooga, and Mait remembered the beauty of the preruined village. The community center, in a sense, was to reincarnate its old beauty and orderliness. Slowly, the center became a place where everyone could come for learning (such as through computer, English, and Estonian classes) and for play. Children had a safe place to go after school. Teenagers gathered there too, and the center housed holiday celebrations for the whole community.

The process of achieving agreement about what to focus on, learning to work together, finding a building, and navigating the bureaucratic hurdles required to renovating it and turn it into the community center was not always smooth. There were occasions when personal or ethnic identity conflicts and other "hidden" sentiments and thoughts got in the way and needed to be brought into the open. Participants in the Klooga Group initially were very concerned with crime in Klooga. If they opened a community center, furnished it, and put computers in it, they were afraid that criminals would steal them. Thus they proposed asking some members of Kaitseliit for protection.

Since I had never heard of Kaitseliit, I quickly gathered information about it. Kaitseliit is the name given to a type of Estonian militia, something like a national guard. As the Soviet government collapsed, some Estonian members of the Soviet army did not give up their weapons. Instead, they organized, I believe with the blessing of the Estonian government, into a kind of militia organization. Their original aim appeared to be to serve as a line of defense should Russia attempt to invade Estonia. In those days the shared feeling of "disappearing" was reflected in societal/military activities. Now Kaitseliit members were everywhere. They practiced target shooting, and they could be hired for protection from the mafia organizations that had emerged during the uncertain days after Estonia's reindependence.

Some Estonian participants in the Klooga Group wanted to turn to Kaitseliit for protection from the "criminal elements," but the local Russian members perceived this as a threatening move. Kaitseliit was basically anti-Russian. But the community, including the Russians in it, needed its help. I sensed that the Russians in Klooga were finding themselves having to choose between two devils—the mafia and Kaitseliit— and this issue had emotional repercussions.

During a visit in January 1997, the CSMHI facilitating group suggested that the Russian members of the Klooga Group speak openly about their dilemma during their group meetings. When this occurred, there was a kind of relief among the Russian as well as Estonian members who regularly met. The Russians did not need to like Kaitseliit, but under these circumstances they might depend on it because for them the mafia was worse than Kaitseliit. Estonians, of course, had no objections to using Kaitseliit to help protect against the criminal element.

A Russian speaker within the Klooga Group offered to be the organizer of the future community center and to be in charge of planned community activities. When I was there I noted that the Klooga Group had already discussed his candidacy for this job and accepted him as a kind of program director. I also sensed that this was a compromise. The future program director was not going to be an ethnic Estonian or an ethnic Russian, but a Russian speaker, an ethnic Armenian. He offered to

stay in the future community building only during the daytime. He said
that if he stayed at the building at night, he could be killed by the local
mafia. When this issue came up, no one in the Klooga Group expected
the Armenian member to be a hero or risk death. At first they thought
that some members of Kaitseliit would stay at the building after dark and
protect it. During these discussions, I noted that the Klooga Group was
becoming more and more a working group, mostly due to Endel and his
assistants' regular visits there. This was a very significant development.
As I indicated in the previous chapter, the internalization of the Soviet
system had made ordinary persons living under this system unable to
negotiate issues among themselves in a democratic fashion and to come
up with compromise formations without loosing their integrity.

The Klooga Group did not ask CSMHI's advice for solving the security matter. In any case, they knew more about the local criminal elements
than we could. Later, as I learned from Endel, who kept me and my
CSMHI colleagues in Charlottesville informed through telephone calls
and mail, opening up the discussion of Kaitseliit and discussing identity
issues created more closeness among the members of the Klooga Group.
In the end, the group agreed to work "hand-in-hand," without asking for
help from Kaitseliit. In fact, this is the name they gave their new NGO,
"Hand-in-Hand."

When I interviewed Endel after our Klooga project was over, he told
me of an unusual "test" for future success that had just taken place only a
few weeks before our January 1997 trip to Klooga, at a time when the
Klooga Group was still wondering if they should ask for Kaitseliit's help.
In order to illustrate the newly found "coexistence" in their village, the
Klooga Group decided to have a common outdoor Christmas tree. Some
people from the village got together and decorated the Christmas tree
with fifty light bulbs. According to Endel, everyone in Klooga, including
him, was anxious. They considered decorating the outdoors Christmas
tree as a test: if the bulbs on the tree were not stolen by the next day or
throughout the Christmas season, it would mean that village people
working together would triumph over the threatening criminal elements.
The next day the village people rushed to the decorated Christmas tree.
They counted the bulbs. There were forty-nine bulbs. They were enor-
mously relieved. Only one bulb had been stolen and this "token" theft was
not threatening. They had passed the test. This test encouraged them to
continue working together.

I should state that Klooga was a "hot" location for a historical reason.
Not only had it once housed the "occupiers" (Soviet army), but it had also

been the site of a Nazi concentration camp. When we were there, the only remaining physical signs of the camp were a few stones here and there that were identified as having been part of it. In fact, we were told of only two Estonians from this area who could recall the existence of the concentration camp, although I never met them. During WWII, Estonians were divided in their loyalties: some fought with the Nazis, some with the Soviets, and others remained Estonian nationalists. When Estonia became independent again, these former divisions were hidden sensitive issues and nearly impossible to talk about. When a small country like Estonia regains its independence, the population sees itself as "one nation." As they minimize the differences among themselves to shore up their national identity, they typically increase their projections onto others. In this case, the Estonians who fought with Nazis and their descendents joined with Estonians who fought with the Soviets and their offspring to create a "new" Estonian identity, and this most likely increased their projections onto the minority, Russians and Russian speakers.

During CSMHI's psychopolitical dialogues in Estonia, issues concerning Estonians' divided loyalties during WWII came up and were discussed in some of the small groups. In Klooga, however, neither CSMHI nor Endel were able to create an atmosphere where WWII-related divisions and events could be discussed in-depth. Ethnic issues were often discussed outside of the official business of the Klooga Group, but they would eventually come to Endel's attention and then he would deal with them. All members of the community were far more focused on basic survival needs, such as security and warm shelter, than they were on history. But repercussions of the past were active all the same. One person from the CSMHI team, psychoanalyst Maurice Apprey, began to look into derivatives of Klooga's past—the "poison" of its being a place where there was a Nazi concentration camp—and shared it with Endel, so that he, in turn, would be sensitive to the villagers' possible reaction to living in such a place.

The fledgling Estonian military was using a field adjacent to Klooga for live target practice, a situation which greatly concerned Klooga's inhabitants, both Estonian and Russian, because it posed a real danger to them and to their children. This issue was brought to Endel's attention very early in his involvement with Klooga. A hidden script went something like this: "We Estonians can now identify with our aggressors. Intellectually, we know that today Klooga is home to Estonian citizens and Estonian children, too, but in our minds we continue to see this place as a Soviet military base. Thus, we bomb it, repeatedly."

There were no facilities—houses or clubs—in the field adjacent to Klooga where the military would gather with their equipment and "bomb." Therefore, they could have chosen any other place in Estonia for their target practice. But they insisted on "bombing" Klooga, the "Russian village," even though it was no longer Russian in reality. The almost daily heavy artillery fire on the field neighboring Klooga was truly dangerous.

The field where live ammunition fell was separated from the village by a twenty-foot-wide dirt road. We were afraid that children playing nearby could be injured or killed. There was one incident when an Estonian villager tried to take a shortcut and went through the field with his old tractor, and his tractor was hit. Incredibly, he survived. Initially, the military would inform the village people when the "bombs" were to be dropped, but eventually they began to perform their target practice without giving notice. This made the situation worse.

So, we had to devise a plan to directly illustrate to Estonian authorities the danger that existed. On July 4, 1997, CSMHI threw a big community-wide party in Klooga. (As noted earlier in this chapter, we had earlier held a Fourth of July party in Mustvee.) We made no fuss about the United States and its independence, but everyone was told what the Fourth of July was all about. We also invited several of the Estonian and Russian speaking participants from the original psychopolitical dialogue series, including some parliamentarians, to come with their families. Most of them lived in Tallinn, and we were aware that they had never been to Klooga before. The Russian embassy even sent their second-ranking diplomat. In any event, the stage was set.

After the party, I invited our guests on a walk around the village, directing them to take the dirt road that separated the village from the field where the live artillery fell. I hoped that the "bombing" practice would resume so that our guests could experience what it was like to live in Klooga—a "hot" village that was under "siege." It was truly a place of intense aggression and mixed emotions. Sure enough, the deafening explosions soon began. The target practice was impossible to ignore and provided unmistakable evidence as to what Klooga's inhabitants lived with every day. However, in spite of seeing the dangers of this practice for themselves, our guests from the parliament still could not bring themselves to do anything about it. It appeared that to do so would have been politically difficult and would have conflicted with their image of Klooga as an "enemy" place, even though they actually witnessed some Estonian kids playing there.

Among the parliamentarians who came to our party that day was

Arvo Haug. Haug practiced psychiatry before becoming a politician and had been an invaluable member of our original psychopolitical dialogue series. I found him to be a most likeable person. We also got to know his wife, a beautiful lady who was the lead singer in the Estonian opera's chorus section. I fondly recall being invited to the dressing-room area of the opera building in Tallinn and mingling with the artists. As we got to know her, we learned that Mrs. Haug was also very sensitive to children's welfare. As we walked around the field that was being "bombed," I could see she was disturbed by it, while her husband, a big man, had to protect his nationalist pride. We counted on Mrs. Haug to speak further about Klooga in private with her husband. During our next trip to Estonia, however, we learned that the "bombing" of Klooga was still going on.

In March 1998, I made another trip to Estonia alone without the members of my team. The reason for this was to increase our presence in order to have more face-to-face dialogues with Endel and his assistants. I was informed that the "bombs" were still falling on Klooga. On March 24, Endel and I visited Tiit Mae, who then was the chief officer of Keila County, which includes Klooga. Since I was very concerned that someone, especially a child, might be hurt or killed, I went against our general principle of not giving advice to local organizations we work with and advised Mae to help us stop the shelling of Klooga. He agreed that to have military exercises that could hurt people was illogical and that there was no reason to shoot without warning or to expose people to the noise of heavy guns. But, in the long run, Mae, too, was unable to assist us. Then I tried to talk to some parliamentarians from Tallinn (some of them participants from the original dialogue series, including Arvo Haug), but I found great resistance to stopping the "bombing" of Klooga. As one parliamentarian put it, "This place now belongs to us. We can do whatever we want there. The Estonian Army is our pride and joy." I was very impressed with how the Estonians still held onto the image of Klooga as a Russian place. This phenomenon shows the power of the unconscious in societal, political, and military affairs.

I had talks with Endel about the psychology of humiliation and the wish to reverse it even in strange and sometimes dangerous ways. We also discussed the concept of identification with the aggressor.[213] My hope was that somehow Endel would pass such understanding to the Klooga NGO and help them reverse their passivity. Endel worked further on increasing the NGO's political consciousness and organizing skills. My colleagues and I were very pleased when we later learned that Mait Prass had initiated a political process: one hundred Klooga residents wrote a letter to then Estonian president Lennart Meri and asked that the shooting stop. Living in the United States, we may think that this was a natural, in fact, easy thing to do. Living under communism and assimilating the rules and regulations of that political system, however, made this effort by the villagers a drastic one. Meanwhile, Tiit Mae passed a local law prohibiting military activities on county property. But the military responded by saying that the property belonged to them. They accused Mait of being a Russian spy and ordered the finance department to audit his and his wife's finances (more identification with the aggressor or oppressor). By that time, Klooga began to receive national attention. Later, I heard that a television station sent its reporters and cameras to the village, and there was a big fuss about the "bombing" of Klooga. Our little community, we noticed, had learned how to be assertive and use political and media pressure for its benefit. Ultimately, the villagers succeeded in stopping the "bombing." The original image of Klooga as a place of aggression thus began to be modified.

Another unexpected but major factor for our success in the libidinalization of the regressed Klooga community was the making of a documentary film on our project. Award-winning Canadian filmmaker Allan King, who is known by many as the "father of film vérité," had become interested in CSMHI's work in the Baltics and had attended one of the psychopolitical dialogue workshops in 1994. After several years of research, development, and fundraising for the film, Allan traveled to the Baltics and spent seven weeks filming in Klooga in the summer of 1997. The result is the film *The Dragon's Egg: Making Peace on the Wreckage of the Twentieth Century*, which offers a vivid illustration of the community-building process in Klooga and of CSMHI's methodology.[214]

The Dragon's Egg has no narrator or script and consists only of the words, activities, and meetings of the Klooga Group as its members worked together, argued, cleaned their village, struggled, and triumphed in the process of forming an NGO, electing a local leader, renovating the community center, and seeking a better life for themselves and their children. The film movingly illustrates Olga Kamyshan's inner struggles with her ethnic identity (her father was an ethnic Estonian who had served in the Soviet army and had been "Russified"), and her assuming the leadership role, and Endel's tactful handling of local conflicts as well as ethnic conflicts. While the members of CSMHI appear briefly in this film, it is about the people, including children, living in Klooga at that time. For me, it tells heart-warming stories of human dignity, while it also shows the ugly side of human nature.

The filmmaking added a dimension to the process in Klooga that was very beneficial. The experience of being followed around and filmed for seven weeks gave Klooga Group members a sense that someone cared about Klooga, that what they did mattered and could make a difference. Allan is a kind man with white hair and a white beard; he is like a slim and fit Santa Claus. The villagers responded to him in a trusting manner, and they did not feel that he was intruding into their privacy.

On March 8, 1999, some of my colleagues from CSMHI joined Allan for the world premiere of the *The Dragon's Egg*, which was shown in the beautifully restored building of the Klooga Community Center. The center was like a jewel, polished and ready to exhibit the pride of the village. Many people in Klooga had volunteered their time to make it beautiful. The villagers painted the inside wall with soothing pastel colors. Where the children would gather, paintings of tigers and trees were added to the walls. There were rooms for future computer classes. One big room would be used for community dances. Earlier, both Estonians and Russians from Klooga had many occasions to get together for joint festivities outdoors, but now the community center gave them an opportunity to get together indoors during cold weather.

The premiere of Allan's film would take place in the big community room. Allan, myself and others from CSMHI, Endel, and some members of the original Klooga Group arrived at the community center an hour or so before the showing of the film. I had not seen the completed renovation of the building until then. We went from room to room, appreciating how much love was invested in this building. Allan was as nervous as a young child who for the first time would appear on the stage of a kindergarten play. It was a cold and snowy night. What if no one showed up for the premiere? What if only a few people came? How would the audience react seeing themselves on the screen? Allan kept looking outside into the darkness, waiting for people to come. Suddenly, only fifteen or so minutes prior to the showing of the film, Klooga inhabitants began to come out of the darkness into their new community center, filling all the available chairs and then some. Their delight in seeing themselves and their Klooga home on film confirmed that what they had accomplished was real, and that this community would be forever changed because of it.[215]

What has happened in Klooga is a symbol of what has happened in Estonia in general. Estonia has evolved as a strong democracy and prospered economically. In early summer of 2003, I went back to Estonia to take part in a gathering of the Eastern European Psychoanalytic Institute, which had been established a few years earlier under the sponsorship of

246 • KILLING IN THE NAME OF IDENTITY

the International Psychoanalytical Association. Its students came from Russia, from the Baltic Republics, and from Eastern European states formerly under communist rule. Students, called "psychoanalytic candidates," and their teachers would meet in different countries for joint classes. This time they were meeting in Haapsalu, a small town in Estonia. I was a guest faculty member and Endel, who played a major role in organizing this meeting, was an official psychoanalytic candidate. One day before and one day after the meeting in Haapsalu, I stayed in Tallinn, which had changed greatly since the first time I had been there in 1996. The "old city" in the center of Tallinn was renovated beautifully and it looked like something from a fairy tale. Tourists were everywhere.

Endel was extremely busy in Haapsalu. But he had enough time to tell me more about a tragic event of which I was already aware: the death of Olga Kamyshan's teenage son in a traffic accident. Olga, the "star" of the Allan King film, had turned out to be a very effective community leader in Klooga. In March of 1999, she ran for a seat in the Estonian parliament. While she did not win, the very fact that she became part of a larger political process was an enormous step, hardly imaginable a few years earlier. When I heard this, I thought that her example was more proof that the Tree Model had been effective in Klooga. Then came the tragedy. When I close my eyes, I see Olga's son in Allan's film talking with other boys about young girls. Endel told me how devastated Olga was after her son's death and how her leadership role was missed. The community center was no longer functional. As Estonia adjusted more and more to its reindependence, the postindependence anxiety about "coexistence" in Klooga was gone. I understood that the place became another typical Estonian village with both its good and bad aspects.

The day after the meeting in Haapsalu was over, I took a lonely walk in Tallinn's beautiful old city. That day my mind was busy thinking about our former activities there at a time when the city—and country—was trying to come back to life after many years of Soviet-era neglect. I passed by a coffee shop and recalled how some years earlier I had seen Arnold Rüütel sitting there by himself. I remembered pulling up a chair and sitting next to him, even though he did not speak English and I did not speak Estonian or Russian. We spoke with hand gestures. He was now, I thought, sitting in the presidential palace. I thought about Ants Paju and others. I wanted to find Peeter Vares, a very kind scholar, who had been the deputy director of the Institute for International and Social Studies in Tallinn while he was attending the psychopolitical dialogue series. Peeter and his people were responsible for organizing our meetings and all the practical things that needed to be done. I realized that I missed them. I also felt nostalgia about my private times with Jaan Kaplinski, an unusual poet in search of the child in himself while valuing everything around him, from his childhood teddy bear to the soil of his farm to the souls of people from diverse backgrounds. I also wanted to go to Klooga and sit by Olga in silence. But I knew that I did not have time to see anybody and I should not call and bother Endel as he was still too busy to assist me.

I amused myself remembering how many Estonian friends used to tell us that they would put up our statues in the old city of Tallinn because of how much we invested in them. But there I was, some years later, walking alone in the old city of Tallinn, just one person of many on the street whom no one paid any particular attention to. Suddenly, my psychoanalytic identity took over. I sensed that I was experiencing a feeling that used to come over me at the end of my analysands' analyses. If their analyses were successful, they would leave me like youngsters, psychologically separating from their parents to find their own autonomy and identities. I knew, however, that unlike youngsters who grow up and still continue relationships with their parents, my analysands who successfully completed their analyses would repress most aspects of their intimate relationship with me. Through various unconscious identifications with me, they would carry me within themselves for the rest of their lives without being aware of doing so. They would not be in physical contact with me any longer or even call me, as should be the case. This realization made me feel good. Somehow, I thought, I existed somewhere in this beautiful country just as I exist in my former analysands, and somehow Estonia would exist in me the rest of my life.

Notes

Chapter 1

1. See Vamık D. Volkan, *The Need to Have Enemies and Allies: From Clinical Practice to International Relationships* (Northvale, NJ: Jason Aronson, 1988).

2. Ibid. In 1988 I developed a concept that connects human societies' need to have enemies and allies to individual childhood development. While growing up, every child attempts to evolve a cohesive sense of self (and a cohesive sense of others, such as his or her mother). A very young child cannot fully experience him or herself as one person: a child has a "good" self when comfortable, well fed, and well cared for. When frustrated, angry, and abandoned, the child has a "bad" self. Around the age of three, the child, for all practical purposes, develops an ability to make "grey" out of the black ("bad") and white ("good") selves: the child develops an integrated, cohesive self. For details on this see: Edith Jacobson, *The Self and the Object World* (New York: International Universities Press, 1964); Margaret S. Mahler, *On Human Symbiosis and the Vicissitudes of Individuation* (New York: International Universities Press,1968); Erik H. Erikson, *Identity and the Life Cycle* (New York: International Universities Press, 1959); Otto F. Kernberg, *Borderline Conditions and Pathological Narcissism* (New York: Jason Aronson, 1975) and *Internal World and External Reality* (New York: Jason Aronson, 1980).

I proposed that this integration is not total. Some "good" and "bad" images remain unintegrated for everyone. To experience them within would induce distress. Children are forced to do something about their unintegrated parts. One of the ways they deal with this problem is to search for permanent "reservoirs" for their unintegrated aspects. Such permanent "reservoirs" are often found in the "cultural amplifiers" of the large group to which the child belongs. (For more on cultural amplifiers see John Mack, "Cultural Amplifiers of Ethnic-Nationalistic Affiliation and Differentiation," paper read at the Committee on International Relations at the Fall Meeting of the Group for the Advancement of

Psychiatry, Cherry Hill, NJ, November 10, 1984.) As they grow, children learn to put (externalize) their unintegrated parts into such reservoirs. For example, the sauna serves as a good "reservoir" for Finnish children, while a pig serves as a "bad" reservoir for Muslim children. Shared and permanent "good" reservoirs prepare a foundation for "we-ness" and permanent and shared "bad" reservoirs become the starting point for a need for societal enemies.

Obviously, large groups have many other reasons for needing enemies and allies, and I have examined many of them in my previous psychopolitical books, such as *The Need to Have Enemies and Allies; Bloodlines: From Ethnic Pride to Ethnic Terrorism* (New York: Farrar, Straus & Giroux, 1997); *Blind Trust: Large Groups and Their Leaders in Times of Crises and Terror* (Charlottesville, VA: Pitchstone Publishing, 2004). My purpose in referring to the earliest motivations for such needs is to remind the reader that, as far as I am concerned, our preoccupations with societal enemies and allies and also with large-group identity issues are very much psychologically determined.

3. Georgia is an ancient country with a history that spans 3,000 years. Anthropologically, Georgians are people unique to the Caucasus. Their language, with its distinctive alphabet (one of fourteen different alphabets in the world), existed in written form as early as 400 CE and is linguistically distant from Slavic and Turkic languages. Christianity, embraced by Georgia in the fourth century, was a milestone in the development of the people's spiritual culture. Between the fourth and seventh centuries, Georgia was a source of contention between the Byzantine and Sassanid Empires, just as it was between the Byzantines and Arabs from the seventh to tenth centuries. The eleventh to thirteenth centuries witnessed Georgia's "golden age," ushered in by the reign of David the Builder, and later, Queen Tamara, when a Georgian-dominated imperium was created that stretched from the Black Sea to the Caspian Sea and included commercial links with both Europe and the Orient.

The invasion of the Caucasus by the Mongols from 1220 onward brought an end to Georgia's renaissance. The fall of Constantinople (today's Istanbul) to the Ottoman Turks in 1453 isolated Georgia from Christendom, and for the next three centuries it became a country over which the Persian and Ottoman Empires competed. In 1783, east Georgia, in accordance with the Georgievsk Treaty, came under Russia's protection. In 1801, Paul I of Russia brought east Georgia under direct Russian rule. As a result of Russo-Turkish and Russo-Persian wars, by the 1870s west Georgian territories also were absorbed by the Russian Empire.

The Russian and Georgian aristocracies were considerably integrated during this period, and absorption into the Russian Empire had certain positive effects, such as higher standards of living, a steadily increasing Georgian population, and infrastructure expansion. But absorption also had negative effects, which continued into the Soviet era. The Georgian Orthodox Church lost its independence to Russian Orthodoxy, though somehow much of the Georgian language and belief systems survived the pressure of "Russification." Georgians, who are themselves divided into different "tribes" or "clans," remained proud of their ancient culture and unique alphabet.

Soon after the 1917 Bolshevik Revolution in Russia, Georgia gained its independence in 1918, although only briefly. It became a Soviet republic in 1921 through the collaboration of the Red Army and local Bolshevik organizations. Georgia, Armenia, and Azerbaijan later were linked as the Transcaucasian Federation, which joined the Soviet Union on December 30, 1922. This federation was dissolved in 1936, and each Transcaucasian republic became a direct member of the Soviet Union.

Though Georgians played a significant role in Soviet politics—Josef Stalin was from Georgia—Georgians were robbed of the experience of administering their own internal and international affairs. Like almost every Soviet republic, Georgia had autonomous ethnic formations within its own territory: Abkhazia, Ajaria, and South Ossetia. The problems associated with reindependence reactivated ethnopolitical tensions between ethnic Georgians and two non-Georgian groups, the Abkhazians and South Ossetians. In 1990, the accumulated grievances and identity-driven political aims of the Abkhazians and South Ossetians resulted in their de facto declarations of independence from Georgia. Their secessionist attempts took place within the context of aggravated Georgian nationalism.

Few people paid serious attention to their claims since a "parade of identity-driven sovereignties" was occurring at this time, with various union republics and their smaller regions and areas proclaiming their presidents one after another. Within Georgia, however, the situation became tragic as two severe ethnic conflicts eventually broke out, first in South Ossetia and then in Abkhazia. As a result, people began killing other people in the name of large-group identity and thousands of people were killed, hundreds of thousands became refugees, and Georgian society as a whole was deeply traumatized.

4. For details see S. Neil MacFarlane, Larry Minear, and Stephen D. Shanfield, *Armed Conflict in Georgia: A Case Study of Humanitarian Action and Peacekeeping* (Providence, RI: Thomas J. Watson, Jr. Institute for International Studies, 1996).

5. When this incident was examined in Moscow, no apology was offered.

6. See Volkan, *Bloodlines* and Joyce Neu and Vamık D. Volkan, *Developing a Methodology for Conflict Prevention: The Case of Estonia* (Atlanta, GA: Carter Center Special Report Series, Winter 1999).

Chapter 2

7. In collecting data from individuals who belong to a traumatized society, I have developed a technique that I call "therapeutic data collection." I tell people that by hearing their life story, I am allowed a better understanding of what has happened to their people. I also guide them as they narrate the milestones of their lives. My aim is not to make a full diagnosis of an individual's personality organization, symptom formation, or psychosexual fixation points. Rather, I seek a better understanding of the intertwining of their internal worlds and the mental representations of external events, mainly events that have been traumatic for these individuals and their group. The perception and experience of shared trauma echoes in traumatized individuals' internal worlds and reflects psychological processes. Often such individual psychological processes are shared across the traumatized group. Bringing them to the surface can assist an analyst in developing strategies that respond to the psychological and realistic needs of those who belong to the group. (For an example, see note 9.) When appropriate, the interviewer may also share with the traumatized individual his or her findings on the psychological processes initiated by the traumas that have been "hidden." This is done when the interviewer feels it will help increase the traumatized individual's coping mechanisms. I must emphasize here that "therapeutic data collection" should only be carried out by professional persons with proper psychoanalytic or psychodynamic training.

8. For political reasons, Abkhazian-language schools were closed in the 1940s.

9. This aspect of the interview with Dali brought attention to a psychological difficulty among the IDPs that would likely not have been identified through a simple question-and-answer form of data collection. Subsequently, through our Georgian hosts, we initiated a process that would allow IDPs who had lost their original identity cards to secure new ones from the authorities in Tbilisi, emphasizing that they should be issued in a respectful manner so as not to induce humiliation. We further suggested that the new identification cards should denote the IDP's original place of birth or residence.

10. Vamık D. Volkan, *Cyprus—War and Adaptation: A Psychoanalytic History of Two Ethnic Groups in Conflict* (Charlottesville, VA: University of Virginia Press, 1979).

11. Michael Sebek describes an identical phenomenon that occurred under a totalitarian regime in Czechoslovakia. See Michael Sebek, "Anality in the Totalitarian System and the Psychology of Post-Totalitarian Society," *Mind and Human Interaction* 4 (1992): 52–59.

Chapter 3

12. The psychological literature refers to a phenomenon called the "replacement child." Several authors have noted that after the death of a child, a mother who has been guilt-ridden, depressed, phobic, or compulsive may replace her lost child with another who still lives. E. O. Poznanski wrote, "Replacing a child with another allows the parents partially to deny the first child's death. The replacement child then acts as a barrier to the parental acknowledgement of death, since the real child exists who is a substitute." E. O. Poznanski, "The 'Replacement Child': A Saga of Unresolved Parental Grief," *Behavioral Pediatrics* 81 (1972): 1090–1193. Vamık D. Volkan and Gabriele Ast in *Siblings in the Unconscious and Psychopathology* (Madison, CT: International Universities Press, 1997) describe how a mother who had lost a child may "deposit" the mental representation of the dead child into the developing self-representation of the second child. Replacement children can deal with what had been "deposited" in them in various ways, some of them adaptive and others pathological.

13. Sigmund Freud's early theories refer to external trauma as the main factor of psychopathology. Sigmund Freud, "Project for a Scientific Psychology," in *The Origins of Psycho-Analysis*, 347–351 (New York: Basic Books, 1893–1954); "Introductory Lectures to Psychoanalysis," in vol. 15 of *The Standard Edition of the Complete Psychological Works of Sigmund Freud*, ed. James Strachey, 5–239 (London: Hogarth Press, 1917–1964); and "Beyond the Pleasure Principle" in vol. 18 of *The Standard Edition of the Complete Psychological Works of Sigmund Freud*, ed. James Strachey, 1–65 (London: Hogarth Press, 1920–1955). Subsequently, Freud focused on inner fantasy that becomes connected with the traumatic event. In "Inhibitions, Symptoms, and Anxiety" in vol. 20 of *The Standard Edition of the Complete Psychological Works of Sigmund Freud*, ed. by James Strachey, 75–175 (London: Hogarth Press, 1926–1959), Freud described trauma as a state of psychic helplessness, which is actually experienced. Thus, he differentiated traumatic events from situations where there is an expectation of danger.

Most psychoanalysts after Freud focused on the inner fantasy that becomes connected with the trauma and not on the external trauma itself. Thus, until the last decade or so, psychoanalysts did not pay enough attention to external events. This situation has now changed.

14. Howard F. Stein, "Personal Thoughts on the Journey from Trauma to Resilience," *Mind and Human Interaction* 13 (2003): 90–98.

15. In 2004, well-known child psychoanalyst Henri Parens in *Renewal of Life:*

Healing from the Holocaust (Rockville, MD: Schreiber Publishing, 2004) gave us a clear example of creative response to trauma. Parens, in the seventh decade of his life, introduced us to a special child—himself at age twelve as he escapes from Rivesaltes, a concentration camp in Vichy, France. We meet his mother, also in Rivesaltes and later murdered in Auschwitz, who found the courage to let her son go, encouraging him to escape. This mother's courage, I think, remained alive in her son as he transformed an existence burdened by unspeakable trauma and loss into a life of caring, healing, and creativity. As a psychoanalyst, Parens worked with children and contributed greatly to the question of how aggression develops and how it is shaped in each of us. See Henri Parens, *The Development of Aggression in Early Childhood* (New York: Jason Aronson, 1979).

16. For an extensive study of trauma and dissociation, see Ira Brenner, *Psychic Trauma: Dynamics, Symptoms and Treatment* (New York: Jason Aronson, 2004).

17. Vamık D. Volkan, "Traumatized Societies and Psychological Care: Expanding the Concept of Preventive Medicine," *Mind and Human Interaction* 11 (2000): 177–194.

18. Here I do not deal with children's reactions to loss. Until a child firmly establishes mental representations of others and thus can hold on to others' various images when he or she is physically separated from them, the dynamics of the child's mourning is different than the dynamics of an adult's mourning. For a review see Vamık Volkan, *Linking Objects and Linking Phenomena: A Study of the Forms, Symptoms, Metapsychology and Therapy of Complicated Mourning* (New York: International Universities Press, 1981).

19. Veikko Tähkä, "Dealing with Object Loss," *Scandinavian Psychoanalytic Review* 1 (1984): 13–33.

20. When identifications with the images and functions of what has been lost are selective and "healthy," the mourning process is considered "normal." The mourner, after going through the pain of grief and after spending considerable energy reviewing the mental representation of the lost person or thing, "gains" something from his or her experiences. Most of the identifications take place unconsciously.

Unhealthy identifications can also occur. If a mourner related to the lost person or thing with excessive ambivalence while this person was still alive or the thing still existed, and if the loss is associated with trauma and helpless rage, the mourner may end up identifying with the representation of the lost item in an unhealthy manner. Such a mourner is unable to create a selective and enriching identification. Instead, they assimilate the representation of the lost item "in toto" into their self-representation. See Joseph Smith, "On the Work of Mourning," in *Bereavement: Its Psychological Aspects,* ed. B. Scoenberg, I. Gerber, A. Weiner, et. al., 18–25 (New York: Columbia University Press, 1975). Accordingly, the love and the hate (ambivalence) that originally connected the mourner to the lost person or thing now turn the mourner's self-representation into a battleground. The struggle between love and hate is now felt within the mourner's self-representation that assimilated the ambivalently related representation of the lost item through a total identification with it. Sigmund Freud called this condition "melancholia." Sigmund Freud, "Mourning and Melancholia," vol. 14 of *The Standard Edition of the Complete Psychological Works of Sigmund Freud,* ed. by James Strachey, 243–258 (London: Hogarth Press, 1917–1957).

When hate toward the assimilated representation of the lost person or thing becomes dominant, some mourners may even attempt to kill themselves (suicide) in order to "kill" the assimilated mental representation. In other words, they want to blast off or choke, psychologically speaking, the mental representation of the lost item within their self-representation, and accordingly shoot or hang themselves. Melancholia (depression) after a loss can be fatal for the mourner.

21. To a great extent, a person who is destined to be a perennial mourner cannot identify with the selected enriching aspects of the mental representation of the lost person or thing. On the other hand, the mourner does not end up identifying totally with the representation of the lost item. In other words, the mourner cannot go through a "normal" mourning process or cannot develop melancholia (depression). Instead, the mourner keeps the mental representation of the lost item as a specific and unassimilated "foreign body" and constantly relates to it. The perennial mourner is torn between a strong yearning for a restored presence of the lost person or thing and an equally deep dread that the lost item might be confronted. The presence of this "foreign body" (psychoanalysts call this an introject) provides an illusion of choice, and in this way it reduces anxiety. But having such a "foreign body" within oneself means a continuation of an internal struggle with it.

22. I coined the term "linking objects" in 1972. See Vamık D. Volkan, "The Linking Objects of Pathological Mourners," *Archives of General Psychiatry* 27 (1972): 215–222.

23. Linking objects should not be confused with childhood transitional objects such as a teddy bear. See Donald Winnicott, "Transitional Objects and Transitional Phenomena," *International Journal of Psycho-Analysis* 34 (1953): 89–97. A transitional object, psychologically speaking, represents the first not-me, but it is never totally not-me. It links not-me with mother-me and it is a temporary construction toward a sense of reality. See Phyllis Greenacre, "The Fetish and the Transitional Object," in *Emotional Growth* 1, 315–334 (New York: International Universities Press, 1969–1974).

Linking objects contain high-level symbolism. They must be thought of as tightly packed symbols whose significance is bound up in the conscious and unconscious nuances of the relationship that preceded the loss. A linking object is an external bridge between the mental representations of the mourner and that of the lost person or thing, just as the introject serves as an internal bridge.

There are various types of items that can evolve into linking objects, such as personal possessions of the deceased or an actual piece of the lost thing; a gift or a symbolic farewell note; something that the lost person used to extend his or her senses or body functions such as a camera; or a "last-minute object," which is something that was at hand when the mourner learned of the death of an important someone or the disappearance of a significant item. Some mourners create their own linking objects, such as a painting (or Khundadze's poems) and still others utilize living linking objects.

24. Initially in my decades-long study on grief and mourning, I focused on the pathological aspects of linking objects. In other words, I considered their existence only as a sign of a mourner's "freezing" his or her mourning process. I later wrote about the linking object as a source of inspiration that gave direction to creativity in some individuals. Complicated mourning still remains in such individuals, but now it is expressed in art forms. It is not proper, I think, to refer to someone who created such a thing as the Taj Mahal as "pathological." See Vamık Volkan and Elizabeth Zintl, *Life After Loss: The Lessons of Grief* (New York: Charles Scribner's Sons, 1993).

25. Donald W. Winnicott states that "in playing, and perhaps only in playing, the child or adult is free to be creative." Donald W. Winnicott, *Playing and Reality* (London: Tavistock Publications, 1971), 53. Also see P. B. Neubaurer, "Playing: Technical Implications," in *The Many Meanings of Play*, ed. by Albert J. Solnit, D. J. Cohen, and P. B. Neubaurer, 100–122 (New Haven, CT: Yale University Press, 1993). Gabriele Ast, a psychoanalyst practicing in Munich Germany, worked with a young woman named "Gitta" who was born with many physical deformities and who had gone through nearly two dozen surgical procedures from babyhood until she was in her early twenties. Surgical procedures and long and extremely difficult hospitalizations traumatized Gitta. As a result, she had a defective body image. During her treatment, she "played" for nine months by fixing her apartment. Her treatment clearly illustrated how her repairing of her external environment was connected with her efforts to repair her internal world and her defective body image. Vamık D. Volkan and Gabriele Ast, "Curing Gitta's

'Leaking Body:' Actualized Unconscious Fantasies and Therapeutic Play," *Journal of Clinical Psychoanalysis* 10 (2001): 557–596. The meaning of the Kachavara family's building "our Vamık's room" is similar to Gitta's work on her apartment.

26. The concept "survivor syndrome," which includes guilt, was first described by William Niederland after his extensive studies of Holocaust survivors. See William Niederland, "The Problem of the Survivor," *Journal of Hillside Hospital* 10 (1961): 233–247.

27. Özker Yashın, *Oglum Savas'a Mektuplar (Letters to My Son Savas)* (Nicosia: Çevre Yayınları, 1965), 18.

28. Özker Yashın, *Kıbrıs Mektubu (The Cyprus Letter)* (Istanbul: Varlık Yayınları, 1958) and *Kanlı Kıbrıs (Bloody Cyprus)* (Istanbul: Varlık Yayınları, 1964). For further information about the events in Cyprus, see Volkan, *Cyprus— War and Adaptation.*

29. Tähkä, "Dealing with Object Loss."

Chapter 4

30. See Volkan, *Blind Trust,* in which I study the development of large-group identity in detail.

31. Donald Winnicott, "Transitional Objects and Phenomena." A transitional object occupies a space between "not-me" and "mother-me." Also see Phyllis Greenacre, "The Transitional Object and the Fetish: With Special Reference to the Use of Illusion," *International Journal of Psycho-Analysis* 51 (1970): 447–456.

32. There are too many references to such studies for me to identify here. A good review of such studies can be found in Vamık D. Volkan, Gabriele Ast, and William Greer, *The Third Reich in the Unconscious: Transgenerational Transmission and its Consequences* (New York: Brunner-Routledge, 2002).

33. John Wilson and Boris Drozdek, eds., *Broken Spirits: The Treatment of Traumatized Asylum Seekers, Refugees, War and Torture Victims* (New York: Brunner-Routledge, 2004).

34. For example, in 1974, A. Cesar Garza-Guerrero wrote about the psychology of voluntary immigration, and in 1979 I studied forced dislocation. A. Cesar Garza-Guerrero, "Culture Shock: Its Mourning and Vicissitudes of Identity,"

Journal of the American Psychoanalytic Association 22 (1974): 408–429 and Volkan, *Cyprus—War and Adaptation*.

35. Leon Grinberg and Rebecca Grinberg, *Psychoanalytic Perspectives on Immigration and Exile*, trans. N. Festinger. (New Haven, CT: Yale University Press, 1989).

36. Ibid., 67.

37. Volkan, *The Need to Have Enemies and Allies*.

38. Demetrios A. Julius, "Biculturalism and International Interdependence," *Mind and Human Interaction* 3 (1992): 53–56

39. Martin Wangh, "Being a Refugee and Being an Immigrant," *International Psychoanalysis* (Winter 1992): 15–17.

40. Melanie Klein, "Mourning and Its Relation to Manic-Depressive States," in *Contributions to Psychoanalysis, 1921–1945*, 331–338 (London: Hogarth Press, 1940) and "Notes on Some Schizoid Mechanisms," in *Development in Psychoanalysis*, ed. J. Riviere, 292–320 (London: Hogarth Press, 1946).

41. Leon Grinberg, *Guilt and Depression*, trans. C. Trollope (London: Karnac Books, 1992), 79.

42. Salman Akhtar, *Immigration and Identity: Turmoil, Treatment and Transformation* (Northvale, NJ: Jason Aronson, 1999).

43. Margaret S. Mahler, *On Human Symbiosis and the Vicissitudes of Individuation* (New York: International Universities Press, 1968).

44. For Argentina, see Antonius C. G. Robben, "The Assault on Basic Trust: Disappearance, Protest, and Reburial in Argentina," in *Cultures Under Siege: Collective Violence and Trauma*, ed. by Antonius C. G. Robben and Marcello M. Suarez-Orozco, 70–101 (Cambridge: Cambridge University Press, 2000). See also Marcelo M. Suarez-Orozco, "The Heritage of Enduring a 'Dirty War': Psychological Aspects of Terror in Argentina, 1976–1988," *Journal of Psychohistory* 18 (1991): 469–505.

For Croatia, see Slavica Jurcevic and Ivan Urlic, "Linking Objects in the Process of Mourning for Sons Disappeared in War," *Croatian Medical Journal* 43 (2001): 234–239.

45. Today, the ownership of the properties left behind by the Cypriot Greeks in North Cyprus after 1974 is a very complicated legal and political issue, as the Turks and Greeks are still struggling to find a solution to the Cyprus problem.

46. Volkan, *Cyprus—War and Adaptation*, chap. 6.

47. I must add here that I did not carry out any studies in Fallujah. Using my knowledge gained elsewhere, I am predicting what will happen psychologically to the inhabitants of that city.

48. Wolf Werdigier, *Hidden Images: Palestinians and Israelis—An Archeology of the Unconscious* (Vienna: Cultural Department, Austrian Federal Ministry of Education, 2003).

49. Obviously, this "minor" difference is important. I will use "Tskhinvali" here as it is the more common name appearing in international publications.

50. Volkan, *The Need to Have Enemies and Allies; Bloodlines;* and *Blind Trust.*

51. Sigmund Freud, "Group Psychology and the Analysis of the Ego" in vol. 18 of *The Standard Edition of the Complete Psychological Works of Sigmund Freud,* ed.James Strachey, 65–143 (London: Hogarth Press, 1921–1955).

Chapter 5

52. This kind of individual-to-individual "conflict resolution" has become popular in recent years. Supported by a number of international organizations in the United States and Europe, various initiatives, for example, have brought together youths from opposing groups in order to "promote understanding through interaction," as one such program put it. Without careful preparation and an informed strategy, however, such encounters may do more harm than good. For instance, imagine that a teenage group of Cypriot Turks and Greeks was brought to a camp in the United States before the border between the two sides was opened in 2004. Under the pressure of their foreign caretakers—whose logical aim is to make the children "love" each other—the children played together at the camp and came to see each other as human individuals. Then, after a few weeks, they returned to Cyprus where the political reality would not allow them any further communication, except perhaps by e-mail. The children would easily become confused: the U.S. camp had fostered a state of mind that literally could not be sustained at home. They often felt like traitors if they spoke of having had fun or if they continued e-mail contact with the "enemy" children. Thus, without careful consideration of the children's long-term psychological contexts, such encounters may actually yield negative results and may even confuse and embitter the young people involved.

53. During my visits to Georgia beginning in May 1998, I closely observed how FDHR evolved into a strong tool for addressing posttraumatic societal issues. Nodar Sharveladze and his colleagues, in addition to opening dialogues with their South Ossetian counterparts, have developed programs for Georgian IDPs in Tbilisi and Gori. Whenever new skirmishes have broken out along the Georgia-Abkhazia "border" and a new wave of traumatized individuals and refugees have emerged, FDHR has been available to deal with their acute situations. Nodar himself joined other Georgians in participating in face-to-face interactions with Abkhazians. And when the Russians overran Chechnya, some eight thousand Chechen refugees fled to northern Georgia, joining some seven thousand Chechens already there. Even though traveling to northern Georgia was quite dangerous, Nodar and his colleagues found ways to provide assistance to them. To this day, they continue to devote their considerable energies to what they call the "social rehabilitation" of their profoundly traumatized region.

54. Traumatized children often dream about urinating on a fire, which is another symbol of anger. These dreams reflect such children's desire to discharge and thereby to eliminate their own anger. It also reflects their mental defense against sensing and knowing their anger: water (urine) puts out the fire (anger).

Chapter 6

55. J. Anderson Thomson has a good review of this diagnostic concept. See J. Anderson Thomson, "Terror, Tears and Timelessness: Individual and Group Responses to Trauma," *Mind and Human Interaction* 11 (2000): 162–176. For psychophysiological reactions and neuroendocrine responses associated with PTSD, see Bessel van der Kolk, "Post Traumatic Stress Disorder and the Nature of Trauma," Dialogues in *Clinical Neuroscience* 2 (2002): 7–22 and Bessel van der Kolk, J.W. Hopper, and J. E. Osterman, "Exploring the Nature of Traumatic Memory," *Journal of Aggression, Maltreatment and Trauma* 4 (2001): 9–31.

56. Concerning the Kennedy assassination, see Martha Wolfenstein and G. Kliman, eds., *Children and the Death of a President: Multi-disciplinary Studies* (Garden City, NY: Doubleday, 1965). About the Rabin assassination, see H. Shumuel Erlich, "Adolescents, Reactions to Rabin assassination: A Case of Patricide?" in *Adolescent Psychiatry: Developmental and Clinical Studies,* ed. A. Esman, 189–205 (London: The Analytic Press, 1998); A. Raviv, A. Sadeh, O Silberstein, and O. Diver, "Young Israelis' Reactions to National Trauma: the Rabin Assassination and Terror Attack," *Political Psychology* 21 (2000): 299–3221 and Rena Moses-Hrushovski, *Grief and Grievance: The Assassination of Yitzhak Rabin* (London: Minerva Press, 2000).

57. While my focus in this chapter is on societal responses to massive trauma, it will be useful to give a couple of examples of individualized responses. When the *Challenger* disaster occurred, one of my analysands felt devastated and entered into an acute grief. She had had an older sister who was a teacher, like Christa McAuliffe was, and who for all practical purposes had mothered and nurtured my patient throughout her difficult childhood. My analysand had come to analysis four years before the *Challenger* disaster after her older sister had died in a car accident. The loss of her sister had induced in her such anxiety; it was as if she would never find a beam of light in the darkness for the rest of her life. During the first four years of her analysis my analysand "learned" how to let her sister's mental image "die." In fact, she had begun to speak of the termination of our work and began mourning appropriately over loosing her analyst. The *Challenger* disaster was unexpected and dramatic. It opened her wounds. The extreme pain returned. It was necessary to deal with her acute grief prior to her going back to "routine" analytic work.

For one of my male analysands, his individualized reaction to the *Challenger* disaster was centered on something completely different. This young man had a great deal of anxiety-provoking competitive feelings with older men who were father figures. He had unresolved oedipal problems and saw his father, and later those who represented his father for him, as rivals in his affection toward his mother. As he began his analysis, he perceived it as a basketball game between two people, himself and an older man (the analyst). Soon, he began to refer to me as the "terrible Turk" who, he thought, had a long saber and who might cut his head off if he continued to be aggressive. As his analysis progressed, he began to see a connection between the competitive unfinished business of his childhood and the expression of this within the analysand-analyst relationship. At this time, the *Challenger* tragedy occurred. For my analysand, the space shuttle stood for his own phallus, his manhood. The explosion induced in him what we psychoanalysts call "castration anxiety": the expectation of punishment at the hands of the analyst/father because of the patient's wish to defeat him. The night of the tragedy my analysand dreamed that he was flying an airplane that exploded. In his dream, he parachuted down to safety, but when he looked down between his legs, he saw a snake (symbolically representing his penis) with its head cut off. My analysand could not have genuine grief over the loss of human life in the *Challenger* disaster since his psyche, at this time in his life, preoccupied him with machinery that symbolically stood for his phallus, which could be lost (castrated).

58. Volkan, *Blind Trust;* Norman Itzkowitz, "Enver Hoxha's Albania," paper read at a panel on Terror and Societal Regression, American Psychoanalytic Association's Winter Meeting, New York, January 23, 2005.

59. Nancy Hollander, *Love in Time of Hate: Liberation Psychology in Latin America* (New Brunswick, NJ: Rutgers University Press, 1997) and "Frozen Grief and the Transitional Transmission of Trauma," paper read at a panel onTerror and Societal Regression, American Psychoanalytic Association's Winter Meeting, New York, January 23, 2005.

60. Michael Casey, "Aceh Hostilities on Hold; Sri Lanka Split," Associated Press, December 29, 2004.

61. Tim Sullivan, "A Civil War, a Tsunami, a Lost Opportunity: Sri Lanka Descends into 'Shadow War,'" Associated Press, September 18, 2005.

62. For a detailed study of the Kardak/Imia incident and for a comparison between the Turkish and Greek large-group identities, see Volkan, *Bloodlines*.

63. David L. Phillips, "Track Two: Beyond Traditional Diplomacy," *State Magazine* (2000): 26–29.

64. In *Blind Trust* (p. 84), I wrote: "Observations of young children show that they are interested in what comes out of their bodies—feces and urine—but are not necessarily interested in blood. Through injuries that bleed, however, children gradually become aware that there is something 'alive' under their skin, at a time when their core identity is developing. The child's sense of self, which, like blood, is also 'alive' within him or her, becomes intertwined with the idea of blood: blood and identity become linked."

65. Kai Erikson, "Loss of Community at Buffalo Creek," *American Journal of Psychiatry* 133 (1975): 302–325; J. L. Tichener and F. Kapp, "Disaster at Buffalo Creek: Family and Character Change," *American Journal of Psychiatry* 133 (1976): 295–299; Robert J. Lifton and E. Olson, "The Human Meaning of Total Disaster: The Buffalo Creek Experience," *Psychiatry* 39 (1976): 1–18; and Leo Rangell, "Discussion of the Buffalo Creek Disaster: The Course of Psychic Trauma," *American Journal of Psychiatry* 133 (1976): 313–316.

The survivors were awarded $13.5 million, $6 million of which was distributed on the basis of a point system as compensation for psychological damage. For the first time, individuals who were not present at the scene of the disaster were allowed to recover for mental injuries. "Psychic impairment" was the term coined for the injuries of survivors-plaintiffs.

66. Erikson, "Loss of Community at Buffalo Creek."

67. R. M. Williams and C. Murray Parkes, "Psychosocial Effects of Disaster: Birth Rate in Aberfan," *British Medical Journal* 2 (1975): 303–304.

68. Rafael Moses, "An Israeli Psychoanalyst Looks Back in 1983," in Psychoanalytic Reflections on the Holocaust: Selected Essays, ed. S. A. Luel and

P. Marcus, 52–69 (New York: KTAV Publishing, 1984).

69. Williams and Parkes, "Psychosocial Effects of Disaster: Birth Rate in Aberfan."

70. Ibid.

71. Volkan, *Cyprus—War and Adaptation.*

72. Robert J. Lifton, *Death in Life: Survivors of Hiroshima* (New York: Random House, 1968).

73. Moses-Hrushovski, *Grief and Grievance.*

74. Ehud Sprinzak, *Brother Against Brother: Violence and Extremism in Israeli Politics from Altena to the Rabin Assassination* (New York: Free Press, 1999), xi.

75. Ibid., 253–254.

76. Ibid., 277

77. Avner Falk, "A Psychohistory of Political Assassination: The Cases of Lee Harvey Oswald and Yigal Amir," paper presented at the Twenty-Second Annual Scientific Meeting of the International Society of Political Psychology, Amsterdam, July 18–21, 1999. For a shorter version, see Avner Falk, "Political Assassination and Personality Disorder: The Cases of Lee Harvey Oswald and Yigal Amir," *Mind and Human Interaction* 12 (2001): 2–34.

78. Falk notes that Haggai envied Yigal for being their mother's favorite son, but repressed this envy and worshiped his younger brother. Later, as the two brothers awaited their assassination trial, Haggai wrote to his parents angrily from the jail: "Yigal has done a great deal. He did it only for Heaven's sake. He wanted to succeed, and he did, for not a hair fell off his head. If it were only for this, I shall admire him for the rest of my life. . . . I shall not accept even a trace of disavowal of Gali on your part. He is bigger than me and you." From *Yediot Aharonot*, December 21, 1995, translated by Avner Falk.

79. Falk, "A Psychohistory of Political Assassination."

80. Ibid.

81. Ibid.

82. Ibid.

83. Irene Misselwitz, "German Reunification: A Quasi Ethnic Conflict," *Mind and Human Interaction* 13 (2003): 77–86. Also see Wolf Wagner, who shows how each side continues to regard its behavior as naturally right while secretly rejecting that of others. Wagner's extensive studies illustrate that almost a decade after the reunification, many former East and West Germans' approaches to routines and daily behavior patterns remain dissimilar. For example, a former West German shakes hands at formal presentations, while former East Germans shake hands with one another when they first meet each day. Wolf Wagner, *Kulturschock Deutschland 1 (Culture Shock Germany 1)* (Hamburg: Rotbuch-Verlag, 1996) and *Kulturschock Deutschland; Der zweite Blick (Culture Shock Germany: The Second View)* (Hamburg: Rotbuch-Verlag, 1998).

84. Viola W. Bernard, Perry Ottenberg, and Fritz Redl, "Dehumanization: A Composite Psychological Defense in Relation to Modern War," in *Sanctions for Evil: Sources of Social Destructiveness*, ed. N. Sanford and C. Comstock, 102–124 (San Francisco: Jossey-Bass, 1973). Also see Salman Akhtar, "Dehumanization: Origins, Manifestations, and Remedies," in *Violence or Dialogue: Psychoanalytic Insights on Terror and Terrorism*, ed. Sverre Varvin and Vamık D. Volkan, 131–145 (London: International Psychoanalytic Association, 2003).

Chapter 7

85. No child's mind or sense of identity develops in a vacuum. The development of an individual's mind and his or her consistent sense of sameness (identity) and the maturation of mental functions depend, to a great extent, on the nature of childhood interactions with parents, siblings, and other important people in the child's environment. There are some specific kinds of interactions with fathers that are necessary for any child's mental growth.

Until they go through the adolescence passage, children's mourning processes are different than an adult's mourning process. See Martha Wolfenstein, "Loss, Rage and Repetition," *Psychoanalytic Study of the Child* 24 (1969): 432–460. The adult mourning process refers to his or her relating to the collection of images (the mental representation) of the deceased and the taming of this internal relationship with this mental representation in the course of "normal" mourning. Children, until the age of two or two-and-a-half, cannot maintain the mental representation of others. Imagine a small child in a room playing. His mother is in the next room, a kitchen, cooking. The child at play can stay alone as long as the mental representation—a kind of mental double—of his mother is present in is mind. As soon as the mother's mental double starts fading away, however, the child says "Mom!" and his mother answers. Or, the child runs to the kitchen, touches the mother, and then returns to the first room and resumes play. We say that the child "refuels" himself with the mother's mental double by the actual and repeated contacts with the real mother. See Margaret Mahler, *On*

Human Symbiosis and the Vicissitudes of Individuation. At the age of two or two-and-a-half, the child begins to maintain the mental representation of the important other (psychoanalysts call this the establishment of object constancy), but this mental double remains "fragile" for some time. This mental representation is shaped according to the child's needs and wishes as well as his or her actual experiences with the other. Such needs and wishes have to be gratified one way or another for the child to assimilate the tasks the adult provides. All of us remain as searchers for providers for our needs and wishes, to one degree or another, for the rest of our lives.

A small child needs to assimilate the functions of a loving mother in order to learn how to love him or herself. The child also needs to have a father who responds to specific needs and wishes. Think also of the oedipal passage; the resolution of it depends on competition with the father and identification with him for boys, and receiving "verification" of womanhood for girls. If there is no father around in reality, children still mentally have to deal with their oedipal passage by having a "fantasized" father figure.

86. Tähkä, "Dealing with Object Loss."

87. Ann Bennett Mix's remarks appear on the AWON website.

88. Hollander, *Love in Time of Hate: Liberation Psychology in Latin America.*

89. Ann Bennet Mix, *Touchstones: A Guide to Records, Rights and Resources for Families of American World War II Causalities* (Indianapolis, IN: James Publishers, 2003); Susan Johnson Hadler and Ann Bennett Mix, *Lost in Victory: Reflections of American War Orphans of World War II* (Denton, TX: University of North Texas Press, 1998).

90. Tom Brokaw, *The Greatest Generation Speaks: Letters and Reflections* (Norwalk, CT: Easton Press, 1999). Also see an enlarged second version, Tom Brokaw, *The Greatest Generation* (New York: Random House, 2004).

91. James E. Young, *The Texture of Memory: Memorials and Meaning* (New Haven: Yale University Press, 1993), 4

92. Jeffrey Karl Ochsner, "A Space of Loss: The Vietnam Veterans Memorial," *Journal of Architectural Education* 10 (1997):156–171, 157

93. Ibid., 168.

94. Ibid., 171.

Chapter 8

95. Vamık D. Volkan, "The Tree Model: A Comprehensive Psychopolitical Approach to Unofficial Diplomacy and the Reduction of Ethnic Tension," *Mind and Human Interaction* 10 (1999): 142–210.

96. For details of the Latvian National Cemetery story, see Volkan, *Bloodlines*, chap. 8.

97. From 1920 to 1940, Estonia had been an independent country. For CSMHI's and the Carter Center's work in Estonia, see Volkan, *Bloodlines*, chap. 13, and Neu and Volkan, *Developing a Methodology for Conflict Prevention.*

98. Volkan, "The Tree Model," 156

99. After a massive trauma at the hands of "others," the affected group may modify its identity and may begin to assimilate a shared sense of victimization. Accordingly, this group may resist changing its "new" identity and not "allow" the other group to show empathy for them. Whenever the Georgian delegates attempted to show empathy for South Ossetians, the South Ossetian delegates would begin to speak about how they, throughout the centuries, have been non-aggressive against their neighbors. South Ossetians would stop Georgians' efforts to be empathic by making themselves "all good" and "innocent" and Georgians "guilty." In other words, if their culture demanded that South Ossetians be always friendly toward "others," only Georgians should be blamed for the conflict and violence.

100. Family violence can emerge due to existing psychopathological forces within the family itself, but it also occurs under the pressures of a societal break-down; often these two causes are intertwined. When a society is destabilized by wars, ethnic tensions, social upheaval, displacement of populations, or changes in the gender balance of the workforce (e.g., women obtaining a higher education or working outside of the home), the family structure that typically strengthens the individual and large-group identities changes and family violence may erupt. Here is an example:

> Salina is a Russian woman married to a South Ossetian who before the war was relatively rich in South Ossetian terms. They have two children. According to family tradition, a wife lives with the husband's extended family. After the war, therefore, when Salina's husband left for Moscow to find work, she had to go live with her husband's family. Because she had no money, she opened a stand and began selling things to make money. But, according to tradition, a woman who works with the public is a "loose"

woman, and Salina was perceived as such, despite the fact that in reality she had been loyal to her husband. Her husband's family contacted the husband in Moscow, where he had a lover, with details of his "loose" wife. Eventually, they made the wife leave the house but kept her children. Salina then went to live in the suburbs, but she would occasionally return to Tskhinvali to gaze at her children from afar. Later on, when the husband returned from Moscow and they tried living together again, he beat her severely, leaving her little recourse other than acceptance of her mistreatment.

This extract is from Vamık D. Volkan, Nino Makhashvili, Nodar Sharveladze, and Isıl Vahip, "IREX Black and Caspian Sea Collaborative Research Program: Gender Issues and Family Violence," a Center for the Study of Mind and Human Interaction document (Charlottesville, VA: Center for the Study of Mind and Human Interaction, July 2002), 8.

101. Ochsner, "A Space of Loss," 159

102. Ibid.

103. Carol Vogel, "Maya Lin's World of Architecture, or Is It Art?" *New York Times,* May 9, 1994.

104. Robert Campbell, "An Emotive Apart," *Art in America* (May 1983): 150–151.

105. Ibid.

106. Kurt Volkan, "The Vietnam War Memorial," *Mind and Human Interaction* 3 (1992): 73–77. For the controversy over black granite of the memorial, see Jan C. Scruggs and Joel L. Swerdlow, *To Heal a Nation: The Vietnam Veterans Memorial* (New York: Harper and Row, 1985).

107. Jan Scruggs, a rifleman during the Vietnam War, was the person who thought of building a monument for those who served in Vietnam that would have the names of everyone killed during that conflict carved on it. For his story, see Scruggs and Swerdlow, *To Heal a Nation.*

108. When the memorial was planned, the completion brief gave 57,692 as the number of dead and missing to be named. Later, additional names were added. Now, more than 58,000 names are displayed.

109. Ochsner, "A Space of Loss," 159.

110. K. Volkan, "The Vietnam War Memorial," 75.

111. Ibid.

112. Ibid.

113. There are a few exceptions. See Rafael Moses and Rena Moses-Hrushovski, "Two Powerful Tools in Human Interactions: To Accept One's Fault and to Ask for Forgiveness," in *Psikopatoloji ve Psikoanalitik Teknik (Psychopathology and Psychoanalytic Technique)*, ed. Ayhan Egrilmez and Isıl Vahip (Izmir, Turkey: Meta, 2002); Volkan, *Bloodlines*; and Salman Akhtar, *New Clinical Realms: Pushing the Envelope of Theory and Technique* (Northvale, NJ: Jason Aronson, 2003). Joseph V. Montville, a career diplomat with great insights about political psychology, also wrote about "apology" and "forgiveness." See Joseph V. Montville, "Justice and the Burdens of History," in *Reconciliation, Coexistence, and Justice in Interethnic Conflict: Theory and Practice*, ed. Mohammed Abu Nimr, 129–144 (Lanham, MD: Lexington Books, 2001) and "Religion and Peacemaking," in *Forgiveness and Reconciliation: Religion, Public Policy, and Conflict Transformation*, ed. Raymond G. Hemlick and Rodney L. Peterson, 97–116 (Philadelphia: Tempelton Foundation Press, 2001). Also see *Journal of the American Psychoanalytic Association* 53, no. 2 (2005), which is devoted to "love, shame, revenge, and forgiveness."

114. Willy Brandt, *Erinnerungen: Mit den Notizen zum Fall G* (Berlin: Ullstein, 1994).

115. The concept of "forgiveness" is included in the Christian religion. For example, a Catholic person at confession may ask for "forgiveness" for his or her sins. The Buddhist concepts *metta* and *karuna* (loving kindness and compassion) may be interpreted as forgiveness. See C. Mahendran, "Forgiveness Between Nations: Eastern Perspectives," *International Minds* 5 (1994): 12–13. I was present at a diplomatic meeting attended by Christian and Muslim diplomats. Muslim participants insisted that the concepts of "apology" and "forgiveness" are not part of their religious culture.

116. For the Serbian sense of being victims, see Marko S. Markovic, "The Secret of Kosovo," in *Landmarks in Serbian Culture and History*, trans. C. Kramer, ed. V. D. Mihailovich, 111–131 (Pittsburgh, PA: Serb National Foundation, 1983); Prince Lazarovich-Hrebelianovich and Eleanor Calhoun, *The Serbian People*, vol. 1 (New York: Scribner's, 1910). For Armenians' response to a collective sense of loss during the last years of the Ottoman Empire and massacres and displacements before World War I, see Gerard Jinair Libaridian, ed., *Armenia at the Crossroads: Democracy and Nationhood in the Post-Soviet Era* (Watertown, MA: Blue Cross Books, 1991).

117. Volkan, *Bloodlines*.

118. Nikos Kazantzakis, *Report on Greco*, trans. P.A. Bien (New York: Simon and Schuster, 1965).

119. A group of Kurds in Turkey under the leadership of Abdullah Öcalan in 1978 named themselves the PKK (Kurdish Workers' Party) and in 1984 launched a campaign of terror, which ultimately resulted in tens of thousands of deaths. For a psychobiographical examination of Abdullah Öcalan, see Volkan, Bloodlines, chap. 11. After this campaign of terror, ethnic differences among citizens of Turkey came to public awareness more clearly. The 2005 television season in Turkey enraptured audiences with a slew of series dealing with matters of national identity and politics. The shows dealt with serious national issues once deemed too delicate for prime time viewing: Greek-Turkish relations, sectarian tensions, the rise of Islam, the Kurdish question, and the Right-Left wars of the 1970s. See Agence France Presse, March 12, 2005.

120. These numbers are taken from Justin McCarthy's research. Justin McCarthy, *Death and Exile* (Princeton: Darwin Press,1995).

121. For a review, see Judith Kestenberg and Ira Brenner, *The Last Witness* (Washington, D.C.: American Psychiatric Press, 1996); Ilany Kogan, *The Cry of Mute Children: A Psychoanalytic Perspective of the Second Generation of the Holocaust* (London: Free Association Books, 1995); Volkan, Ast, and Greer, *The Third Reich in the Unconscious.*

122. Vamık D. Volkan, "On Chosen Trauma," *Mind and Human Interaction* 4 (1991): 3–19; Volkan, *Bloodlines*; and Volkan, *Blind Trust.*

123. Robert D. Kaplan, *Balkan Ghosts: A Journey Through History* (New York: Vintage Books, 1993); Volkan, *Blind Trust.* See also, Vamık D. Volkan and Norman Itzkowitz, *Turks and Greeks: Neighbours in Conflict* (Cambridgeshire, England: Eothen Press, 1994).

Chapter 9

124. Anna Freud and Dorothy Burlingham, *War and Children* (New York: International Universities Press, 1942).

125. Harry S. Sullivan, *Schizophrenia as a Human Process* (New York: W. W. Norton, 1962).

126. Mahler, *On Human Symbiosis and the Vicissitudes of Individuation.*

127. Daniel N. Stern, *The Interpersonal World of the Infant* (New York: Basic Books, 1985); Stanley I. Greenspan, *The Development of the Ego: Implications for Personality Theory, Psychopathology and the Psychotherapeutic Process* (Madison,

CT: International Universities Press, 1989); and Robert N. Emde, "Positive Emotions for Psychoanalytic Theory: Surprises from Infancy Research and New Directions," *Journal of the American Psychoanalytic Association* 39 (Supplement 1991): 5–44.

128. Johannes Lehtonen, "Research: The Dream Between Neuroscience and Psychoanalysis: Has Feeding an Impact on Brain Function and the Capacity to Create Dream Images in Infants?" *Psychoanalysis in Europe* 57 (2003): 175 –182; Johannes Lehtonen, M. Kononen, M. Purhonen, J. Partanen, S. Saarikoski, and K. Launiala, "The Effect of Nursing on the Brain Activity of the Newborn," *Journal of Pediatrics* 132 (1998): 646–651; Johannes Lehtonen, M. Kononen, M. Purhonen, J. Partanen, S. Saarikoski, and K. Launiala "The Effects of Feeding on the Electroencephalogram in 3- and 6-Month Old Infants," *Psychophysiology* 39 (2002): 73–9 and M. Purhonen, A. Pääkkönen, H. Yppärilä, Johannes Lehtonen, and J. Karhu, "Dynamic Behavior of the Auditory N100 Elicited by a Baby's Cry," *International Journal of Psychophysiology* 41(2001): 271–278.

129. Vamık D. Volkan and As'ad Masri, "The Development of Female Transsexualism," *American Journal of Psychotherapy* 43 (1989): 92–107.

130. Robert Zuckerman and Vamık D. Volkan, "Complicated Mourning over a Body Defect: The Making of a 'Living Linking Object,'" in *The Problem of Loss and Mourning: Psychoanalytic Perspectives,* ed. by D. Deitrich and P. Shabad, 257–274. (New York: International Universities Press. 1988).

131. Psychic borders can also be permeable in a relationship between a grown child and parent or caretaker, or between two adults when they relate to each other under regressed or partially regressed states. Since analysands regress therapeutically and analysts also regress "in the service of the other," permeability of borders between two adults can also be observed during analytic sessions. See Stanley L.Olinick, *The Therapeutic Instrument* (New York: Jason Aronson, 1980), 7. Based on such observations, Harold F. Searles wrote about "driving the other crazy" and Sheldon Heath examined how depressed individuals can pass their depression on to their analysts. Harold F. Searles, "The Effort to Drive the Other Person Crazy: An Element in the Aetiology and Psychotherapy of Schizophrenia," in *Collected Papers on Schizophrenia and Related Subjects,* 254–283 (New York: International Universities Press, 1959) and Sheldon Heath, *Dealing with the Therapist's Vulnerability to Depression* (Northvale, NJ: Jason Aronson, 1991).

132. "Depositing" is a lasting and very special kind of projective identification. See Vamık D. Volkan, *Six Steps in the Treatment of Borderline Personality*

Organization (Northvale, NJ: Jason Aronson, 1987) and Volkan, Ast, and Greer, *The Third Reich in the Unconscious.*

133. The experiences that created these mental images in the adult are not "accessible" to the child. Yet those mental images are deposited or pushed into the child, but without the experiential/contextual "framework" that created them. For example, the child might not actually know the individual whose mental image is planted into the child's self-representation. Judith Kestenberg's term "transgenerational transportation," I believe, refers to "depositing images." Judith Kestenberg, "A Psychological Assessment Based on Analysis of a Survivor's Child," in *Generations of the Holocaust,* ed. by M. S. Bergmann and M. E. Jucovy, 158–177 (New York: Columbia University Press, 1982).

134. A. C. Cain and B. S. Cain, "On Replacing a Child," *Journal of the American Academy of Child Psychiatry* 3 (1964): 443–456; Poznanski, "The 'Replacement Child'"; and Volkan and Ast, *Siblings in the Unconscious and Psychopathology.*

135. If this task is not successful, the replacement child may develop an unintegrated self-representation and therefore a borderline or narcissistic personality organization. See Volkan, *Six Steps in the Treatment of Borderline Personality Organization.*

136. A total account of Peter's analysis was published earlier in German. Vamık D. Volkan and Gabriele Ast, *Spektrum des Narzissmus* (Göttingen: Vanderhoeck & Ruprecht, 1994).

137. Volkan, *Six Steps in the Treatment of Borderline Personality Organization.*

138. During the terminal period of Peter's analysis, he clearly perceived the analyst as a "new person" (technically called a "new object"), whereas in the earlier phases of his analysis he perceived the analyst as his own "hungry" self and as representing the images of his childhood important others. For more on "new objects," see Hans Loewald, "On the Therapeutic Action of Psychoanalysis," *International Journal of Psycho-Analysis* 41 (1960): 16–33.

139. A. A. Bocksel, *Rice, Men and Barbed Wire: A True Epic of Americans as Japanese POW's* (Hauppage, NY: Michael B. Glass & Associates, 1991) and S. Stewart, *Give Us This Day* (New York: Avon Books, 1990).

140. Erik H. Erikson, *Childhood and Society* (New York: W. W. Norton, 1950).

141. A. Hopkins, "Pearl Harbor, Day of Infamy," *Time Magazine,* December 2, 1991.

Chapter 10

142. Vamık D. Volkan and Norman Itzkowitz, "Istanbul, not Constantinople: The Western World's View of 'the Turk,'" *Mind and Human Interaction* 4 (1993): 129–134, and *Turks and Greeks: Neighbours in Conflict.*

143. Robert Schwoebel, *The Shadows of the Crescent: The Renaissance Image of the Turk, 1453–1517* (New York: St. Martin Press, 1967).

144. Ibid., 14.

145. Kenneth Young, *The Greek Passion: A Study in People and Politics* (London: J. M. Dent & Sons, 1969).

146. References to Giovanni Maria Filelfo can be found in *Monumenta Hungariae, XXIII,* part one, no. 9, 308, 309, 405, and 453 and to Felix Fabri in *Evagatorium III,* 236–239. See also Schwoebel, *The Shadows of the Crescent.*

147. Niyazi Berkes, *Türk Düsününde Batı Sorunu (The Western Question in Turkish Thought)* (Ankara: Bilgi Yayınevi, 1988).

148. T. de Motolinia, *History of Indians of New Spain,* trans. F. B. Steck (Washington, D.C.: Academy of American Franciscan History, 1951).

149. Max Harris, "Hidden Transcripts in Public Places," *Mind and Human Interaction* 3 (1992): 63–69.

150. Volkan and Itzkowitz, *Turks and Greeks: Neighbours in Conflict* and Talat Halman, "Istanbul," in *The Last Lullaby,* 8–9 (Merrick, NY: Cross Cultural Communications, 1992).

151. Michael Herzfeld, *Ours Once More: Ideology and the Making of Modern Greece* (New York: Pella, 1986).

152. Nikolaos G. Politis, "Khelidhonisma" (Swallow Song), *Neoelinika Analekta* 1 (1872): 354–368; *Introductory Lecture for the Class in Hellenic Mythology* (in Greek) (Athens, Greece: Aion, 1882); Spyridon Zamblios, "Some Philosophical Researches on the Modern Greek Language" (in Greek), *Pandora* 7 (1856): 369–380, 484–489 and *Whence the Vulgar Word Traghoudho? Thoughts Concerning Hellenic Poetry* (in Greek), (Athens, Greece: P. Soutsas and A. Ktenas, 1859).

153. Paschalis M. Kitromilides, "'Imagined communities' and the Origins of the National Question in the Balkans," in *Modern Greek Nationalism and Nationality,* ed. by M. Blickhorn and T. Veremis, 23–65 (Athens, Greece: Sage-Eliamep, 1990), 35.

154. Kyriacos C. Markides, *The Rise and Fall of the Cyprus Republic* (New Haven, CT: Yale University Press, 1977), 10.

155. Ibid.

156. M. S. Markovic, "The Secret of Kosovo."

157. Roy Gutman, *Witness to Genocide: The 1993 Pulitzer Prize-Winning Dispatches on the "Ethnic Cleansing" of Bosnia* (New York: Maxwell Macmillan International, 1993), x.

158. Ibid.

159. Ibid.

160. Beverly Allen, *Rape Warfare: The Hidden Genocide in Bosnia-Herzegovina and Croatia* (Minneapolis, MN: University of Minnesota Press, 1946).

161. Volkan, *Blind Trust.*

162. Ibid.

Chapter 11

163. Erik H. Erikson, *Identity: Youth and Crises* (New York: W.W. Norton, 1968), 41.

164. J. Anderson Thomson, "Killer Apes on American Airlines, or: How Religion Was the Main Hijacker on September 11," in *Violence or Dialogue? Psychoanalytic Insights on Terror and Terrorism,* ed. Sverre Varvin and Vamık D. Volkan, 73–84 (London: International Psychoanalysis Library, 2003). See also Richard Wrangham, "Is Military Incompetence Adaptive? Apes and the Origins of Human Violence," *Evolution and Human Behavior* 20 (1999): 3–17; Richard Wrangham and D. Peterson, *Demonic Males* (Boston: Houghton Mifflin, 1996). David M. Buss and Joshua D. Duntley of the University of Texas–Austin also wrote on this topic: "Murder by Design: The Evolution of Homicide" (in press).

165. Ronald P. Barston, *Modern Diplomacy* (New York: Longman, 1988).

166. In psychoanalysis, the concept of morality is related to the concept "superego." One's morality depends not only on what parents and teachers insist upon or on religious admonitions. Students of human development see the superego, which can be equated loosely with "a conscience," as arising from a combination of compromise formations dealing with mental conflicts that crystallize mostly during the oedipal phase of life. Imagine a boy at the oedipal age.

His oedipal conflicts bring fears of loosing loved ones and/or their love and being punished and castrated. He then becomes "moral" in a way his fantasies dictate, in order to minimize anxiety and other uncomfortable feelings. He may identify with his perception of a forbidding parent or remove himself from competition in an effort to avoid expected punishment. Since the beginning of morality is linked to unconscious fear (anxiety) and other uncomfortable feelings, the more anxiety and bad affects the child has, the stricter superego he or she may develop. Psychoanalytic investigations tell us that the compelling sense of morality a person has is equal to the compelling need to avoid punishment. Based on psychoanalytic observations, we should not be surprised to find that the moral sense is not to be relied upon in situations in which there are regressive tendencies in the individual. The same thing can be said about societies when the large-group identity is threatened. In order to protect the large-group identity, moral corruption may appear within the society.

Of course, in "normal" development, a child does not remain in the oedipal phase but develops a more integrated superego and more benign moral code as well as more sophisticated mental mechanisms to protect his integrated superego and benign moral code. Unfortunately, under certain circumstances, regressions occur both in individuals and societies. Psychoanalysts are not surprised when they notice the corruption of so-called national values and other ideals under certain threatening political and international conditions.

167. Sigmund Freud also "speculated" about early human groups. For example, he wrote about how early humans developed the incest taboo. Sigmund Freud, "Totem and Taboo," vol. 13 of *The Standard Edition of the Complete Psychological Works of Sigmund Freud,* ed. James Strachey, 1–162. (London: Hogarth Press, 1913–1955).

168. Harold H. Saunders, "Official and Citizens in International Relationships: The Dartmouth Conference," in *The Psychodynamics of International Relationships,* vol. 2, *Unofficial Diplomacy at Work,* ed. Vamık D. Volkan, Joseph V. Montville, and Demetrios A. Julius, 41–69 (Lexington, MA: Lexington Books,1991).

169. Abba Eban, *The New Diplomacy: International Affairs in the Modern Age* (New York: Random, 1983).

170. Harold Nicholson, *Diplomacy* (London: Oxford University Press, 1963)

171. Eban, *The New Diplomacy,* 386.

172. I established CSMHI in 1987 and directed it until 2002. During this time period, a former assistant secretary of state during the Carter administration, Harold Saunders, was a member of CSMHI's advisory board. Saunders participated in the Dartmouth Conference series and I heard from him about the inner workings of these meetings. (The name of these series came from the fact that the first meeting took place at Dartmouth College in Hanover, NH.) Certain concepts dealing with the human dimensions of the U.S.-USSR conflict, such as one robbing the other of having an enemy, found echoes in official statements and speeches, especially by Mikhail Gorbachev. Another CSMHI advisory board member, Rita Rogers, regularly attended the Pugwash Conferences, which became important when the Soviets began sending scholars with political clout. Both conferences functioned as bridges in diplomatic negotiations, especially between the United States and USSR. In the introduction, I referred to activities at the Esalen Institute which were also significant in keeping meaningful links between East and West during difficult times.

173. Charles Levinson, *Vodka Cola* (London: Gordon and Cremonesi, 1978); Marshall I. Goldman, *Détente and Dollars: Doing Business with Soviets* (New York: Basic Books, 1975); Maureen R. Berman and Joseph E. Johnson, eds., *Unofficial Diplomats* (New York: Columbia University Press, 1977).

174. John Scali, "Backstage Mediation in the Cuban Missile Crises," in *Conflict Resolution: Tract Two Diplomacy*, ed. John W. McDonald, Jr. and D. B. Bendahmane (Washington, D.C.: Center for the Study of Foreign Affairs, 1987).

175. Herbert Kelman, "Interactive Problem Solving: The Uses and Limits of a Therapeutic Model for the Resolution of International Conflict" in *The Psychodynamics of International Relationships*, vol. 2, ed. Volkan, Montville, and Julius, 145–160.

176. Joseph V. Montville, "The Arrow and the Olive branch. A Case for Tract Two Diplomacy," in *Conflict Resolution: Tract Two Diplomacy*, ed. John McDonald and D. B. Bendahmane, 5–20 (Washington, D.C.: U.S. Government Printing Office, 1987).

177. Harold H. Saunders, *The Other Walls: The Politics of the Arab-Israeli Peace Process* (Washington, D.C.: American Enterprise Institute, 1985).

178. See http://www.usip.org.

179. The participants of this meeting included diplomats, political scientists, psychologists, psychoanalysts, and sociologists. They were Richard Arndt, Edward Azar, John Burton, Stephen Cohen, Harriett Crosby, Demetrios Julius, Herbert Kelman, James Laue, Joseph Montville, Harold Saunders, and Vamık Volkan. Retired ambassador Samuel Lewis, then president of the United States Institute of Peace, attended as an observer.

180. Two volumes were published from the presentations at this gathering.

Vamık D. Volkan, Joseph V. Montville and Demetrius Julius, eds., *The Psychodynamics of International Relations,* vol. 1, *Concepts and Theories,* (Lexington, MA: Lexington Books, 1990) and Volkan, Julius and Montville, eds., *The Psychodynamics of International Relationships,* vol. 2. For many years these two volumes were used by many "students" in their attempts to clarify the concept of "unofficial diplomacy."

John W. Burton, who was the permanent head of the Australian Foreign Office in 1947 and high commissioner for Ceylon in 1955, was influenced by theories of "human needs." John W. Burton, "Conflict Resolution as a Political System," in *The Psychodynamics of International Relations,* vol. 2, ed. Volkan, Montville, and Julius, 71–92 (Lexington, MA: Lexington Books, 1991). Burton believed human participants in conflict situations are "compulsively struggling in their respective institutional environments at all social levels to satisfy primordial and universal needs—needs such as security, recognition, and development" (ibid, 83). His "conflict resolution" attempts, therefore, primarily addressed demands for institutional reorganizations rather than for altered attitudes and enforced conformity within given norms of behavior. Burton saw two types of disputes: "interest-based disputes" and "value- or needs-based disputes." Interest-based disputes are not deep rooted "for no one wishes to die in a fight over wages as such" (ibid). Burton contended that a variety of legal, arbitration, and other dispute-resolution techniques could deal with this type of conflict. Value- or needs-disputes, on the other hand, reflect demands that are not negotiable. According to Burton, it is impossible to barter with values and needs. He wrote that sufficient coercion or bargaining power sometimes leads to suppression and "settles" value- or needs-based disputes. Psychoanalytic insights have little or no relevance to Burton's ideas. His "unofficial" approach to diplomacy is parallel to "official" rational-actor models of diplomacy. Burton's approach has been the focus of the Institute for Conflict Analysis and Resolution (ICAR) at George Mason University in northern Virginia where Burton worked from the mid-1950s to the late 1980s. ICAR, a well-known training site for aspiring unofficial diplomats, has expanded on Burton's ideas.

Herbert C. Kelman, a social psychologist, who was a professor of social ethics at Harvard University when he attended the 1987 gathering at CSMHI, drew heavily on the pioneering efforts of John Burton with a focus on human needs. Jerome Frank, a psychiatrist who studied social processes and utilized some psychoanalytic concepts, also influenced Kelman. Frank borrowed the idea of "corrective emotional experience" from psychoanalysts Franz Alexander and Thomas French, who were influential and controversial psychoanalytic teachers in the United States in the 1940s. See Franz Alexander and Thomas French, *Psychoanalytic Theory* (New York: Ronald Press, 1946). The term corrective emotional experience was first used in the clinical setting to describe when a psychoanalyst deliberately behaves differently in a situation from the patient's important childhood figures. Frank used this concept in his group therapy sessions and in turn influenced Kelman's work. See Herbert C. Kelman, "Interactive Problem Solving."

Harold Saunders called attention to the dangers and limitations as well as the value of contributions by unofficial individuals and organizations, whether they work with influential members of opposing large groups or focus on grassroots movements. Saunders believed that unofficial diplomacy gatherings can play a crucial role in providing "ideas in the air." See Harold Saunders, "Officials and Citizens in International Relationships," 61. Once an official diplomatic policy has been developed, political leaders and other official decision makers do not usually seek advice from those outside their circles. (This has been the case, for example, in the Bush administration.) However, if a policy does not work once it has been implemented, political leaders may have to then listen to ideas in the air. Saunders suggested that Gorbachev's speech to the United Nations on December 1988 reflected ideas in the air that were articulated during the Dartmouth Conference dialogues.

181. Such ideas were put forward long ago and remained influential for many decades. See, for example, Henry Morgenthau, *Politics Among Nations* (New York: Knopf, 1954).

182. Donald L. Horowitz, *Ethnic Groups in Conflict* (Berkeley: University of California Press, 1985), 140.

183. Horowitz, *Ethnic Groups in Conflict.*

Chapter 12

184. Funds also came from other sources. For example, CSMHI received additional funds from the United States Institute of Peace during the assessment phase of this project and then received funds from and collaborated with the Carter Center in Atlanta during the psychopolitical-dialogue phase of the project. (The Carter Center received funds for the Estonian project from the Charles Stewart Mott Foundation.) The PEW Charitable Trust gave CSMHI a grant to bring the project to the grassroots level.

185. When physicians face an acute situation in which a patient is bleeding to death, the first thing they do is attempt to stop the bleeding, leaving a complete assessment of the cause of bleeding to a later time. Similarly, we cannot imagine that slow-moving unofficial diplomacy such as the Tree Model will be effective in an acute and bloody large-group conflict. However, some concepts that evolved from the application of the Tree Model are useful in assessing acute international problems and developing specific strategies for them.

186. For details, see Volkan, *Bloodlines*. See also Neu and Volkan, *Developing a Methodology for Conflict Prevention.*

187. See, for example, Demetrios Julius, "The Practice of Tract Two Diplomacy in the Arab-Israeli Conferences" in *The Psychodynamics of International Relationships,* vol. 2, ed. Volkan, Montville, and Julius, 193–205.

188. During my tenure as the head of CSMHI, we never supplied financial support for individuals who participated in its unofficial diplomacy activities, except for covering the expense associated with meetings. This was also true for the CSMHI faculty. Whenever the representatives of opposing large groups whom we brought together learned that the CSMHI faculty was not making money by facilitating the meetings, they were positively impressed. CSMHI faculty who were full-time faculty members of the University of Virginia received their routine salaries. I appreciate very much the support CSMHI received from the then dean of the medical school, Robert Carey; he allowed CSMHI activities to be counted as routine medical school activities for the full-time faculty members.

189. There were many occasions, however, when the veterans of the psycho-political dialogues series would become influential politicians in their countries or locations, even reaching top positions, such as Arnold Rüütel, a veteran of our Estonia series who was elected president of Estonia on September 21, 2001.

190. For small group psychodynamics, see S. H. Foulkes and E. James Anthony, *Group Psychotherapy: The Psychoanalytic Approach* (London: Penguin, 1964); Wilfred R. Bion, *Experiences in Groups and Other Papers* (London: Tavistock Publications, 1961); D. Wilfred Abse, *Clinical Notes on Group-Analytic Psychotherapy* (Charlottesville: University Press of Virginia, 1974); and Malcolm Pines, ed., *The Evolution of Group Analysis* (London: Routledge & Kegan Paul, 1983). See also, Earl Hopper, *Traumatic Experience in the Unconscious Life of Groups: The Fourth Basic Assumption: Incohesion: Aggregation/Massification or (ba) I: A/M* (London: Jessica Kingsley Publishers, 2003). Besides writing about small groups, Hopper offers a new understanding of the dynamics of group-like social systems.

191. For further detailed descriptions of the "anatomy" of such meetings, see: Vamık D. Volkan and Max Harris, "Negotiating a Peaceful Separation: A

Psychopolitical Analysis of Current Relationships Between Russia and Baltic Republics," *Mind and Human Interaction* 4 (1992): 20–29 and "The Psychodynamics of Ethnic Terrorism," *International Journal of Group Rights* 3 (1995): 145–159.

192. *Palestinian Weekly,* December 6, 1985.

193. David Rothstein, "The Assassin and the Assassinated: As Nonpatient Subject of Psychiatric Investigation" in *Dynamics of Violence,* ed. J. Fawcett, 145–155 (Chicago: American Medical Association, 1972).

194. Melanie Klein, "Notes on Some Schizoid Mechanisms," in *Development in Psychoanalysis,* ed. J. Riviere, London: Hogarth Press.

195. Facilitators, of course, need to deal with this when it happens by illustrating "gray areas" between "black" and "white." Dialogue facilitators may have also become the targets of participants' externalizations and projections. That is, facilitators may appear to be blamed or criticized for things the participants are upset about. When this happens, facilitators with clinical experience have an advantage because they are accustomed to receiving and dealing with their patients' externalizations and projections (transference). Countertransference— irrational expectations on the part of the facilitators—may also surface. Rubbing elbows with politically important individuals, for example, may give the facilitators a sense of undeserved omnipotence. Experienced mental health professionals are cognizant of this phenomenon and, after decades of work in the field, are less likely to succumb to damaging countertransference responses.

196. John Mack, "Foreword," in *Cyprus: War and Adaptation* by Vamık D. Volkan, (Charlottesville, VA: University Press of Virginia, 1979), ix–xxi.

197. The concept of "minor differences" was described by Sigmund Freud. See Sigmund Freud, "Taboo of Virginity," vol. 11 of *The Standard Edition of the Complete Psychological Works of Sigmund Freud,* ed. James Strachey, 191–208. (London: Hogarth Press, 1917–1955) and *Group Psychology and the Analysis of the Ego.* For "minor differences" in international relationships, see Volkan, *The Need to Have Enemies and Allies, Bloodlines,* and *Blind Trust.*

198. Maurice Apprey describes the importance of differences among members of one team concerning large-group identity issues. See Maurice Apprey, "Heuristic Steps for Negotiating Ethno-National Conflicts: Vignettes from Estonia," *New Literary History* 27 (1996): 199–212.

If the Tree Model is progressing as expected, the personal stories appear spontaneously. In cases where meetings occur less than three times a year because of lack of funds, the facilitators themselves may "push" the participants from opposing teams to tell their stories pertaining to large-group conflict. If enough background for personal and emotional security is established, this may work. Otherwise, it becomes a "forced" duty and does not work.

199. Neu and Volkan, *Developing a Methodology for Conflict Prevention.*

200. Volkan, *Blind Trust.*

201. In 1999, CSMHI became involved in unofficial diplomacy activities between influential Greeks and Turks. It is most interesting that in this series, too, the elephant-rabbit metaphor surfaced.

202. Sigmund Freud, *Mourning and Melancholia;* George Pollock, *The Mourning and Liberation Process,* 2 vols. (Madison, CT: International Universities Press, 1989); Volkan, *Linking Objects and Linking Phenomena;* Volkan and Zintl, *Life After Loss.*

203. During the Estonia dialogues, CSMHI experimented with looking at how different generations perceived Estonian-Russian relations. Accordingly, we chose four Estonian college students and four Russian-Estonian college students and conducted small group sessions with them. Toward the latter part of the original psychopolitical dialogue series, we invited the students to join the elders at one of the gatherings. When they were first brought in, the students were seated in the middle of a plenary room and the elder participants sat in chairs surrounding the young people and two CSMHI facilitators, psychoanalyst Maurice Apprey and myself. The facilitators engaged the students in discussion among themselves while the elder participants just listened. Our aim was to see whether there were generational differences in perceptions of the enemy and approaches to peace. We wanted to investigate whether it was true—as was generally believed—that members of the younger generation did not think like their elders and that they were more moderate and willing to accept change. During these discussions, we discovered that, if one looks below the surface, there are surprising similarities between the generations on topics related to "hot" large-group identity issues and conflicts.

As the young participants discussed their views, one Estonian resolutely declared that her generation was very different from that of her grandfather who was very anti-Russian. She felt that she and her peers were better at dealing with the problems of integrating Russian speakers in Estonia. As the dialogue progressed, however, and she was encouraged to examine her own perceptions and feelings toward Russians living in Estonia, she found herself expressing some of the societal traumas of her grandfather's generation. She then recognized that she was unconsciously her grandfather's "spokesperson" and that despite some real differences in their generations, shared images of traumas and corresponding attitudes had been passed onto her. This shocked her but paradoxically helped her find her own less contaminated views about Russians.

Though we found that members of the younger generation indeed carried some of the same historical images as their parents, the intergenerational format had some positive results. We observed that showing the older generation how their historical burdens persist in the younger generation was itself a motivating factor for the elders. It encouraged those in influential positions to do some soul-searching themselves and gave them more of an impetus to act. It had pained them to see what had been inflicted on their children. While as facilitators we experimented with this issue only once, I believe that this method of intergenerational discussion could be a useful tool for other situations.

204. Eban, *The New Diplomacy.*

205. While some of this is reminiscent of John Burton's ideas on institution-building described in chapter11, in CSMHI's methodology, the psychopolitical dialogues must be allowed to take their course before institution-building can be successful. The psychopolitical dialogues provide the necessary groundwork and shifts in attitudes and understanding that prepare the way for programs and other structural changes within the society.

Chapter 13

206. Timing is very important when building such new NGOs. Premature efforts to create interethnic institutions can be counterproductive in the long run if members succumb to malignant ethnic, nationalistic, religious, or ideological attitudes. After the Soviet Union collapsed, concepts such as personal property, individual thinking and responsibility, community service, civil law, and regulation needed time to evolve in the postcommunist world and to be experienced enough to be assimilated.

207. In Estonia, the leader of our Contact Group was psychologist Endel Talvik. In addition to having experienced CSMHI's psychopolitical dialogues from 1994 to 1996, Talvik received training from CSMHI in Estonia and in the United States. With support from Harold Saunders, he (as well as Alexei Semionov, one of the leaders of Russians in Estonia) traveled to Dayton, Ohio, and participated in a community-building seminar organized by the Kettering Foundation. Later, Talvik received psychoanalytic training in Finland and from of the Eastern European Psychoanalytic School of the International Psychoanalytical Association (IPA). Today, Talvik is a psychoanalyst certified by the IPA.

208. Stories of these locations were previously told in my book, *Bloodlines*. but our work there continued after my writing of *Bloodlines,* so here I am able to report more complete stories.

209. A dedicated Estonian educator, Ly Krikk, provided leadership in preparing these textbooks. She was assisted by her own staff, as well as by Endel Talvik and psychoanalyst Maurice Apprey, historian Norman Itzkowitz, and psychiatric nurse and mediator Margie Howell of CSMHI.

210. This process is described by Michael Sebek. See Sebek, "Anality in the Totalitarian System and the Psychology of Post-Totalitarian Society."

211. There is, however, one statistical evaluation of our work in Mustvee. Maurice Apprey, in collaboration with Ly Krikk, Victor Apprey, and Endel Talvik, "From the Heuristic to the Empirical: Integrating Inter-Ethnic Kindergartens." *Mind and Human Interaction* 11, no. 3 (2000): 194–205.

212. Here is a short list of achievements:

1. While the psychopolitical dialogue series was continuing, Vladimir Homyokov, as a representative of the Russian and Russian speakers in Estonia, was invited to the Riigikogu. He addressed the parliament so that the Estonian deputies might better understand their concerns.

2. During the fifth psychopolitical dialogue, three Russian Duma representatives who participated in the dialogue series were invited to Riigikogu, where they met with their Estonian counterparts. They had a productive talk.

3. Jaan Kaplinski, a 1995 candidate for the Nobel Prize in Literature and a well-known figure, wrote several articles for Estonian newspapers to influence the public and to promote peaceful coexistence between ethnic Estonians and others living in Estonia.

4. Mustamäe's NGO, Käsikäes, has designed, written, and published textbooks, a teacher's manual, and accompanying materials for teaching Estonian language and culture to Russian-speaking children. Such teaching materials did not exist prior to this project. The textbook is an important tool for realistically promoting coexistence of Russian speakers and Estonians in Estonia. By introducing children of both groups to one another and giving them the language and the opportunity to interact, the Estonian and Russian organizers and participants began changing their pat-

terns of interaction and behavior and charting a way to peaceful coexistence.

5. The Mustamäe NGO has obtained funding for their language teachers and program directors to train teachers in other parts of Estonia on their Estonian language and culture curriculum. They have also requested the participation of Endel Talvik to address the psychological issues involved.

6. Mustvee developed an information center to help tourists visiting the town and printed material in several languages describing sites to visit. NGO members have gained sufficient confidence and experience in program planning and implementation to seek new funding on their own for further enhancements to the town's facilities for tourists and visitors. For example, they have received funding from the Soros Foundation.

7. Since the completion of CSMHI's project in Estonia, Endel Talvik has been hired as an expert on "integration" projects in the Narva-Jõesuu and Aseri localities of Estonia, a consultation requested as a direct result of his experience and achievements with the three CSMHI-sponsored community projects.

8. Ly Krikk, the Mustamäe project coordinator, has produced videos from actual footage of their Estonian language-teaching program in Russian-speaking schools and their joint Estonian-Russian children's gatherings. These videos have been used to alleviate misconceptions and fears concerning Russian-Estonian interaction and are proving that visual demonstration of integration in action is indeed a powerful tool for reducing resistances to such programs.

9. Paul Lettens, a participant in the 1994–96 psychopolitical dialogue series, was put on the board of the Estonian Integration Foundation. He was instrumental in promoting the Mustamäe language project to other members of the Integration Foundation board. His efforts resulted in Mustamäe receiving a grant from the foundation.

10. Sergei Ivanov, then Estonia's leading Russian-speaking parliamentarian, carried insights from CSMHI activities to his community.

11. Arnold Rüütel was elected president of Estonia on September 21, 2001. We assume that he has carried his experiences in the CSMHI activities with him into his office.

After our work in Estonia was completed, we tried to apply the Tree Model in the Republic of Georgia (see chapters 1–3). It become clear that in order to apply the methodology to other locations and circumstances, certain modifications must be made. In particular, the entry point—the point through which the facilitating team first gains access and becomes involved with members of the opposing groups—is critical and will vary greatly according to political, social, and other factors. For example, in many situations, it is neither feasible nor even desirable to start by bringing together senior level decision makers from both sides (as CSMHI did in Estonia).

During the diagnostic phase, facilitators should evaluate and decide on the best context in which to become involved in the intergroup tensions or conflicts. Thus, in some situations, initiating dialogues at the local or grassroots level may be the most effective entry point. No matter where they start, however, the facilitators will ultimately seek a ripple effect that creates critical contacts and meeting points with officialdom and that influences policy, thinking, and behavior on many levels. If one begins at the top, eventually one will need to spread insights and activities downward to the community level. If one begins on the local level, one will need to find ways of communicating results and insights to higher political echelons. Regardless of the entry point, the general philosophy of the Tree Model remains the same.

213. The concept "identification with aggressor" was first described by Anna Freud. See Anna Freud, *The Ego and the Mechanisms of Defense* (New York: International Universities Press, 1936–1946).

214. See http://www.allankings.com for information on Allan King's *The Dragon's Egg.*

215. Klooga received some program funds from the Organization for Security and Cooperation in Europe (OSCE) for activities in their community center. The Klooga NGO and other residents organized a variety of events and activities at the center that would not have been possible before its creation. These included after-school children's activities, Estonian language classes (for Russians), joint English language classes for Estonians and Russians, computer classes for adolescents and others, and community-wide social gatherings and holiday celebrations.

Bibliography

Abse, D. Wilfred. *Clinical Notes on Group-Analytic Psychotherapy.* Charlottesville: University Press of Virginia, 1974.

Akhtar, Salman. "Dehumanization: Origins, Manifestations, and Remedies." In *Violence or Dialogue: Psychoanalytic Insights on Terror and Terrorism.* Edited by Sverre Varvin and Vamık D. Volkan, 131–145. London: International Psychoanalytic Association, 2003.

———. *Immigration and Identity: Turmoil, Treatment and Transformation.* Northvale, NJ: Jason Aronson, 1999.

———. *New Clinical Realms: Pushing the Envelope of Theory and Technique.* Northvale, NJ: Jason Aronson, 2003.

Alexander, Franz, and Thomas F. French. *Psychoanalytic Theory.* New York: Ronald Press, 1946.

Allen, Beverly. *Rape Warfare: The Hidden Genocide in Bosnia-Herzegovina and Croatia.* Minneapolis, MN: University of Minnesota Press, 1946.

Apprey, Maurice. "Heuristic Steps for Negotiating Ethno-National Conflicts: Vignettes from Estonia." *New Literary History* 27 (1996): 199–212.

Apprey, Maurice. "From the Heuristic to the Empirical: Integrating Inter-Ethnic Kindergartens." In collaboration with Ly Krikk, Victor Apprey, and Endel Talvik. *Mind and Human Interaction* 11(2000): 194–205.

Barston, Ronald P. *Modern Diplomacy.* New York: Longman, 1988.

Berkes, Niyazi. *Türk Düşününde Batı Sorunu (The Western Question in Turkish Thought).* Ankara: Bilgi Yayınevi, 1988.

Berman, Maureen R., and Joseph E. Johnson, eds. *Unofficial Diplomats.* New York: Columbia University Press, 1977.

Bernard, Viola W., Perry Ottenberg, and Fritz Redl. "Dehumanization: A Composite Psychological Defense in Relation to Modern War." In *Sanctions for Evil: Sources of Social Destructiveness.* Edited by N. Sanford and C.

Comstock, 102–124. San Francisco: Jossey-Bass, 1973.

285

Bion, Wilfred R. *Experiences in Groups and Other Papers.* London: Tavistock Publications, 1961.

Bocksel, A.A. *Rice, Men and Barbed Wire: A True Epic of Americans as Japanese POW's.* Hauppage, NY: Michael B. Glass & Associates, 1991.

Brandt, Willy. *Erinnerungen: Mit den Notizen zum Fall G.* Berlin: Ullstein, 1994.

Brenner, Ira. *Psychic Trauma: Dynamics, Symptoms and Treatment.* New York: Jason Aronson, 2004.

Brokaw, Tom. *The Greatest Generation.* New York: Random House, 2004.

———. *The Greatest Generation Speaks: Letters and Reflection.* Norwalk, CT: Easton Press, 1999.

Burton, John W. "Conflict Resolution as a Political System." In *The Psychodynamics of International Relations.* Vol. 2, *Unofficial Diplomacy at Work.* Edited by Vamık D. Volkan, Joseph V. Montville, and Demetrios A. Julius, 71–92. Lexington, MA: Lexington Books, 1991.

Cain, A. C., and B.S. Cain. "On Replacing a Child." *Journal of the American Academy of Child Psychiatry* 3 (1964): 443–456.

Campbell, Robert. "An Emotive Apart." *Art in America* (May 1983): 150–151.

Chinard, G. *The Letters of Lafayette and Jefferson.* New York: Arno Press. 1979.

Eban, Abba. *The New Diplomacy: International Affairs in the Modern Age.* New York: Random, 1983.

Emde, Robert N. "Positive Emotions for Psychoanalytic Theory: Surprises from Infancy Research and New Directions." *Journal of the American Psychoanalytic Association* 39 (Supplement 1991): 5–44.

Erikson, Erik H. *Childhood and Society.* New York: W. W. Norton, 1950.

———. *Identity and Life Cycle.* New York: International Universities Press, 1959.

———. *Identity: Youth and Crises.* New York: W.W. Norton, 1968.

Erikson, Kai. "Loss of Community at Buffalo Creek." *American Journal of Psychiatry* 133 (1975): 302–325.

Erlich, H. Shumuel. "Adolescents' Reactions to Rabin's Assassination: A Case of Patricide?" In *Adolescent Psychiatry: Developmental and Clinical Studies.* Edited by A. Esman, 189–205. London: The Analytic Press, 1998.

Falk, Avner. "A Psychohistory of Political Assassination: The Cases of Lee Harvey Oswald and Yigal Amir." Paper read at the Twenty-Second Annual Scientific Meeting of the International Society of Political Psychology, Amsterdam, July 18–21, 1999.

———. "Political Assassination and Personality Disorder: The Cases of Lee Harvey Oswald and Yigal Amir." *Mind and Human Interaction* 12 (2001): 2–34.

Foulkes, S. H., and James Anthony. *Group Psychotherapy: The Psychoanalytic Approach.* London: Penguin, 1964.

Freud, Anna. *The Ego and the Mechanisms of Defense.* New York: International Universities Press, 1936–1946.

Freud, Anna, and Dorothy Burlingham. *War and Children.* New York: International Universities Press, 1942.

Freud, Sigmund. "Beyond the Pleasure Principle." Vol. 18 of *The Standard Edition of the Complete Psychological Works of Sigmund Freud.* Edited by James Strachey, 1–64. London: Hogarth Press, 1920–1955.

———. "Group Psychology and the Analysis of the Ego." Vol. 18 of *The Standard Edition of the Complete Psychological Works of Sigmund Freud.* Edited by James Strachey, 65–143. London: Hogarth Press, 1921–1955.

———. "Inhibitions, Symptoms and Anxiety." Vol. 20 of *The Standard Edition of the Complete Psychological Works of Sigmund Freud.* Edited by James Strachey, 75–175. London: Hogarth Press, 1926–1959.

———. "Introductory Lectures on Psycho-Analysis." Vol. 15 of *The Standard Edition of the Complete Psychological Works of Sigmund Freud.* Edited by James Strachey, 5–239. London: Hogarth Press, 1917–1964.

———. "Mourning and Melancholia." Vol.14 of *The Standard Edition of the Complete Psychological Works of Sigmund Freud.* Edited by James Strachey, 243–258. London: Hogarth Press, 1917–1957.

———. "Project for a Scientific Psychology." In *The Origins of Psycho-Analysis,* 347–351. New York: Basic Books, 1893–1954.

———. "Taboo of Virginity." Vol. 11 of *The Standard Edition of the Complete Psychological Works of Sigmund Freud.* Edited by James Strachey, 191–208. London: Hogarth Press, 1917–1955.

———. "Totem and Taboo." Vol. 13 of *The Standard Edition of the Complete Psychological Works of Sigmund Freud.* Edited by James Strachey, 1–162. London: Hogarth Press, 1913–1955.

Garza-Guerrero, A. Cesar. "Culture Shock: Its Mourning and Vicissitudes of Identity." *Journal of the American Psychoanalytic Association* 22 (1974): 408–429.

Goldman, Marshal I. *Détente and Dollars: Doing Business with the Soviets.* New York: Basic Books, 1975.

Greenacre, Phyllis. "The Fetish and the Transitional Object." In *Emotional Growth.* Vol. 1, 315–334. New York: International Universities Press, 1969–1974.

———. "The Transitional Object and the Fetish: With Special Reference to the Use of Illusion." *International Journal of Psycho-Analysis* 51 (1970): 447–456.

Greenspan, Stanley I. *The Development of the Ego: Implications for Personality Theory, Psychopathology and the Psychotherapeutic Process.* Madison, CT: International Universities Press, 1989.

Grinberg, Leon. *Guilt and Depression*. Translated by C. Trollope. London: Karnac Books, 1992.

Grinberg, Leon, and Rebecca Grinberg. *Psychoanalytic Perspectives on Migration and Exile*. Translated by N. Festinger. New Haven, CT: Yale University Press, 1989.

Gutman, Roy A. *Witness to Genocide: The 1993 Pulitzer Prize-Winning Dispatches on the "Ethnic Cleansing" of Bosnia*. New York: Maxwell Macmillan International, 1993.

Hadler, Susan Johnson, and Ann Bennett Mix. *Lost in Victory: Reflections of American War Orphans of World War II*. Denton, TX: University of North Texas Press, 1998.

Halman, Talat S. "Istanbul." In *The Last Lullaby*, 8–9. Merrick, NY: Cross Cultural Communications, 1992.

Heath, Sheldon. *Dealing with the Therapist's Vulnerability to Depression*. Northvale, NJ: Jason Aronson, 1991.

Herzfeld, Michael. *Ours Once More: Ideology and the Making of Modern Greece*. New York: Pella, 1986.

Hollander, Nancy. "Frozen Grief and the Transitional Transmission of Trauma." Paper read at a panel on Terror and Societal Regression, American Psychoanalytic Association's Winter Meeting, New York, 23 January, 2005.

———. *Love in Time of Hate: Liberation Psychology in Latin America*. New Brunswick, NJ: Rutgers University Press, 1997.

Hopper, Earl. T*raumatic Experience in the Unconscious Life of Groups: The Fourth Basic Assumption: Incohesion: Aggregation/Massification or (ba) I: A/M*. London: Jessica Kingsley Publishers, 2003.

Horowitz, D. L. *Ethnic Groups in Conflict*. Berkeley: University of California Press, 1985.

Itzkowitz, Norman. "Enver Hoxha's Albania." Paper read at a panel on Terror and Societal Regression, American Psychoanalytic Association's Winter Meeting, New York, 23 January, 2005.

Jacobson, Edith. *The Self and the Object World*. New York: International Universities Press, 1964.

Julius, Demetrios A. "Biculturalism and International Independence." *Mind and Human Interaction* 3 (1992): 53–56.

———. "The Practice of Tract Two Diplomacy in the Arab-Israeli Conferences." In *The Psychodynamics of International Relationships*. Vol. 2, *Unofficial Diplomacy at Work*. Edited by Vamık D. Volkan, Joseph V. Montville, and Demetrios A. Julius, 193–205. Lexington, MA: Lexington Books, 1991.

Jurcevic, Slavica, and Ivan Urlic. "Linking Objects in the Process of Mourning for Sons Disappeared in War: Croatia 2001." *Croatian Medical Journal* 43 (2001): 234–239.

Kaplan, Robert D. *Balkan Ghosts: A Journey Through History.* New York: Vintage Books, 1993.

Kazantzakis, Nikos. *Report on Greco.* Translated by P.A. Bien. New York: Simon and Schuster, 1965.

Kelman, Herbert C. "Interactive Problem Solving: The Uses and Limits of a Therapeutic Model for the Resolution of International Conflict." In *The Psychodynamics of International Relationships.* Vol. 2, *Unofficial Diplomacy at Work.* Edited by Vamık D. Volkan, Joseph V. Montville, and Demetrios A. Julius, 145–160. Lexington, MA: Lexington Books, 1965.

Kernberg, Otto F. *Borderline Conditions and Pathological Narcissism.* New York: Jason Aronson, 1975.

———. *Internal World and External Reality.* New York: Jason Aronson, 1980.

Kestenberg, Judith S. "A Psychological Assessment Based on Analysis of a Survivor's Child." In *Generations of the Holocaust.* Edited by M. S. Bergmann and M. E. Jucovy, 158–177. New York: Columbia University Press, 1982.

Kestenberg, Judith, and Ira Brenner. *The Last Witness.* Washington, D.C.: American Psychiatric Press, 1996.

Kitromelides, Paschalis M. "'Imagined communities' and the Origins of the National Question in the Balkans." In Modern Greek Nationalism and Nationality. Edited by M. Blickhorn and T. Veremis, 23–65. Athens, Greece: Sage-Eliamep, 1990.

Klein, Melanie. "Mourning and Its Relation to Manic-Depressive States." In *Contributions to Psychoanalysis, 1921 –1945,* 331–338. London: Hogarth Press, 1940.

———. "Notes on Schizoid Mechanisms." In *Development in Psychoanalysis.* Edited by J. Riviere, 292–320. London: Hogarth Press, 1946.

Kogan, Ilany. *The Cry of Mute Children: A Psychoanalytic Perspective of the Second Generation of the Holocaust.* London: Free Association Books,1995.

Lazarovich-Hrebelianovich, Prince, and Eleanor Calhoun. *The Serbian People.* Vol. 1. New York: Scribner's, 1910.

Lehtonen, Johannes. "Research: The Dream Between Neuroscience and Psychoanalysis: Has Feeding an Impact on Brain Function and the Capacity to Create Dream Images in Infants?" *Psychoanalysis in Europe* 57 (2003): 175–182.

Lehtonen, Johannes, M. Kononen, M. Purhonen, J. Partanen, S. Saarikoski, and K. Launiala. "The Effects of Feeding on the Electroencephalogram in 3- and 6-Month Old Infants." *Psychophysiology* 39 (2002): 73–9.

———. "The Effect of Nursing on the Brain Activity of the Newborn." *Journal of Pediatrics* 132 (1998): 646–651.

Levin, S. "On Psychoanalysis of Attitudes of Entitlement." *Bulletin of the Philadelphia Association of Psychoanalysis* 20 (1970):1–10.

Levinson, Charles. *Vodka Cola.* London: Gordon and Cremonesi, 1978.

Libaridian, Gerard Jinair, ed. *Armenia at the Crossroads: Democracy and Nationhood in the Post-Soviet Era.* Watertown, MA: Blue Cross Books, 1991.

Lifton, Robert J. *Death in Life: Survivors of Hiroshima.* New York: Random House, 1968.

Lifton, Robert J., and E. Olson. "The Human Meaning of Total Disaster: The Buffalo Creek Experience." *Psychiatry* 39 (1976): 1–18.

Loewald, H. "On the Therapeutic Action of Psychoanalysis." *International Journal of Psycho-Analysis* 41 (1960): 16–33.

Loewenberg, Peter. *Fantasy and Reality in History.* New York: Oxford University Press, 1995.

———. "Uses of Anxiety." *Partisan Review* 3 (1991): 514–525.

MacFarlane, S. Neil, Larry Minear, and Stephen Shenfield. *Armed Conflict in Georgia: A Case Study in Humanitarian Action and Peacekeeping.* Providence, RI: Thomas J. Watson, Jr. Institute for International Studies, 1996.

Mack, John E. "Cultural Amplifiers in Ethno-Nationalistic Affiliation and Differentiation." Paper read at the Committee on International Relations at the Fall Meeting of the Group for the Advancement of Psychiatry, Cherry Hill, NJ, 10–12 November, 1984.

———. "Foreword." In *Cyprus—War and Adaptation,* by Vamık D. Volkan, ix–xxi. Charlottesville, VA: University Press of Virginia, 1979.

McCarthy, Justin. *Death and Exile.* Princeton: Darwin Press, 1995.

Mahendran, C. "Forgiveness Between Nations: Eastern Perspectives." *International Minds* 5 (1994): 12–13.

Mahler, Margaret S. *On Human Symbiosis and the Vicissitudes of Individuation.* New York: International Universities Press, 1968.

Markides, Kyriacos C. *The Rise and Fall of the Cyprus Republic.* New Haven, CT: Yale University Press, 1977.

Markovic, Marko S. "The Secret of Kosovo." In *Landmarks in Serbian Culture and History,* translated by C. Kramer. Edited by V. D. Mihailovich, 111–131. Pittsburgh, PA: Serb National Foundation, 1983.

Misselwitz, Irene. "German Reunification: A Quasi Ethnic Conflict." *Mind and Human Interaction* 13 (2003): 77–86.

Mix, Ann Bennet. *Touchstones: A Guide to Records, Rights and Resources for Families of American World War II Casualties*. Indianapolis, IN: James Publishers, 2003.

Montville, Joseph V. "The Arrow and the Olive Branch: A Case for Tract Two Diplomacy." In *Conflict Resolution: Tract Two Diplomacy*. Edited by John McDonald and D. B. Bendahmane, 5–20. Washington: U.S. Government Printing Office, 1987.

———. "Justice and the Burdens of History." In *Reconciliation, Coexistence, and Justice in Interethnic Conflict: Theory and Practice*. Edited by Mohammed Abu Nimr, 129–144. Lanham, MD: Lexington Books, 2001.

———. "Religion and Peacemaking." In *Forgiveness and Reconciliation: Religion, Public Policy, and Conflict Transformation*. Edited by Raymond G. Hemlick and Rodney L. Peterson, 97–116. Philadelphia: Tempelton Foundation Press, 2001.

Morgenthau, Henry. *Politics Among Nations*. New York: Knopf, 1954.

Moses, Rafael. "An Israeli Psychoanalyst Looks Back in 1983." In *Psychoanalytic Reflections on the Holocaust: Selected Essays*. Edited by S. A. Luel and P. Marcus, 52–69. New York: KTAV Publishing, 1984.

Moses, Rafael, and Rena Moses-Hrushovski. "Two Powerful Tools in Human Interactions: To Accept One's Fault and to Ask for Forgiveness." In *Psikopatoloji ve Psikoanalitik Teknik (Psychopathology and Psychoanalytic Technique)*. Edited by Ayhan Egrilmez and Isıl Vahip. Izmir, Turkey: Meta, 2002.

Moses-Hrushovski, Rena. *Grief and Grievance: The Assassination of Yitzhak Rabin*. London: Minerva Press, 2000.

Motolinia, T. de. *History of Indians of New Spain*. Translated by F. B. Steck. Washington, D.C.: Academy of American Franciscan History, 1951.

Neu, Joyce, and Volkan, Vamık D. *Developing a Methodology for Conflict Prevention: The Case of Estonia*. Atlanta, GA: Carter Center Special Report Series, Winter, 1999.

Neubaurer, P. B. "Playing: Technical Implications." In *The Many Meanings of Play*. Edited by Albert J. Solnit, D. J. Cohen, and P. B. Neubaurer, 100–122. New Haven, CT: Yale University Press, 1993.

Nicholson, Harold. *Diplomacy*. London: Oxford University Press, 1963.

Niederland, William C. "The Problem of the Survivor." *Journal of Hillside Hospital* 10 (1961): 233–247.

Ochsner, Jeffrey, Karl. "A Space of Loss: The Vietnam Veterans Memorial." *Journal of Architectural Education* 10 (1997):156–171.

Olinick, Stanley L. *The Therapeutic Instrument*. New York: Jason Aronson, 1980.

Parens, Henri. *The Development of Aggression in Early Childhood*. New York: Jason Aronson, 1979.

————. *Renewal of Life: Healing from the Holocaust*. Rockville, MD: Schreiber Publishing, 2004.

Phillips, David L. "Track Two: Beyond Traditional Diplomacy." *State Magazine* (2000) 26–29. Washington, D.C.: United States Department of State.

Pines, Malcolm, ed. *The Evolution of Group Analysis*. London: Routledge & Kegan Paul, 1983.

Politis, Nikolaos G. *Introductory Lecture for the Class in Hellenic Mythology* (in Greek). Athens, Greece: Aion, 1882.

————. "Khelidhonisma" (Swallow Song). Neoelinika Analekta, 1 (1872): 354–368.

Pollock, George H. *The Mourning and Liberation Process*. 2 vols. Madison, CT: International Universities Press, 1989.

Poznanski, E. O. "The 'Replacement Child': A Saga of Unresolved Parental Grief." *Behavioral Pediatrics* 81 (1972): 1190–1193.

Purhonen, M., A. Pääkkönen, H. Yppärilä, J. Lehtonen, and J. Karhu. "Dynamic Behavior of the Auditory N100 Elicited by a Baby's Cry." *International Journal of Psychophysiology* 41 (2001): 271–278.

Rangell, Leo. "Discussion of the Buffalo Creek Disaster: The Course of Psychic Trauma." *American Journal of Psychiatry* 133 (1976): 313–316.

Raviv, A., A. Sadeh, O. Silberstein, and O. Diver. "Young Isrealis' Reactions to National Trauma: Rabin Assassination and Terror Attacks." *Political Psychology* 21 (2000): 299–322.

Robben, C. G. Antonius. "The Assault on Basic Trust: Disappearance, Protest, and Reburial in Argentina." In *Cultures Under Siege: Collective Violence and Trauma*. Edited by Antonius C. G. Robben and Marcello M. Suarez-Orozco, 70–101. Cambridge: Cambridge University Press, 2000.

Rothstein, David A. "The Assassin and the Assassinated: As Nonpatient Subject of Psychiatric Investigation." In *Dynamics of Violence*. Edited by J. Fawcett, 145–155. Chicago: American Medical Association, 1972.

Saunders, Harold H. "Officials and Citizens in International Relationships: The Dartmouth Conference." In *The Psychodynamics of International Relationships*. Vol. 2, *Unofficial Diplomacy at Work*. Edited by Vamık D. Volkan, Joseph V. Montville, and Demetrios A. Julius, 41–69. Lexington, MA: Lexington Books, 1991.

————. *The Other Walls: The Politics of the Arab-Israel Peace Process*. Washington, D.C.: American Enterprise Institute, 1985.

Scali, John. "Backstage Mediation in the Cuban Missile Crises." In *Conflict Resolution: Tract Two Diplomacy*. Edited by John W. McDonald, Jr. and D. B. Bendahmane. Washington, DC: Center for the Study of Foreign Affairs, 1987.

Schwoebel, Robert. *The Shadows of the Crescent: The Renaissance Image of the Turk, 1453–1517.* New York: St. Martin Press, 1967.

Scruggs, Jan C., and Joel L. Swerdlow. *To Heal a Nation: The Vietnam Veterans Memorial.* New York: Harper and Row, 1985.

Scruton, Roger. *A Dictionary of Political Thought.* New York: Harper & Row, 1982.

Searles, Harold F. "The Effort to Drive the Other Person Crazy: An Element in the Aetiology and Psychotherapy of Schizophrenia." In *Collected Papers on Schizophrenia and Related Subjects,* 254–283. New York: International Universities Press, 1959.

Sebek, Michael. "Anality in the Totalitarian System and the Psychology of Post-Totalitarian Society." *Mind and Human Interaction* 4 (1992): 52–59.

Smith, J.H. "On the Work of Mourning." In *Bereavement: Its Psychological Aspects.* Edited by B. Scoenberg, I. Gerber, A. Weiner, et al.,18–25. New York: Columbia University Press, 1975.

Sprinzak, Ehud. *Brother Against Brother: Violence and Extremism in Israeli Politics from Altena to the Rabin Assassination.* New York: Free Press, 1999.

Stein, Howard F. "Personal Thoughts on the Journey from Trauma to Resilience." *Mind and Human Interaction* 13 (2003): 90–98.

Stern, Daniel N. *The Interpersonal World of the Infant.* New York: Basic Books, 1985.

Stewart, S. *Give Us This Day.* New York: Avon Books, 1990.

Suarez-Orosco, Marcello, M. "The Heritage of Enduring a 'Dirty War': Psychological Aspects of Terror in Argentina, 1976–1988." *Journal of Psychohistory* 18 (1991): 469–505.

Sullivan, Harry S. *Schizophrenia as a Human Process.* New York: W. W. Norton, 1962.

Tähkä, Veikko. "Dealing with Object Loss." *Scandinavian Psychoanalytic Review* 1 (1984): 13–33.

Thomson, J. Anderson. "Killer Apes on American Airlines, or: How Religion Was the Main Hijacker on September 11." In *Violence or Dialogue? Psychoanalytic Insights on Terror and Terrorism.* Edited by Sverre Varvin and Vamık D. Volkan, 73–84. London: International Psychoanalysis Library, 2003.

———. "Terror, Tears, and Timelessness: Individual and Group Responses to Trauma." *Mind and Human Interaction* 11 (2000):162–176.

Tichener, J. L., and F. Kapp. "Disaster at Buffalo Creek: Family and Character Change." *American Journal of Psychiatry* 133 (1976): 295–299.

van der Kolk, Bessel. "Post Traumatic Stress Disorder and the Nature of Trauma." *Dialogues in Clinical Neuroscience* 2 (2002): 7–22.

van der Kolk, Bessel, J.W. Hopper, and J.E. Osterman. "Exploring the Nature of Traumatic Memory." *Journal of Aggression, Maltreatment and Trauma* 4 (2001): 9–31.

Volkan, Kurt. "The Vietnam War Memorial." *Mind and Human Interaction* 3 (1992): 73–77.

Volkan, Vamık D. *Blind Trust: Large Groups and Their Leaders in Times of Crises and Terror*. Charlottesville, VA: Pitchstone Publishing, 2004.

———. *Bloodlines: From Ethnic Pride to Ethnic Terrorism*. New York: Farrar, Straus & Giroux, 1997.

———. *Cyprus—War and Adaptation: A Psychoanalytic History of Two Ethnic Groups in Conflict*. Charlottesville, VA: University Press of Virginia, 1979.

———. *Linking Objects and Linking Phenomena: A Study of the Forms, Symptoms, Metapsychology and Therapy of Complicated Mourning*. New York: International Universities Press, 1981.

———. "The Linking Objects of Pathological Mourners." *Archives of General Psychiatry* 27 (1972): 215–222.

———. *The Need to Have Enemies and Allies: From Clinical Practice to International Relationships*. Northvale, NJ: Jason Aronson, 1988.

———. "On Chosen Trauma." *Mind and Human Interaction* 4 (1991): 3–19.

———. *Six Steps in the Treatment of Borderline Personality Organization*. Northvale, NJ: Jason Aronson, 1987.

———. "Traumatized Societies and Psychological Care: Expanding the Concept of Preventive Medicine." *Mind and Human Interaction* 11 (2000): 177–194.

———. "The Tree Model: A Comprehensive Psychopolitical Approach to Unofficial Diplomacy and the Reduction of Ethnic Tension." *Mind and Human Interaction* 10 (1999): 142–210.

Volkan, Vamık D., and Gabriele Ast. "Curing Gitta's 'Leaking Body': Actualized Unconscious Fantasies and Therapeutic Play." *Journal of Clinical Psychoanalysis* 10 (2001): 557–596.

———. *Siblings in the Unconscious and Psychopathology*. Madison, CT: International Universities Press, 1997.

———. *Spektrum des Narzissmus*. Göttingen: Vanderhoeck & Ruprecht, 1994.

Volkan, Vamık D., Gabriele Ast, and Willliam Greer. *The Third Reich in the Unconscious: Transgenerational Transmission and its Consequences*. New York: Brunner-Routledge, 2002.

Volkan, Vamık D., and Max Harris. "Negotiating a Peaceful Separation: A Psychopolitical Analysis of Current Relationships Between Russia and Baltic Republics." *Mind and Human Interaction* 4 (1992): 20–29.

———. "The Psychodynamics of Ethnic Terrorism." *International Journal of Group Rights* 3 (1995): 145–159.

Volkan, Vamık D., and Norman Itzkowitz. "Istanbul, not Constantinople: The Western World's View of 'the Turk.'" *Mind and Human Interaction* 4 (1993): 129–134.

———. *Turks and Greeks: Neighbours in Conflict.* Cambridgeshire, England: Eothen Press, 1994.

Volkan, Vamık D., Demetrios Julius, and Joseph V. Montville, eds. *The Psychodynamics of International Relationships.* Vol. 2, Unofficial Diplomacy at Work. Lexington, MA: Lexington Books, 1990.

Volkan, Vamık, Nino Makhashvili, Nodar Sharveladze, and Isıl Vahip. "IREX Black and Caspian Sea Collaborative Research Program: Gender Issues and Family Violence," a Center for the Study of Mind and Human Interaction (CSMHI) document. Charlottesville, VA: Center for the Study of Mind and Human Interaction (CSMHI), July, 2002.

Volkan, Vamık. D., and As'ad Masri. "The Development of Female Transsexualism." *American Journal of Psychotherapy* 43 (1989): 92–107.

Volkan, Vamık D., Joseph V. Montville, and Demetrios Julius, eds. *The Psychodynamics of International Relations.* Vol. l, Concepts and Theories. Lexington, MA: Lexington Books, 1990.

Volkan, Vamık D., and Elizabeth Zintl. *Life After Loss: The Lessons of Grief.* New York: Charles Scribner's Sons, 1993.

Wagner, Wolf. *Kulturschock Deutschland 1 (Culture Shock Germany 1).* Hamburg: Rotbuch-Verlag, 1996.

———. *Kulturschock Deutschland; Der zweite Blick (Culture Shock Germany: The Second View).* Hamburg: Rotbuch-Verlag, 1998.

Wangh, Martin. "Being a Refugee and Being an Immigrant." *International Psychoanalysis,* Winter issue (1992): 15–17.

Werdigier, Wolf. *Hidden Images: Palestinians and Israelis: An Archeology of the Unconscious.* Vienna: Cultural Department, Austrian Federal Ministry of Education, 2003.

Williams, R. M. and Murray C. Parkes. "Psychosocial Effects of Disaster: Birth Rate in Aberfan." *British Medical Journal* 2 (1975): 303–304.

Wilson, John and Boris Drozdek, eds. *Broken Spirits: The Treatment of Traumatized Asylum Seekers, Refugees, War and Torture Victims.* New York: Brunner-Routledge, 2004.

Winnicott, Donald W. *Playing and Reality.* London: Tavistock Publications, 1971.

———. "Transitional Objects and Transitional Phenomena." *International Journal of Psycho-Analysis* 34 (1953): 89–97.

Wolfenstein, Martha. "Loss, Rage and Repetition." *Psychoanalytic Study of the Child* 24 (1969): 432–460.

Wolfenstein, Martha, and G. Kliman, eds. *Children and the Death of a President: Multi-disciplinary Studies*. Garden City, NY: Doubleday, 1965.

Wrangham, Richard. "Is Military Incompetence Adaptive? Apes and the Origins of Human Violence," *Evolution and Human Behavior* 20 (1999): 3–17.

Wrangham, Richard, and D. Peterson. *Demonic Males*. Boston: Houghton Mifflin, 1996.

Yasın, Özker. *Kanlı Kıbrıs (Bloody Cyprus)*. Istanbul: Varlık Yayınları, 1964.

———. *Kıbrıs Mektubu (The Cyprus Letter)*. Istanbul: Varlık Yayınları, 1958.

———. *Oglum Savas'a Mektuplar (Letters to My Son Savas)*. Nicosia: Çevre Yayınları, 1965.

Young, James E. *The Texture of Memory: Memorials and Meaning*. New Haven: Yale University Press, 1993.

Young, Kenneth. *The Greek Passion: A Study in People and Politics*. London: J. M. Dent & Sons, 1969.

Zamblios, Spyridon. "Some Philosophical Researches on the Modern Greek Language" (In Greek). *Pandora* 7 (1856): 369–380, 484–489.

———. *Whence the Vulgar Word Traghoudho? Thoughts Concerning Hellenic Poetry* (in Greek). Athens, Greece: P. Soutsas and A. Ktenas, 1859.

Zuckerman, Robert, and Vamık D. Volkan. "Complicated Mourning over a Body Defect: The Making of a 'Living Linking Object.'" In *The Problem of Loss and Mourning: Psychoanalytic Perspectives*. Edited by D. Deitrich & P. Shabad, 257–274. New York: International Universities Press, 1988.

Index

297

About the Author

Vamık D. Volkan, M.D., is an emeritus professor of psychiatry and the founder of the Center for the Study of Mind and Human Interaction (CSMHI) at the University of Virginia School of Medicine. He was the director of CSMHI from 1987 until his retirement in 2002. CSMHI was closed in September 2005.

Dr. Volkan is also the Senior Erik Erikson Scholar at the Austen Riggs Center in Stockbridge, Massachusetts, and an emeritus training and supervising analyst at the Washington Psychoanalytic Institute. He is a past president of both the International Society of Political Psychology and the Virginia Psychoanalytic Society.

In the 1990s, he served as a member of the Carter Center's International Negotiation Network, headed by former U.S. president Jimmy Carter. In 1995, he chaired a Select Advisory Commission to the Federal Bureau of Investigation's Critical Incident Response Group. In 1999, he gave the twenty-seventh Annual Sigmund Freud Lecture in Vienna, Austria. In 2000, he served as an Inaugural Rabin Fellow at the Yitzhak Rabin Center for Israeli Studies in Tel Aviv. In February 2001, he was a visiting professor of law at Harvard University in Cambridge, Massachusetts. In 2003, he was the recipient of the Sigmund Freud Award given by the city of Vienna in collaboration with the World Council of Psychotherapy. In 2005, he received an honorary doctorate degree from the Kuopio University, Finland. In 2006, he will be a Fulbright and Sigmund Freud-Privatstiftung Visiting Scholar of Psychoanalysis in Vienna, Austria.

For nearly three decades, Dr. Volkan led his interdisciplinary team from CSMHI to various trouble spots around the world and brought high-level "enemy" representatives together for years-long unofficial dialogues. His work in the trenches resulted in his developing new theories about large-group behavior in times of peace and war.